VARIATIONS ON A THEME PARK

VARIATIONS ON

Michael Sorkin

EDITOR

HILL AND WANG

A THEME PARK

The New American City and the End of Public Space

The Noonday Press • *New York*

Printed in the United States of America
Published simultaneously in Canada by HarperCollinsCanadaLtd
Designed by Victoria Wong
This edition first pubished in 1992 by The Noonday Press
Third printing, 1993

Library of Congress Cataloging-in-Publication Data
Variations on a theme park : The New American City and the End of Public Space /
edited and with an introduction by Michael Sorkin. — 1st ed.
p. cm.
1. Cities and towns—United States. 2. City planning—United
States. 3. City and town life—United States. 4. Public spaces—
United States. I. Sorkin, Michael.
HT123.V37 1992   307.76'0973—dc20   91-22976   CIP

We wish to thank the Collection Centre Canadien d'Architecture/Canadian Centre
for Architecture, Montréal, for permission to reproduce Leopoldo Alinari's
Ponte Vecchio, Florence, Italy.

To Joan

This book has been a long time coming. Originally commissioned by Sara Bershtel at the old Pantheon, it survived the purge there thanks to her dedication and thanks to Hill and Wang, which has provided both Sara and this collection with a fine new home. I'm most grateful to Sara for her friendship, perseverance and skill, and to Hill and Wang for their commitment to being a publisher of ideas. Thanks also to David Frederickson for his fine copy editing and to Sally Singer for her feats of coordination.

Contents

MICHAEL SORKIN

Introduction: Variations
on a Theme Park

With the precise prescience of a true Master of the Universe, Walter
Wriston recently declared that "the 800 telephone number and the
piece of plastic have made time and space obsolete." Wriston ought
to know. As former CEO of the suggestively named Citicorp, he's
a true Baron Haussmann for the electronic age, plowing the boulevards of capital through the pliant matrix of the global economy.

This comparison isn't meant to be flip: Wriston's remark begs
fundamental questions about urbanity. Computers, credit cards,
phones, faxes, and other instruments of instant artificial adjacency
are rapidly eviscerating historic politics of propinquity, the very
cement of the city. Indeed, recent years have seen the emergence
of a wholly new kind of city, a city without a place attached to it.

This ageographical city is particularly advanced in the United
States. It's visible in clumps of skyscrapers rising from well-wired
fields next to the Interstate; in huge shopping malls, anchored by
their national-chain department stores, and surrounded by swarms
of cars; in hermetically sealed atrium hotels cloned from coast to
coast; in uniform "historic" gentrifications and festive markets; in
the disaggregated sprawl of endless new suburbs without cities;
and in the antenna bristle of a hundred million rooftops from
Secaucus to Simi Valley, in the clouds of satellite dishes pointed
at the same geosynchronous blip, all sucking Arsenio and the
A-Team out of the ether.

In fact, the structure of this city is a lot like television. TV's
main event is the cut, the elision between broadcast bits, the seam-

less slide from soap opera to docudrama to a word from our sponsor. The "design" of television is all about erasing differences among these bits, about asserting equal value for all the elements in the net, so that any of the infinite combinations that the broadcast day produces can make "sense." The new city likewise eradicates genuine particularity in favor of a continuous urban field, a conceptual grid of boundless reach. It's a process of erasure much noted. In the 1950s and 1960s, the alarm was sounded over "urban sprawl" and "Megalopolis," the spread of an uninterrupted zone of urbanization along the American Northeast coast, a city become region. More recently, attention has focused on the explosion of so-called "suburban cities" on the fringes of existing metropolises. In this vast, virtually undifferentiated territory—stretching from Fairfax County, Virginia, to Orange County, California—homes, offices, factories, and shopping malls float in a culturing medium, a "non-place urban realm" that provides the bare functions of a city, while doing away with the vital, not quite disciplined formal and social mix that gives cities life.

The city described in this book, though, is not simply a phenomenon of extent. Its growth no longer merely physical—a matter of egregious densities or metastasizing reach—the new city also occupies a vast, unseen, conceptual space. This invisible Cyburbia—so aptly evoked by Wriston—takes form as necessary, sprouting like sudden mushrooms at capital's promiscuous nodes. What's missing in this city is not a matter of any particular building or place; it's the spaces in between, the connections that make sense of forms.

The history of cities is embedded in the ways their elements are juxtaposed, the structures of art and regulation that govern urban amalgamation. Questions both of what goes with what and what yields to what are at the basis of urban form-making. Traditional cities have adjudicated such questions via relations to central places. Whether agora, castle, piazza, or downtown, the idea of a city of centers stands, at a minimum, for the idea of a spatial city, a city in which order is a function of proximity. This physical city has historically mapped social relations with a profound clarity, imprinting in its shapes and places vast information about status and order. Whether "the other side of the tracks" in a small town, the New England commons, or the bar-graph of real estate values visible in the Manhattan skyline, social order has long been legible in urban form. In the new, recombinant city, however, the legibility of these orders has been dramatically manipulated, often completely obscured. Here, anything seems to go with anything—hierarchies are both reinforced and concealed, at once fixed and despatialized. Value is still a function of location, but the invisible hand has learned a new geometry. As phone and modem render the street irrelevant, other dimensions become preeminent. Main Street is now the space between airports, the fiber-optic cables linking the fax machines of the multinational corporations' far-flung offices, an invisible worldwide skein of economic relations. Liberated from its centers and its edges by advances in communication and mobility and by a new world order bent on a single citizenship of consumption, the new city threatens an unimagined sameness even as it multiplies the illusory choices of the TV system.

Three salient characteristics mark this city. The first is the dissipation of all stable relations to local physical and cultural geography, the loosening of ties to any specific space. Globalized capital, electronic means of production, and uniform mass culture abhor the intimate, undisciplined differentiation of traditional cities. The new city replaces the anomaly and delight of such places with a universal particular, a generic urbanism inflected only by appliqué. Here, locality is efficiently acknowledged by the inclusion of the croque-monsieur at the McDonald's on the Boul' Miche or the Cajun Martini at the airport lounge in New Orleans (and you're welcome to keep the glass). This "place" is fully ageographic: it can be inserted equally in an open field or in the heart of town; the inward-looking atrium hotel is as apt to the featureless greensward as it is to teeming unreclaimed downtowns. With its components reduced to a repetitive minimum, space is departicularized. Obsessed with the point of production and the point of sale, the new city is little more than a swarm of urban bits jettisoning a physical view of the whole, sacrificing the idea of the city as the site of community and human connection.

A second characteristic of this new city is its obsession with "security," with rising levels of manipulation and surveillance over its citizenry and with a proliferation of new modes of segregation. The methods are both technological and physical. The former consist of invasive policing technologies—domesticated versions of the "electronic battlefield"—and a growing multitude of daily connections to the computer grid, ranging from encounters with the automated teller to the full-blown regulatory environment of the electronic workplace. The physical means are equally varied: parallel, middle-class suburban cities growing on the fringes of old centers abandoned to the poor; enclaved communities for the rich; gentrification; the globe-girdling cocoon that envelops the business traveler as he or she encounters the same airport, hotel, and office building from Denver to Dubai; the lacework of overhead and underground circulation systems imposed in Minneapolis or Edmonton to permit shoppers and office workers to circulate in climate-regulated security through threatening urban territory. This impulse to a new urban segregation seems ubiquitous: throughout America, city planning has largely ceased its historic role as the integrator of communities in favor of managing selective development and enforcing distinction.

Finally, this new realm is a city of simulations, television city, the city as theme park. This is nowhere more visible than in its architecture, in buildings that rely for their authority on images drawn from history, from a spuriously appropriated past that substitutes for a more exigent and examined present. In most American cities, the "historic" has become the only complicit official urban value. The result is that the preservation of the physical remnants of the historical city has superseded attention to the human ecologies that produced and inhabit them. Today, the profession of urban design is almost wholly preoccupied with reproduction, with the creation of urbane disguises. Whether in its master incarnation at the ersatz Main Street of Disneyland, in the phony historic festivity of a Rouse marketplace, or the gentrified architecture of the "reborn" Lower East Side, this elaborate apparatus is at pains to assert its ties to the kind of city life it is in the process of obliterating.

Here is urban renewal with a sinister twist, an architecture of deception which, in its happy-face familiarity, constantly distances itself from the most fundamental realities. The architecture of this city is almost purely semiotic, playing the game of grafted signification, theme-park building. Whether it represents generic historicity or generic modernity, such design is based in the same calculus as advertising, the idea of pure imageability, oblivious to the real needs and traditions of those who inhabit it. Welcome to Cyburbia.

   This book is not an attempt to theorize this new city but to describe it. The sites discussed are representative; they do not simply typify the course of American urbanism but are likely to be models for urban development throughout the world. The frame of reference is thus limited: it is not about Soweto, the South Bronx, or Dhaka. Nor is it directly about Urbino, Paris, or Savannah, those pleasant centers of traditional urbanity. And yet it is. The danger in this new city is in its antithesis: in Victor Hugo's famous phrase, "This will destroy that." The new city has the power simply not only to bypass the traditional scenes of urbanity but to co-opt them, to relegate them to mere intersections on a global grid for which time and space are indeed obsolete.

   "City air makes people free," goes a medieval maxim. The cautionary essays collected here describe an ill wind blowing through our cities, an atmosphere that has the potential to irretrievably alter the character of cities as the preeminent sites of democracy and pleasure. The familiar spaces of traditional cities, the streets and squares, courtyards and parks, are our great scenes of the civic, visible and accessible, our binding agents. By describing the alternative, this book pleads for a return to a more authentic urbanity, a city based on physical proximity and free movement and a sense that the city is our best expression of a desire for collectivity. As spatiality ebbs, so does intimacy. The privatized city of bits is a lie, simulating its connections, obliterating the power of its citizens either to act alone or to act together.

   This is the meaning of the theme park, the place that embodies it all, the ageographia, the surveillance and control, the simulations without end. The theme park presents its happy regulated vision of pleasure—all those artfully hoodwinking forms—as a substitute for the democratic public realm, and it does so appealingly by stripping troubled urbanity of its sting, of the presence of the poor, of crime, of dirt, of work. In the "public" spaces of the theme park or the shopping mall, speech itself is restricted: there are no demonstrations in Disneyland. The effort to reclaim the city is the struggle of democracy itself.

VARIATIONS ON A THEME PARK

MARGARET CRAWFORD

The World in
a Shopping Mall

Larger than a hundred football fields, the West Edmonton Mall is, according to the *Guinness Book of Records*, the largest shopping mall in the world. At 5.2 million square feet, the world's first megamall is nearly twice as large as the runner-up, the Del Amo Mall in Los Angeles, which covers only 3 million square feet. Other *Guinness* titles the mall holds are World's Largest Indoor Amusement Park, World's Largest Indoor Water Park, and World's Largest Parking Lot. Besides its more than 800 shops, 11 department stores, and 110 restaurants, the mall also contains a full-size ice-skating rink, a 360-room hotel, a lake, a nondenominational chapel, 20 movie theaters, and 13 nightclubs. These activities are situated along corridors of repeated storefronts and in wings that mimic nineteenth-century Parisian boulevards and New Orleans's Bourbon Street. From the upper stories of the mall's hotel, the glass towers of downtown Edmonton are just visible in the distance.

Seen from above, the mall resembles an ungainly pile of oversized boxes plunked down in the middle of an enormous asphalt sea, surrounded by an endless landscape of single-family houses. Inside, the mall presents a dizzying spectacle of attractions and diversions: a replica of Columbus's *Santa Maria* floats in an artificial lagoon, where real submarines move through an impossible seascape of imported coral and plastic seaweed inhabited by live penguins and electronically controlled rubber sharks; fiberglass columns crumble in simulated decay beneath a spanking new Victorian iron bridge; performing dolphins leap in front of Leather

World and Kinney's Shoes; fake waves, real Siberian tigers, Ching-dynasty vases, and mechanical jazz bands are juxtaposed in an endless sequence of skylit courts. Mirrored columns and walls further fragment the scene, shattering the mall into a kaleidoscope of ultimately unreadable images. Confusion proliferates at every level; past and future collapse meaninglessly into the present; barriers between real and fake, near and far, dissolve as history, nature, technology, are indifferently processed by the mall's fantasy machine.

Yet this implausible, seemingly random, collection of images has been assembled with an explicit purpose: to support the mall's claim to contain the entire world within its walls. At the opening ceremony aboard the *Santa Maria*, one of the mall's developers, Nader Ghermezian, shouted in triumph, "What we have done means you don't have to go to New York or Paris or Disneyland or Hawaii. We have it all here for you in one place, in Edmonton, Alberta, Canada!"[1] Publicity for the Fantasyland Hotel asks, "What country do you want to sleep in tonight?"—offering theme rooms based not only on faraway places such as Polynesia and Hollywood, and distant times such as ancient Rome and Victorian England, but also on modes of transportation, from horse-drawn carriages to pickup trucks.

The developer's claims imply that the goods for sale inside the mall represent the world's abundance and variety and offer a choice of global proportions. In fact, though, the mall's mixture of American and Canadian chains, with a few local specialty stores, rigorously repeats the range of products offered at every other shopping mall. Internal duplication reduces choice even further, since many stores operate identical outlets at different points in the mall. Despite the less than worldwide selection, shoppers still come from all over the world (70 percent of the mall's visitors are from outside Alberta) and spend enough to generate profits of $300 per square foot—more than twice the return of most malls. The West Edmonton Mall (WEM) dominates the local commercial economy. If superimposed onto downtown Edmonton, the mall and its parking lot would span most of the central business district. Commercially overshadowed by the mall, long-established downtown stores now open branches in the mall. As a gesture of urban goodwill, the WEM's developers have agreed to build another mall downtown

West Edmonton Mall

to replace some of the revenue and activity drained off by the
megamall.[2]

The inclusion of more and more activities into the mall has
extended its operating day to twenty-four hours: a chapel offers
services before shops open, nightclubs draw customers after they
close, and visitors spend the night at the mall's hotel. The mall is
also a workplace, with more than fifteen thousand people employed
in its shops, services, and offices, many of whom also eat and spend
their free time there. In the suburbs of Minneapolis, the WEM's
developers are now erecting an even larger complex, the Mall of
America, complete with office towers, three hotels, and a convention
center. Orange County's Knott's Berry Farm theme park will supply
the mall's entertainment centerpiece, "Camp Snoopy."[3] The mayor
of Bloomington, Minnesota, exults, "Now people can come here
and watch a Vikings game and stay for the weekend. It's a different
world when you have a megamall."[4]

The mall's encyclopedic agglomeration of activities requires
only the addition of housing, already present in other urban mall
megastructures, to become fully inhabitable, a world complete in
itself. In a sense, the fragmented forms and functions of modern
living are being brought together under the mall's skylighted dome.
This suggests the possibility that the unified world of premodern
times might be reconstituted through the medium of consumption,
an ironic reversal of the redemptive design projects imagined by
nineteenth-century utopians such as Fourier and Owen, who sought
unity through collective productive activity and social reorganization. Although Fourier's Phalanstery merged the arcade and the
palace into a prefigurative mall form, its glass-roofed corridors were
intended to encourage social intercourse and foster communal emotions, rather than stimulate consumption.

The Science of Malling

The WEM's nonstop proliferation of attractions, activities, and images proclaims its uniqueness; but, beneath its myriad distractions,
the mall is easily recognizable as an elephantine version of a generic
type—the regional shopping mall. Indeed, the WEM is only the
latest incarnation of a self-adjusting system of merchandising and
development that has conquered the world by deploying standardized units in an extensive network. And, as the state-of-the-art mall

is continually redefined, the WEM's jumbled collection of images is already on the verge of becoming obsolete. More seamless alternative worlds are coming off the drawing boards. Disney "imagineers" have recently designed an entertainment center and shopping mall for Burbank inspired by the "lure and magic of the movies." The cinematic medium, inherently fragmented and unreal, structures a sophisticated fantasy world that will be both more complex and more coherent than the WEM.[5]

Although it is, for the moment, unrivaled in size and spectacle, the WEM is not exempt from the rules of finance and marketing that govern the 28,500 other shopping malls in North America.[6] These rules date from the golden years between 1960 and 1980, when the basic regional mall paradigm was perfected and systematically replicated. Developers methodically surveyed, divided, and appropriated suburban cornfields and orange groves to create a new landscape of consumption. If a map of their efforts were to be drawn, it would reveal a continent covered by a wildly uneven pattern of overlapping circles representing mall-catchment areas, each circle's size and location dictated by demographic surveys measuring income levels and purchasing power. In a strangely inverted version of central-place theory, developers identified areas where consumer demand was not being met and where malls could fill the commercial voids.[7] Dense agglomerations of malls would indicate the richest markets, and empty spots the pockets of poverty: West Virginia, for example, has the lowest shopping-mall square footage per inhabitant in the country.[8]

The size and scale of a mall, then, reflects "threshold demand"—the minimum number of potential customers living within the geographical range of a retail item to enable it to be sold at a profit. Thus, *neighborhood* centers serve a local market within a two-mile radius; *community* centers draw from three to five miles. The next tier of 2,500 *regional* malls (at least two department stores and a hundred shops) attracts customers from as far as twenty miles away, while an elite group of 300 *super-regional* malls (at least five department stores and up to three hundred shops) serve a larger, often multistate, area within a hundred-mile radius. At the peak of the pyramid sits the West Edmonton megamall, an international shopping attraction. The system as a whole dominates retail sales in the United States and Canada, accounting for more than 53 percent of all purchases in both countries.[9]

The malling of America in less than twenty years was accomplished by honing standard real-estate, financing, and marketing techniques into predictive formulas. Generated initially by risk-free investments demanded by pension funds and insurance companies (sources of the enormous amounts of capital necessary to finance malls) the malling process quickly became self-perpetuating, as developers duplicated successful strategies. Specialized consultants developed techniques of demographic and market research, refined their environmental and architectural analysis, and produced *econometric* and *locational* models. Mall architect Victor Gruen proposed an ideal matrix for mall-building that combined the expertise of real-estate brokers, financial and marketing analysts, economists, merchandising experts, architects, engineers, transportation planners, landscape architects, and interior designers—each drawing on the latest academic and commercial methodologies. Gruen's highly structured system was designed to minimize guesswork and to allow him to accurately predict the potential dollar-per-square-foot-yield of any projected mall, thus virtually guaranteeing profitability to the mall's developers.

In a game with such high stakes, competition became irrelevant. The technical expertise and financial resources required for mall-building restricted participation to a small circle of large developers. The pioneers—DeBartolo, Rouse, Hahn, Bohannon, and Taubman—established their own institutions: the International Council of Shopping Centers and trade journals such as *Shopping Center World* and *National Mall Monitor* insured rapid circulation of investment and marketing information; the Urban Land Institute worked to standardize mall-development procedures. The application of such standardized methods of determining locations, structuring selling space, and controlling customers produced consistent and immense profits. In their first twenty-five years, less than one percent of shopping malls failed; profits soared, making malls, according to DeBartolo, "the best investment known to man."[10]

For the consumer, the visible result of this intensive research is the "mix"—each mall's unique blend of tenants and department-store "anchors." The mix is established and maintained by restrictive leases with clauses that control everything from decor to prices. Even within the limited formula that the mix establishes for each mall, minute variations in the selection and location of stores can be critical. Detailed equations are used to determine exactly how many jewelry or shoe stores should be put on each floor. Since branches of national chains are the most reliable money-makers, individually owned stores are admitted only with shorter leases and higher rents. Mall managers constantly adjust the mix, using rents and leases to adapt to the rapidly changing patterns of consumption. The system operates much like television programming, with each network presenting slightly different configurations of the same elements. Apparent diversity masks fundamental homogeneity.

The various predictable mixes are fine-tuned to the ethnic composition, income levels, and changing tastes of a particular shopping area. Indexes such as VALS (the Values and Life Styles program), produced by the Stanford Research Institute, correlate objective measures such as age, income, and family composition with subjective indicators such as value systems, leisure preferences, and cultural backgrounds to analyze trade areas. For instance, Brooks Brothers and Ann Taylor are usually solid bets for areas populated by outer-directed *achievers* ("hardworking, materialistic, highly educated traditional consumers; shopping leaders for luxury products") and *emulators* ("younger, status-conscious, conspicuous consumers"). But since climate, geography, and local identity also play a role in spending patterns, these stores may not succeed in areas like Orange County, California, where good weather allows more informal dress. *Sustainers* ("struggling poor; anger toward the American system") and *belongers* ("middle-class, conservative, conforming shoppers, low to moderate income"), on the other hand, tend to be "value-oriented," making K mart or J. C. Penney good anchors for malls where these groups predominate. Shoppers' perceptions of themselves and their environment furnish more accurate predictions of shopping habits than income. According to the Lifestyle Cluster system, an alternative index, even with identical incomes, the *black enterprise* and *pools and patios* groups will exhibit very different consumption patterns.[11]

Through a careful study of such spending patterns, mallbuilders can generate a mix that makes the difference between a mere profit-maker and a "foolproof money-machine" such as Southdale, outside of Minneapolis, the most successful of Equitable Life Assurance's one hundred shopping malls. Southdale's managers are constantly adjusting its mix to reflect increasingly refined consumer profiles. They know, for example, that their average customer is a 40.3-year-old female with an annual income of over $33,000, who lives in a household of 1.7 people. She is willing to spend more than $125 for a coat and buys six pairs of shoes a year in sizes 5 to 7. Southdale's mix reflects this ideal consumer; women's clothing stores and upscale boutiques have now replaced Woolworth's and the video arcade. The mall's decor and promotions target her tastes through "psychographics"—the detailed marketing profiles which identify the customer's aspirations as well as her stated needs in order to chart "identity" as well as income.[12]

Such precision in locating and satisfying consumers has become increasingly important since 1980, when malls approached the saturation point. The system demonstrated a surprising adaptability: in spite of its history of rigidly programmed uniformity, new economic and locational opportunities prompted new prototypes. Specialty malls were built without department stores, allowing a more flexible use of space. To fit urban sites, malls adopted more compact and vertical forms with stacked floors of indoor parking, as at the Eaton Center in Toronto and the Beverly Center in Los Angeles. To insure financing in uncertain markets, developers formed partnerships with redevelopment agencies. The Grand Avenue in Milwaukee and the Gallery at Market East in Philadelphia are both joint ventures by HUD, municipal redevelopment agencies, and the Rouse Company. To survive in high-rent downtown locations, malls added hotels, condominiums, and offices to become omni-centers, such as Trump Tower on Fifth Avenue, or Water Tower Place and Chicago Place on North Michigan Avenue.

Existing malls renewed themselves by upgrading their decor and amenities. Future archaeologists will read Orange County's social history in South Coast Plaza's successive levels: the lowest floors, featuring Sears and J. C. Penney's, recall the suburbs' original lower-middle-class roots; the elaborate upper levels, with stores such as Gucci and Cartier, reflect the area's more recent affluence. Open-air plazas, once thought obsolete, have been revived and a new generation of consumers now stroll uncovered walkways.[13] Virtually any large building or historic area is a candidate for reconfiguration into a mall. Americans regularly browse through renovated factories (the Cannery and Ghirardelli Square in San Francisco), piers (North Pier in Chicago), and government buildings (the Old Post Office in Washington, D.C.). The imposing neoclassical space of McKim, Mead, and White's Union Station, which once solemnly celebrated entry into the nation's capital, now contains a shopping mall. The city of New York has even considered developing the Brooklyn Bridge as a historic shopping mall, with the brick arches of its Manhattan approach enclosing retail shops and a health spa.[14]

Although by 1980 the American landscape was crowded with these palaces of consumption, the rest of the world was still open for development. The form could be exported intact into third-world economies, with local developers providing enclosed shopping malls as exotic novelties for upper-class consumers in Caracas or Buenos Aires. Planners of new towns such as Milton Keynes, England, and Marne-la-Vallée, outside Paris, followed the example of Columbia, Maryland, to create state-sponsored social-democratic malls, combining government and community facilities with retail space to create new town centers. Asian versions in Hong Kong and Singapore adapted local marketplace traditions, filling vast malls with small, individually owned shops. The enormous new market opening up in Eastern Europe will surely place Warsaw and Budapest on *Shopping Center World*'s list of hot spots ripe for development. The variations are endless, but whatever form the system adopts, the message conveyed is the same—a repeated imperative to consume.

The Utopia of Consumption

The ethos of consumption has penetrated every sphere of our lives. As culture, leisure, sex, politics, and even death turn into commodities, consumption increasingly constructs the way we see the world. As William Leiss points out, the best measure of social consciousness is now the *Index of Consumer Sentiment*, which charts optimism about the state of the world in terms of willingness to spend. The decision to buy a washing machine or a fur coat depends less on finances than on subjective reactions to everything from congressional debates to crime and pollution.[15] Consumption hierarchies, in which commodities define life-styles, now furnish indications of status more visible than the economic relationships of class positions. Status is thus easy to read, since the necessary information has already been nationally distributed through advertising. Moreover, for many, the very construction of the self involves the acquisition of commodities. If the world is understood through commodities, then personal identity depends on one's ability to compose a coherent self-image through the selection of a distinct personal set of commodities.

As central institutions in the realm of consumption, shopping malls constantly restructure both products and behavior into new combinations that allow commodities to penetrate even further into daily life. Most directly, the mall, as its domination of retail sales indicates, functions as an extremely efficient agent for the circulation of large numbers of goods. However, the rigid financial and merchandising formulas that guarantee and maximize its profits restrict the range and variety of goods it can offer. Retailers and shoppers are equally subject to a commercial logic that forces both to constantly justify themselves by concretely realizing the abstract concept of consumption in money terms. These economic imperatives are clearly expressed in the inescapable measurement of mall success in terms of dollars per square foot.

Faced with such restrictions, the mall can realize its profits only by efficiently mediating between the shopper and the commodity. The process of shopping begins even before the shopper enters the mall, in the commercialized contemporary social environment that William Leiss has characterized as the "high-intensity market setting." Primed by a barrage of messages about what he or she "needs" (before the age of twenty, the average American has seen 350,000 television commercials), the shopper arrives at the mall with "a confused set of wants." Presented with a constantly increasing range of products, each promising specialized satisfaction, the shopper is forced to fragment needs into constantly smaller elements. These are not false needs, distinct from objectively determined "real" needs; rather they conflate material and symbolic aspects of "needing" in an ambiguous, unstable state. Because advertising has already identified particular emotional and social conditions with specific products, the continuous fracturing of emotions and artifacts forces consumers to engage in intensive efforts to bind together their identity and personal integrity. Consumption is the easiest way to accomplish this task and achieve at least temporary resolution.[16]

Similarly fragmented attributes make up the commodities themselves. These bundles of objective and imputed characteristics and signals are in constant flux, rendered even more unstable by the consumer's fluctuating desires. As Leiss observes, "the realm of needs becomes identical with the range of possible objects, while the nature of the object itself becomes largely a function of the psychological state of those who desire it."[17] The shopping mall prolongs this exchange by offering a plethora of possible purchases that continuously accelerate the creation of new bonds between object and consumer. By extending the period of "just looking," the imaginative prelude to buying, the mall encourages "cognitive acquisition" as shoppers mentally acquire commodities by familiarizing themselves with a commodity's actual and imagined qualities. Mentally "trying on" products teaches shoppers not only what they want and what they can buy, but also, more importantly, what they don't have, and what they therefore need. Armed with this knowledge, shoppers can not only realize what they are but also imagine what they might become. Identity is momentarily stabilized even while the image of a future identity begins to take shape, but the endless variation of objects means that satisfaction always remains just out of reach.[18]

The shopping-mall mix is calculated to organize the disorienting flux of attributes and needs into a recognizable hierarchy of shops defined by cost, status, and life-style images. These shops, in turn, reflect the specific consumption patterns of the mall's marketing area. Merchandise contextualized by price and image orients the shopper, allowing the speculative spiral of desire and deprivation to be interrupted by purchases. The necessity of this double action—stimulating nebulous desire and encouraging specific purchases—establishes the mall's fundamentally contradictory nature. To survive profitably, it must operate within the enormous disjuncture created between the objective economic logic necessary for the profitable circulation of goods and the unstable subjectivity of the messages exchanged between consumers and commodities, between the limited goods permitted by this logic and the unlimited desires released by this exchange.

The physical organization of the mall environment mirrors this disjuncture; this is one reason why conventional architectural criticism, a discourse based on visible demonstrations of order, has not been able to penetrate its system. All the familiar tricks of mall design—limited entrances, escalators placed only at the end of corridors, fountains and benches carefully positioned to entice shoppers into stores—control the flow of consumers through the numbingly repetitive corridors of shops. The orderly processions of goods along endless aisles continuously stimulates the desire to buy. At the same time, other architectural tricks seem to contradict commercial considerations. Dramatic atriums create huge floating spaces for contemplation, multiple levels provide infinite vistas from a variety of vantage points, and reflective surfaces bring near and far together. In the absence of sounds from outside, these artful visual effects are complemented by the "white noise" of Muzak and fountains echoing across enormous open courts. The resulting "weightless realm" receives substance only through the commodities it contains.[19]

These strategies are effective; almost every mallgoer has felt their power. For Joan Didion the mall is an addictive environmental drug, where "one moves for a while in an aqueous suspension, not only of light, but of judgment, not only of judgment, but of personality." In the film *Dawn of the Dead*, both zombies and their victims are drawn to the mall, strolling the aisles in numb fascination, with fixed stares that make it difficult to tell the shoppers from the living dead. William Kowinski identified *mal de mall* as a perceptual paradox brought on by simultaneous stimulation and sedation, characterized by disorientation, anxiety, and apathy. The jargon used by mall management demonstrates not only their awareness of these side-effects, but also their partial and imprecise attempts to capitalize on them. The Gruen Transfer (named after architect Victor Gruen) designates the moment when a "destination buyer," with a specific purchase in mind, is transformed into an impulse shopper, a crucial point immediately visible in the shift from a determined stride to an erratic and meandering gait. Yet shoppers do not perceive these effects as negative: the expansion of the typical mall visit from twenty minutes in 1960 to nearly three hours today testifies to their increasing desirability.[20]

Retail Magic

Malls have achieved their commercial success through a variety of strategies that all depend on "indirect commodification," a process by which nonsalable objects, activities, and images are purposely placed in the commodified world of the mall. The basic marketing principle is "adjacent attraction," where "the most dissimilar objects lend each other mutual support when they are placed next to each other."[21] Richard Sennett explains this effect as a temporary suspension of the use value of the object, its decontextualized state making it unexpected and therefore stimulating. Thus, placing an ordinary pot in a window display of a Moroccan harem transforms the pot into something exotic, mysterious, and desirable. This logic of association allows noncommodified values to enhance commodities, but it also imposes the reverse process—previously noncommodified entities become part of the marketplace. Once this exchange of attributes is absorbed into the already open-ended and indeterminate exchange between commodities and needs, associations can resonate infinitely.

At an early stage, malls began to introduce a variety of services, such as movies and restaurants, fast-food arcades, video-game rooms, and skating rinks, which, while still requiring expenditure, signaled the malls' expanded recreational role. As "mall time" has become an increasingly standard unit of measure, more and more promotional activities have appeared; first fashion shows and petting zoos, then symphony concerts (the Chicago Symphony performs regularly at Woodfield Mall), and even high-school proms. Hanging out at the mall has replaced cruising the strip; for teenagers, malls are now social centers, and many even find their first jobs there. Now malls have become social centers for adults as well. The Galleria in Houston has achieved a reputation as a safe and benevolent place for singles to meet, and "mall-walkers"—senior citizens and heart patients seeking a safe place to exercise—arrive at malls before the shops open, to walk a measured route around the corridors. Popular culture also attests to the incorporation of the mall into daily life. Recent films such as *Scenes from a Mall* and *Phantom of the Mall* suggest that virtually any cinematic genre can be successfully transposed to this familiar setting. *Beverly Center*, the first novel named for a shopping mall, recounts the torrid adventures of retail employees in a place "where everything is for sale and nothing comes cheap."[22] Proximity has established an inescapable behavioral link between human needs—for recreation, public life, and social interaction—and the commercial activities of the mall, between pleasure and profit in an enlarged version of "adjacent attraction." As developer Bill Dawson sums it up: "The more needs you fulfill, the longer people stay."[23]

Indirect commodification can also incorporate fantasy, juxtaposing shopping with an intense spectacle of accumulated images and themes that entertain and stimulate and in turn encourage more shopping. The themes of the spectacle owe much to Disneyland and television, the most familiar and effective commodifiers in American culture. Theme-park attractions are now commonplace in shopping malls; indeed, the two forms converge—malls routinely entertain, while theme parks function as disguised marketplaces. Both offer controlled and carefully packaged public spaces and pedestrian experiences to auto-dependent suburban families already primed for passive consumption by television—the other major cultural product of the fifties.

While enclosed shopping malls suspended space, time, and weather, Disneyland went one step further and suspended reality. Any geographic, cultural, or mythical location, whether supplied by fictional texts (Tom Sawyer's Island), historical locations (New Orleans Square), or futuristic projections (Space Mountain), could be reconfigured as a setting for entertainment. Shopping malls easily adapted this appropriation of "place" in the creation of a specialized theme environment. In Scottsdale, the Borgata, an open-air shopping mall set down in the flat Arizona desert, reinterprets the medieval Tuscan hill town of San Gimignano with piazza and scaled-down towers (made of real Italian bricks). In suburban Connecticut, Olde Mystick Village reproduces a New England Main Street, circa 1720, complete with shops in saltbox houses, a waterwheel, and a pond. Again, the implied connection between unexpected settings and familiar products reinvigorates the shopping experience.

The larger the mall, the more sophisticated the simulation. The West Edmonton Mall borrowed yet another design principle from Disneyland: the spatial compression of themes. To simultaneously view Main Street and an African jungle from Tomorrowland was a feat previously reserved for science fiction. By eliminating the unifying concept of "land"—Disneyland's main organizing principle—the WEM released a frenzy of free-floating images. If Disneyland's abrupt shifts of space and time suggested that to change realities could be as easy as changing channels on a television, the WEM, as one writer observed, was more like turning on all the channels at once.[24] Again, the principle of "adjacent attraction" ensures that these images will exchange attributes with the commodities in the mall. The barrage of diverse images, though, may heighten the unstable relationship of commodity and consumer needs to such a degree that the resulting disorientation leads to acute shopper paralysis. This discouraging prospect makes oases of relative calm, such as the water park and the hotel, necessary for recuperation. Even the all-inclusive mall must acknowledge perceptual limits.

The contrived packaging, obvious manipulation, and mass-market imagery of formula malls was not without critics, particularly among affluent and educated shoppers. To please this more demanding audience, developer James Rouse expanded the definition of "adjacent attraction" to incorporate genuinely historic and scenic places into the world of the mall. Rouse's successful packaging of "authenticity" made him a legend in development circles. "Festival marketplaces" such as Faneuil Hall in Boston, Harborplace in Baltimore, and South Street Seaport in Manhattan reject the architectural homogeneity of the generic mall in favor of the unique character of a single location enhanced through "individualized" design. These scenic and historic areas use cultural attractions such as museums and historic ships to enliven predictable shopping experiences. Festival marketplaces, then, reverse the strategy employed at the WEM—imagery is reduced and activities focus on a single theme rooted in a genuine context—but with comparable results, the creation of a profitable marketplace. Faneuil Hall attracts as many visitors each year as Disneyland, confirming Rouse's slogan: "Profit is the thing that hauls dreams into focus."[25]

Public Life in a Pleasure Dome

The shift from a market economy to a consumer culture based on intensified commodity circulation became apparent in the first mass-consumption environment, the Parisian department store, which, after 1850, radically transformed the city's commercial landscape. The enormous number of goods presented in a single location dazzled shoppers accustomed to small shops with limited stocks. By 1870, the largest of the *grands magasins*, the Bon Marché, offered a huge assortment of goods to ten thousand customers a day.[26] Moreover, the department store's fixed prices altered the social and psychological relations of the marketplace. The obligation to buy implied by the active exchange of bargaining was replaced by the invitation to look, turning the shopper into a passive spectator, an isolated individual, a face in the department-store crowd, silently contemplating merchandise. Richard Sennett observed that haggling had been "the most ordinary instance of everyday theater in the city," weaving the buyer and the seller together socially; but the fixed-price system "made passivity into a norm."[27]

Department stores gradually discovered the marketing strategies required by this new passivity and began to theatricalize the presentation of goods. Emile Zola modeled his *Au Bonheur des Dames* on the Bon Marché; it portrays the modern retail enterprise as hardheaded commercial planning aimed at inducing fascination and fantasy. Zola vividly describes the display practices that dazzled and intoxicated the mostly female customers: "Amidst a deep bed of velvet, all the velvets, black, white, colored, interwoven with silk or satin, formed with their shifting marks a motionless lake on which reflections of sky and landscape seemed to dance. Women, pale with desire, leaned over as if to see themselves." Another shopper is "seized by the passionate vitality animating the great nave that day. Mirrors everywhere extended the shop spaces, reflecting displays with corners of the public, faces the wrong way round, halves of shoulders and arms." Zola's retail pleasure dome alternates such disorienting perspectives with comfortable resting places, reading and writing rooms, and a free buffet, countering the escapist fantasy world with comfortable homelike spaces where shoppers could reacquire a sense of control.[28]

In fact, the shopper's dream world was always firmly anchored to highly structured economic relations. The constant and rapid turnover of goods demanded standardized methods of organization, subjecting employees to a factorylike order that extended beyond working hours into the carefully supervised dormitories and eating halls. A strict hierarchy separated the sales clerks, drilled in middle-class manners and housed in attic dormitories, from the proletariat that staffed the workshops and stables and slept wherever they could. Class boundaries also put limits on the "magic" of merchandising. For instance, stores like the Magasins Dufayel and Bazar de l'Hôtel de Ville, located closer to the proletarian northern and eastern suburbs, offered more straightforward selections of inexpensive goods to their working-class clientele.[29]

The possibilities of material abundance and mass consumption first suggested in Zola's department store also inspired a number of other nineteenth-century writers and thinkers. While the naturalist Zola called his novel "a poem of modern life," more speculative thinkers imagined ideal futures in which the problematic realm of production withered away completely, leaving consumption the dominant mode of experience. In America, Edward Bellamy's *Looking Backward* outlined a future in which reorganized production systems efficiently supplied necessities to the entire population, reducing the workday or eliminating the need for work altogether. In this labor-free world of material plenty, the idle masses could now devote themselves to the pursuit of self-realization and aesthetic pleasure as well as the idle rich. Other writers enlarged the miniature dream world of the department store into a full-scale Utopia. Inspired by temples of abundance such as Wanamaker's and Macy's, the novel *The World a Department Store*, written by Ohio department-store owner Bradford Peck, proposed an ideal state modeled after a department store that equitably supplied housing, food, and endless goods to its contented citizens.[30]

America after World War II seemed to promise the realization of many such dreams. The booming consumer economy offered a previously unimaginable prosperity, with full employment supplying consumers for the large-scale distribution of affordable goods, while advertising and planned obsolescence insured their continuous circulation. Standardized work weeks allowed free time for new leisure activities. Jobs and housing quickly migrated to the suburbs, propelled by Federal subsidies and guaranteed mortgage insurance, and highway programs initiated a cycle of growth by stimulating the automobile, oil, and construction industries. In the cities, even the poor had housing and money to spend. On the cities' edges, suburban growth produced an economic landscape of single-family tracts connected by superhighways and punctuated by shopping centers.

With suburbs and automobiles, downtown department stores were no longer relevant. Interstate highways and suburbs created the demand for commercial services in newly developed areas. City stores built suburban branches; roadside strips and strip centers (collections of stores with shared parking) grew up along major routes and at important intersections; and developers continued to construct tasteful shopping centers in upscale suburbs, following earlier prototypes such as the Roland Park Shop Center outside of Baltimore (1907) and Market Square in Lake Forest (1916). All of these forms provided convenient off-street parking.

J. C. Nichols, generally regarded as the father of the shopping center for his role in developing Country Club Plaza in Kansas City (1924), established many of the financial, management, and merchandising concepts that were fundamental to postwar shopping centers.[31] Nichols's 1945 Urban Land Institute publication, *Mistakes We Have Made in Developing Shopping Centers*, codified his experience into a list of 150 maxims, which covered everything from strategies to ensure local political support to adequate ceiling heights. Although Country Club Plaza's elaborate Mediterranean architecture—complete with tiled fountains and wrought-iron balconies—distinguished it from the bland exteriors of later centers, Nichols argued against any unnecessary expenditure on decor. The key to shopping-center success, he claimed, lay in providing abundant, even unlimited, parking. By 1950, as the varieties of neighborhood shopping centers merged into a single new form—the regional mall—Nichols's wisdom was confirmed.

After several false starts, the successful prototype of the classic dumbbell format finally emerged at Northgate in Seattle in 1947: two department stores anchoring the ends of an open-air pedestrian mall, set in the middle of acres of parking. Designed by John Graham, Jr., the innovative combination of easy automobile access and free parking with pedestrian shopping offered both suburban convenience and downtown selection. Graham's mall, a narrow pedestrian corridor modeled after a downtown street, efficiently funneled shoppers from one department store to the other, taking them past every store in the mall.[32] Similar multi-million-dollar malls multiplied, spurred on by the abundance of cornfield sites at agricultural-land prices and encouraged by Reilly's Law of Retail Gravitation, which posits that, all other factors being equal, shoppers will patronize the largest shopping center they can get to easily. This served as the rationale for ever-larger centers optimally located near the exits of new interstate highways.[33]

The consumers were ready, armed with postwar savings and the benefits of recent prosperity—vital necessities in the newly created world of the suburbs, where the new way of life depended on new ways of consuming. The ideal single-family home—inhabited by the ideal family, commuting father, housewife, and two children—demanded an enormous range of purchases: house, car, appliances, furniture, televisions, lawnmowers, and bicycles. The mass production of standardized products found a market of consumers primed by advertising, television, and magazines. In a landscape of stratified subdivisions, status, family roles, and personal identity found further expression in consumption. Without familiar neighborhoods and extended-family networks to set social standards, suburban families used their possessions as a mark of belonging. The suburb itself was a product: nature and community packaged and sold.[34]

Initially, shopping-mall design reinforced the domestic values and physical order of suburbia. Like the suburban house, which rejected the sociability of front porches and sidewalks for private backyards, the malls looked inward, turning their back on the public street. Set in the middle of nowhere, these consumer landscapes reflected the profound distrust of the street as a public arena visible in the work of such dissimilar urbanists as Frank Lloyd Wright and Le Corbusier. Instead, streets, preferably high-speed highways, served exclusively as automobile connections between functionally differentiated zones and structures. Although mall apologists cited earlier marketplace types to establish the mall's legitimacy, they ignored their different consequences for urban life. While Islamic bazaars and Parisian arcades reinforced existing street patterns, malls—pedestrian islands in an asphalt sea—further ruptured an already fragmented urban landscape. As suburbs sprawled, so did their only public spaces; the low-rise, horizontal forms of suburban centers reversed the tightly vertical order of traditional urban space.[35] Informal open areas landscaped with brick flowerbeds and spindly trees echoed frontyard imagery. Malls, composed of rows of basic boxes enlivened with porchlike overhangs, shared the design logic of the suburban tract; economics rather than aesthetics prevailed.

In 1956, the first enclosed mall—Southdale, in Edina, a suburb of Minneapolis—changed all this. Although its central court surrounded by two levels of shopping floors was quickly surpassed by more extravagant developments, Southdale's breakthrough design firmly established Victor Gruen in the pantheon of mall pioneers. By enclosing the open spaces and controlling the temperature, Gruen created a completely introverted building type, which severed all perceptual connections with the mall's surroundings. Inside, the commercial potential of enormous spaces was realized in theatrical "sets" where "retail drama" could occur. Mall developers rediscovered the lesson of the Parisian department store and transformed focused indoor spaces into fantasy worlds of shopping. Southdale was covered for practical reasons; Minnesota weather allows for only 126 outdoor shopping days. The contrast between the freezing cold or blistering heat outdoors and the mall's constant 72 degrees was dramatized by the atrium centerpiece, the Garden Court of Perpetual Spring, filled with orchids, azaleas, magnolias, and palms. Exaggerating the differences between the world outside and the world inside established a basic mall trope: an inverted space whose forbidding exteriors hid paradisiacal interiors. This combination was compelling enough to ensure that enclosed malls soon flourished even in the most temperate climates.

Recreating a "second" nature was only the first step; the next was to reproduce the single element missing in suburbia—the city. The enclosed mall compressed and intensified space. Glass-enclosed elevators and zigzagging escalators added dynamic vertical and diagonal movement to the basic horizontal plan of the mall. Architects manipulated space and light to achieve the density and bustle of a city downtown—to create essentially a fantasy urbanism devoid of the city's negative aspects: weather, traffic, and poor people. The consolidation of space also altered the commercial identity of the mall. Originally built to provide convenient one-stop shopping, newly glamorized malls now replaced stores serving practical needs—supermarkets, drugstores, hardware stores—with specialty shops and fast-food arcades. Infinitely expandable suburban strips became the new loci for commercial functions expelled from the increasingly exclusive world of the shopping mall. Sealed off from the tasks of everyday life, shopping became a recreational activity and the mall an escapist cocoon.

As the mall incorporated more and more of the city inside its walls, the nascent conflict between private and public space became acute. Supreme Court decisions confirmed an Oregon mall's legal right to be defined as a private space, allowing bans on any activity the owners deemed detrimental to consumption. Justice Thurgood Marshall's dissenting opinion argued that since the mall had assumed the role of a traditional town square, as its sponsors continually boasted, it must also assume its public responsibilities: "For many Portland citizens, Lloyd Center will so completely satisfy their wants, that they will have no reason to go elsewhere for goods and services. If speech is to reach these people, it much reach them in Lloyd Center."[36] Many malls now clarify the extent of their public role by posting signs that read: "Areas in this mall used by the public are not public ways, but are for the use of the tenants and the public transacting business with them. Permission to use said areas may be revoked at any time," thus "protecting" their customers from potentially disturbing petitions or pickets. According to the manager of Greengate Mall in Pennsylvania, "We simply don't want anything to interfere with the shopper's freedom to not be bothered and have fun."[37]

Repackaging the city in a safe, clean, and controlled form gave the mall greater importance as a community and social center. The enclosed mall supplied spatial centrality, public focus, and human density—all the elements lacking in sprawling suburbs. The mall served as the hub of suburban public life, and provided a common consumer focus for the amorphous suburbs. In New Jersey—which had already spawned settlements such as Paramus, "the town Macy's built"—the importance of the Cherry Hill Mall as a focal point and an object of considerable local pride led the inhabitants of adjacent Delaware Township to change the name of their town to Cherry Hill. Reversing the centrifugal pattern of suburban growth, malls became magnets for concentrated development, attracting offices, high-rise apartments, and hospitals to their vicinity, thereby reproducing a central business district.

The financial success of the simulated downtown-in-the-suburbs also restimulated the actual downtowns, which had previously been weakened by regional malls. Newly placed urban malls brought their suburban "values" back into the city. In urban contexts the suburban mall's fortresslike structures literalized their meaning, privatizing and controlling functions and activities formerly enacted in public streets. Heavily patrolled malls now provide a safe urban space with a clientele as homogeneous as that of their suburban counterparts. In many cities, the construction of urban malls served to resegregate urban shopping areas. In Chicago, for example, white suburbanites coming into the city flocked to the new Marshall Field's branch inside the Water Tower Place mall on upper Michigan Avenue, effectively abandoning the original Marshall Field's department store in the downtown Loop to mostly black and Hispanic patrons.[38]

In more than one way, downtown malls cash in on the paradoxical prospect of a new order of urban experience, well protected from the dangerous and messy streets outside. Attempting a double simulation of New York, Herald Center, when it opened on 34th Street, offered thematized floors named for the city's familiar sites, such as Greenwich Village, Central Park, and Madison Avenue, which imitated their namesakes with businesses approximating their commercial character: sandal shops, sporting goods, and European boutiques. Not only were the actual places represented in name only, the "typical" goods for purchase reduced to caricature the rich mixtures of a real urban neighborhood. By reproducing the city inside its walls, the mall suggested that it was safer and cleaner to experience New York inside its climate-controlled spaces than on the real streets outside. This particular experiment failed, but did not discourage new efforts. On Times Square, a new mall project designed by Jon Jerde, Metropolis Times Square, tries to upstage the flash and dazzle of its setting with its own indoor light show, featuring hundreds of televisions, neon lights and laser projections. This hyper-real Times Square mall, sanitizing the sleaze and vulgarity outside, offers instead the tamer delights of shops, restaurants, and a cineplex open twenty-four hours a day.[39]

While the city began to incorporate suburban-style development, the suburbs became increasingly urban. Large numbers of jobs have moved to the suburbs, turning these areas into new metropolitan regions, "urban villages" or "suburban downtowns." Superregional malls at freeway interchanges—such as the Galleria outside Houston, South Coast Plaza in Orange County, and Tyson's Corners near Washington, D.C.—became catalysts for new suburban minicities, attracting a constellation of typically urban functions. Their current importance represents the culmination of several decades of suburban growth. The evolution of the Galleria–Post Oaks suburb in Houston, for example, began in the late fifties with shopping centers built to serve affluent residential areas. The construction of the 610 Loop freeway encouraged retail expansion, notably the Galleria, one of the first spectacular multi-use malls, followed by office buildings, high-rise apartments and hotels, and finally corporate headquarters. White-collar and executive employees moved to nearby high-income residential neighborhoods, which generated the critical mass necessary to support restaurants, movie complexes, and cultural centers. The result now surpasses downtown Houston, containing the city's highest concentration of retail space, high-rise apartment units, and hotels as well as the state's third-highest concentration of office space. It is also Houston's most visited attraction.[40]

Although these businesses and residences are concentrated spatially, they maintain the low-density suburban building pattern of isolated single-function buildings. Parallel to the 610 Loop and along Post Oak Boulevard rise clusters of freestanding towers, including the sixty-four-story Transco Tower. Each building stands alone, though, insulated by landscaping, parking, and roads. Sidewalks are rare, making each structure an enclave, accessible only by automobile. In this atomized landscape, the Galleria, pulsing with human activity, has expanded its role as town center even further, providing not only food, shopping, and recreation, but also urban experience. For many suburban inhabitants, the Galleria is the desirable alternative to the socially and economically troubled urban downtowns they fled. President Bush, casting his vote in the presidential election at the Galleria, symbolically verified the mall's status as the heart of the new suburban downtown.[41]

Hyperconsumption: Specialization and Proliferation

Throughout the period of shopping-mall expansion, economic and social changes were significantly altering the character of the consumer market. After 1970, it became evident that the postwar economic and social system of mass production and consumption was breaking down, fragmenting income, employment, and spending patterns into a much more complex mosaic. More flexible types of production appeared, emphasizing rapid cycles of products that quickly responded to the consumer market's constantly changing needs and tastes. Restructured industries and markets in turn produced a differentiated and fragmented labor force. The pyramid model of income distribution that supported the regional mall was being replaced by a configuration more like a bottom-heavy hourglass, with a small group of very high incomes at the top, and the middle disappearing into a much larger group of low incomes. This picture was further complicated by an increasingly uneven geographic distribution of economic development, which produced equally exaggerated differences between zones of prosperity and poverty.

In this unstable situation, the continued development of existing mall types was no longer assured. Heightened competition—between corporations, entrepreneurs, and even urban regions—forced a series of shakedowns in the industry. Although the system of regional malls continued to flourish, it was clear that the generic-formula mix no longer guaranteed profits.[42] (Industry experts agree that there are few regional holes left to fill, although the system can still absorb three or even four more megamalls.) Instead, malls expanded by multiplying and diversifying into as many different fragments as the market. An enormous range of more specialized and flexible mall types appeared, focused on specific niches in the newly dispersed market. Such specialization permitted more coherent matching of consumer desires and commodity attributes at a single location, making consumption more efficient, while greater diversity allowed a much greater collection of commodities to be merchandised than ever before.

Specialization occurs across a wide economic spectrum. In the richest markets, luxury malls, like Trump Tower on Fifth Avenue or the Rodeo Collection in Beverly Hills, offer expensive specialty goods in sumptuous settings, more like luxurious hotels than shopping malls. At the other end of the market, outlet malls sell slightly damaged or out-of-date goods at discount prices; since low cost is the major attraction, undecorated, low-rent buildings only enhance their utilitarian atmosphere. New smaller malls eliminate social and public functions to allow more efficient shopping. Strip malls, with parking in front, are the most flexible type: their false fronts can assume any identity, their format can be adjusted to any site, and they can contain any mix of products. Some strip malls focus on specific products or services—furniture, automotive supplies, printing and graphic design, or even contemporary art. In Los Angeles, more than three thousand minimalls (fewer than ten stores) supply the daily needs of busy consumers with convenience markets, dry cleaners, video stores, and fast-food outlets.[43]

In this overcrowded marketplace, imagery has become increasingly critical as a way of attracting particular shops and facilitating acts of consumption. Through a selective manipulation of images, malls express a broad variety of messages about the world both outside and inside the mall. Large, diverse cities like Los Angeles offer veritable encyclopedias of specialized mall types that cater to recent immigrant groups. Here the images retain a vestige of their cultural heritage: Korean malls have blue-tile temple roofs, Japanese malls combine Zen gardens with slick modernism to attract both local residents and touring Japanese. Minimall developers in Los Angeles also style their malls according to location: postmodern on the affluent Westside, high-tech in dense urban areas, and Spanish in the rest of the city.

Such imagery treads a thin line between invitation and exclusion. But if mall decor and design are not explicit enough to tell young blacks or the homeless that they are not welcome, more literal warnings can be issued. Since statistics show that shopping-mall crimes, from shoplifting and purse-snatching to car theft and kidnapping, have measurably increased, the assurance of safety implied by the mall's sealed space is no longer adequate.[44] At the WEM, the mall's security headquarters, Central Dispatch, is prominently showcased. Behind a glass wall, a high-tech command post lined with banks of closed-circuit televisions and computers is constantly monitored by uniformed members of the mall's security force. This electronic Panopticon surveys every corner of the mall, making patrons aware of its omnipresence and theatricalizing routine security activities into a spectacle of reassurance and deterrence. But the ambiguous attractions of a lively street life, although excluded from the WEM by a strictly enforced code of behavior, are not wholly absent. Rather, they are vicariously acknowledged, at a nostalgic distance to be sure, by Bourbon Street's collection of mannequins, "depicting the street people of New Orleans." Frozen in permanent poses of abandon, drunks, prostitutes, and panhandlers act out transgressions forbidden in the mall's simulated city.

Malls have not only responded to changing market conditions, but have also become trump cards in the increasing competition between developing cities and regions. The enormous success of projects like Faneuil Hall and the WEM have brought in revenue and attracted jobs, residents, and visitors to the cities. In a large-scale version of adjacent attraction, malls lend glamour and success to their urban setting, suggesting that the city is important, exciting, and prosperous.[45] Even if the WEM weakened the commercial power of Edmonton's downtown, as a whole it added luster and money to the urban region overall. Recognizing these potential benefits, cities now court developers with a range of financial incentives, from tax breaks to significant investments, in order to attract major mall projects. Faneuil Hall's success in generating adjacent development, such as condominiums, shops, and offices, led cities from Toledo to Norfolk into private-public ventures with the Rouse Company to build waterfront centers as catalysts for urban revitalization. This strategy can also backfire: Horton Plaza, San Diego's spectacular, enormously profitable, and heavily subsidized "urban theme park" mall has remained a self-contained environment, a city in itself—with little effect on its seedy surroundings.[46]

In Europe, political participation has gone even further. Municipal governments with extensive planning powers have taken over the developer's role themselves, though state sponsorship has produced no changes in the mall form. Thus, the Greater London Council developed festival marketplaces in Covent Gardens and the St. Katharine Docks as the commercial beachheads for larger urban redevelopment schemes. Built over the opposition of residents who demanded local services, the Covent Garden project produces municipal revenue by duplicating commercial formulas that attract tourists and impulse buyers. In Paris, the lengthy political battle over what would replace the razed Les Halles market was resolved by the decision to build a multi-level shopping center clad in the slick architectural modernism that the French state has adopted as its distinctive design image. This mall was the first step in the reorganization of the entire district and now stands at the center of a regional transport network, connected to a sequence of public sport, leisure, and cultural facilities through underground corridors.[47]

The World as a Shopping Mall

The spread of malls around the world has accustomed large numbers of people to behavior patterns that inextricably link shopping with diversion and pleasure. The transformation of shopping into an experience that can occur in any setting has led to the next stage in mall development: "spontaneous malling," a process by which urban spaces are transformed into malls without new buildings or developers. As early as 1946, architects Ketchum, Gina, and Sharp proposed restructuring Main Street in Rye, New York, as a pedestrian shopping mall; later Victor Gruen planned to turn downtown Fort Worth into an enclosed mall surrounded by sixty thousand parking spaces. More recently, a number of cities have reconstituted certain areas as malls simply by designating them as pedestrian zones, which allows the development of concentrated shopping. Self-regulating real-estate values allow these new marketplaces to create their own tenant mix, organized around a unifying theme; this, in turn, attracts supporting activities such as restaurants and cafes. In Los Angeles, even without removing automobiles, urban streets like Melrose Avenue and Rodeo Drive have spontaneously regenerated themselves as specialty malls, thematically based on new-wave and European chic.

Different stimuli can initiate this process. The construction of a regional mall in a rural area of DuPage county, outside Chicago, completely transformed commercial activities in the area. Afraid of losing shoppers to the mall, local merchants in Naperville, an old railroad town, moved to transform its main street into a gentrified shopping area of antique shops and upscale boutiques. By emphasizing Naperville's historical small-town character, providing off-street parking, and offering specialized shops not available in malls, Naperville developed a commercial identity that allowed it to coexist harmoniously with the mall.[48] When its historical center was inundated by tourists, Florence turned the Via Calzaioli between the Duomo and the Piazza Signoria into a pedestrian zone, which soon resembled an outdoor Renaissanceland mall with the two monuments serving as authentic cultural anchors. Shoe and leather shops, fast-food restaurants, and the inevitable Benetton outlets—offering merchandise available at malls all over the world—took over from older stores, as tourists outnumbered local residents. In France, state policies to ensure the preservation of historical centers awarded large subsidies to small cities like Rouen, Grenoble, and Strasbourg. This unintentionally redefined commerce: as pedestrian zones brought more shoppers into the center and greater profits attracted national chains of luxury shops, stores for everyday needs disappeared, replaced by boutiques selling designer clothing, jewelry, and gifts.[49]

Clearly, the mall has transcended its shopping-center origins. Today, hotels, office buildings, cultural centers, and museums virtually duplicate the layouts and formats of shopping malls. A walk through the new additions to the Metropolitan Museum in New York with their enormous internal spaces, scenographic presentation of art objects, and frequent opportunities for purchasing other objects connected to them, produces an experience very similar to that of strolling through a shopping mall. The East Wing of the National Gallery of Art in Washington, D.C., designed by I. M. Pei, is an even closer match. The huge skylighted atrium is surrounded by promenades connected by bridges and escalators; individual galleries open off this space, placed exactly where the shops would be in a mall. Potted plants, lavish use of marble and brass, and, in the neon-lit basement concourse, fountains, shops, and fast-food counters make the resemblance even more striking.[50]

Indeed, as one observer has suggested, the entire Capitol Mall has been malled. A hodgepodge of outdoor displays, a giant dinosaur, a working 1890s carousel, the gothic fantasy of Smithson's sandstone castle, and NASA rockets hint at the range of time and space explored in the surrounding museums. Here, old-fashioned methods of systematically ordering and identifying artifacts have given way to displays intended for immediate sensory impact. Giant collages include authentically historical objects like *The Spirit of St. Louis*, supported by simulated backgrounds and sounds that recall Lindbergh's famous flight. In the Air and Space Museum, airplanes, rockets, and space capsules are suspended inside a huge central court, slick graphics direct visitors to the omni-max theater, and gift shops offer smaller replicas of the artifacts on display.[51] The barrage of images, the dazed crowds, are all too familiar; the museum could easily be mistaken for the WEM. The Museum of Science and Industry in Chicago presents a similar spectacle. Mannequins in glass cases reenact significant moments in the history of science; visitors line up to tour the full-size coal mine; families sample ice cream in the nostalgic ambience of Yesterday's Main Street, complete with cobblestones and gaslights. In the museum shops, posters and T-shirts serve as consumable surrogates for artifacts that stimulate the appetite but cannot themselves be purchased.

If commodities no longer dominate, this is because the salable product no longer carries the same importance, since history, technology, and art, as presented in the museums, have now become commodified. The principle of adjacent attraction is now operating at a societal level, imposing an exchange of attributes between the museum and the shopping mall, between commerce and culture. Even the Association of Museum Trustees, by meeting at Disney World to discuss new research-and-development strategies, acknowledges this new reality. The world of the shopping mall—respecting no boundaries, no longer limited even by the imperative of consumption[52]—has become the world.

Silicon Valley
Mystery House

You can see it to the north of Highway 280 as you drive west through San Jose before swinging northwest toward Palo Alto—a fabulous display of industrial wealth, technical ingenuity, arcane knowledge, creative imagination, devoted teamwork, and a vitality born of obsession. It is the Winchester Mystery House, a bizarre remnant of the Gilded Age, open daily to tourists who marvel at the oddities of the mansion's architectural style: 160 finely crafted rooms arranged in a four-story labyrinth with 10,000 windows, stairways leading nowhere, doors opening onto blank walls, secret corridors, push-button gaslights, and everywhere the number 13 repeated in bathrooms, windowpanes, and delicately inlaid wooden floors and panels. All of this sprang from the tormented vision of Sarah Pardee Winchester, heiress to the fortune left by the manufacturer of the Winchester Repeating Rifle. After her husband died in 1881, Sarah Winchester began to fear that the vengeful ghosts of those killed by Winchester rifles during the settlement of the West were about to descend upon her. At a séance in Boston, a medium advised her to find a house whose design would attract benign spirits and confuse evil ones. In 1884 she moved to San Jose and purchased a nine-room ranch house, which she immediately started to renovate and expand. For the next thirty-eight years Mrs. Winchester employed dozens of carpenters and craftsmen twenty-four hours a day to implement ersatz-Victorian plans she claimed to have received from the spirits. Her death would be forestalled, she believed, as long as the expansion continued; the secret was to keep on building. This strategy worked splendidly until 1922, when Sarah Winchester, eighty-three, died in her sleep and all construction on the mansion ceased.[1]

It seems a relief to step outside the gates of this deranged, haunted monument into the very citadel of cool-headed, post-industrial rationality. Silicon Valley, home to thousands of high-tech firms and tens of thousands of scientific and technical professionals, spreads over the northwest quarter of Santa Clara County, an area once famous as the prune capital of America. Named for the silicon semiconductors that are the heart of the region's industry, it is not a valley at all, but rather the nearly flat area south of San Francisco Bay. Journalists started using the term Silicon Valley in the 1970s to describe the unprecedented concentration of microelectronics firms—Hewlett-Packard, IBM, Intel, National Semiconductor, Amdahl, Rolm, Tandem, Apple, Atari, and countless others—that have headquarters or large branch offices here. Widely celebrated for its technical virtuosity and economic dynamism, Silicon Valley has become a major destination for foreign scientists and entrepreneurs eager to admire its accomplishments and emulate its methods. Along with Manchester of the 1820s, Pittsburgh of the 1890s, and Detroit of the 1920s, the valley of chips stands as one of history's paradigmatic centers of industrial production.

Now several decades old, Silicon Valley offers one working model of what a postindustrial society might look like. While some features of its way of life are clearly particular to a specific time and place, others suggest the shape of things to come. But if Silicon Valley is the model for cities of the future, exactly what is the future it holds in store? Which features of the place are the most salient? Will the *place* itself matter at all?

A Very Clean Orchard

Microelectronics is clearly the dominant industry in and around Santa Clara County. Of the county's one and a quarter million residents, more than 200,000 are employed directly by firms producing semiconductors, computers, software, communication systems, and the like. The rest work primarily in occupations that provide material supplies, advertising, repair, housing, and transportation to the industry, as well as a wide range of financial, legal, custodial, and educational services. Indeed, it is difficult to find a person or family not connected in some way to this all-encompassing industry. Even the largest newspaper in the area, the *San Jose Mercury News*, sees itself as a kind of industrial house organ, giving front-page banner headlines to stories like this one from the mid-1980s: JAPANESE PRODUCE 256K RAM CHIP. To this community, the important world events are those that indicate an upturn or downturn in the electronics business or some innovation that will alter the terms of competition.

Although the valley is the center of a dynamic, worldwide, multi-billion-dollar industry, it has no center of its own. During the post–World War II economic boom that plowed under the orchards and built acres of factories, office buildings, and homes, the identity of separate towns and cities gradually blurred together. Today as one drives from San Jose to Santa Clara, Sunnyvale, Mountain View, and Palo Alto, there is little indication where one town stops and another begins. Shopping malls, industrial parks, fast-food restaurants, and housing tracts blend together into a motley tapestry without clear edges or form. It is as if a reincarnation of Sarah Winchester had been elected head of the county planning commission and decided to extend the structures of the Mystery House into every corner of the land.

There are no serious contenders to become the region's urban focus. San Francisco, thirty miles to the north, is too far away to serve as the valley's economic or cultural hub. San Jose, the county's largest and fastest-growing municipality, seems a possible core, but its awkward spread belies the idea of a city. Silicon Valley, then, is the quintessential example of new California urbanism—a vast suburb with no central city to give it meaning and focus.

The coherence notably absent from the urban landscape, however, is supplied by something else: the microelectronics industry itself, with its laboratories, production facilities, investments, competition, skilled management, driven personalities, and international connections. The material and cultural spaces of the region's towns and cities do not provide a way of living separate but equal to the dominant business. Here the business is everything. Among Silicon Valley residents there is even a certain pride that other human interests have been demoted to secondary concerns; conversations in shops, restaurants, bars, and health clubs incessantly focus upon computers, technological innovation, and money.

Winchester Mystery House

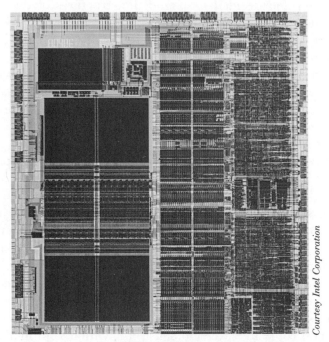

Intel486™ chip

The industry's extraordinary allure shapes not only the community's view of the present, but also its sense of the past. During the 1930s Santa Clara County boasted a hundred thousand acres of orchards and twenty thousand acres of vegetables. Touted as "The Valley of the Heart's Delight," it was a Garden of Eden where perpetual sunshine and the fruit of the trees symbolized a leisurely, gracious, almost Mediterranean way of life. But in a valley renamed for the crystalline structures derived from solid-state physics— transistors, integrated circuits, microprocessors, dynamic RAM chips, and the like—the agricultural past has been largely forgotten, now preserved only as a quaint backdrop for corporate operations.[2]

An example of this peculiar overlay can be seen at the enormous manufacturing and development facilities of IBM at Cottle Road in south San Jose. Occupying 520 acres of what was formerly Rancho Santa Teresa, fertile land first settled by a Spanish soldier in 1826, their primary function is to produce state-of-the-art mass-storage systems for very large capacity mainframe computers. Some of the technically refined operations performed here require "class-100" maintenance—rooms in which airborne particles can be no more than one hundred per cubic foot of air. Workers in these rooms wear sanitized white clothing and masks to ensure they cause no human contamination of delicate circuitry. In fields just across from these high-tech production facilities, IBM has preserved some of the orchards that once supported Rancho Santa Teresa. Essentially ornamental now, the neat rows of fruit trees are absolutely immaculate, perfectly trimmed, watered, and weeded, with not a single blade of grass or dead leaf on the ground beneath them. They exist as rare entities within the realm of vegetable life: state-of-the-art, class-100, clean orchards. The land's organic fertility has been encapsulated, reorganized within the thoroughly rational, hygienic order of the triumphant postindustrial complex.

This ability to absorb and transform knows no boundaries. Nearby communities, even outside Santa Clara County proper, have experienced the strong magnetism of Silicon Valley's wealth and power. A proliferation of microelectronics companies now threatens to consume the identities of a number of neighboring towns and cities, influencing economic development in Fremont and Hayward in the East Bay, the town of Gilroy to the southeast of San Jose, and Scotts Valley, Santa Cruz, and Watsonville over the mountains to the southwest, in Santa Cruz County. Laws restricting growth, like those passed in environmentally conscious Santa Cruz, have done little to slow this momentum. Former artichoke patches along the sandy shores of Monterey Bay are now sprouting the factories, offices, and warehouses of an amorphous development that might be called Silicon Bay. The process of growth follows a typical pattern: A firm starts small with a handful of employees in an inconspicuous rented building. Within a year or two, if all goes well, it expands rapidly, adding facilities and employees. Like the wildly expanding railroads described in Frank Norris's 1901 novel *The Octopus*, a portrait of California a century ago, the microelectronics industry reaches out to claim communities previously shielded from its grasp.[3]

In fact, the dreams and ambitions of Silicon Valley are so contagious that the place has begun to resemble another California dreamscape, Hollywood—that is, less a specific geographical location than a state of mind. In Hollywood, everyone's in show business and everybody's a star. Similarly, the mentality of Silicon Valley encourages aspirants far and wide to imagine themselves the budding stars and moguls of microelectronics, poised to make a killing with a flashy new product. This mystique affects not only individuals and start-up companies, but whole towns and cities as well. During the early 1980s several regions in the U.S. and abroad enthusiastically nominated themselves as contenders for the valley's crown: Silicon Mountain (Denver, Boulder, and Colorado Springs); Silicon Prairie (Dallas–Ft. Worth); Silicon Forest (Portland, Oregon); Silicon Glen (Scotland), as well as a truly legitimate rival, Route 128 circling Boston. Textbooks in business administration now offer step-by-step advice to hopefuls interested in "growing the next Silicon Valley."[4]

To read news reports about the inventions and fortunes of Silicon Valley, one might suppose they sprang up overnight. That mistaken impression overlooks a gestation period of four decades in which there were few headlines at all. The real story behind the success of Silicon Valley tells of a long, slow process involving the ideas and energies of thousands of people. Yet, although there was no grand architect, no master builder, the history of the region points to the defining influence of one man. Frederick Terman, engineering professor at Stanford University, showed what could happen if sophisticated scientific knowledge were to leave the academic sanctuary and apply itself to solid, profit-making concerns. It is the realization of Terman's grand idea that gives the valley its distinctive character and fascination.

A Paradise for Engineers

Born in 1900, Frederick Terman grew up in Palo Alto, the son of the Stanford University psychology professor who invented the Stanford-Binet IQ test and whose lifework was the study of gifted children. Terman graduated from Stanford in 1920 with a degree in chemistry and received his doctorate in electrical engineering from MIT in 1924. Soon he was hired at Stanford and given the task of developing a laboratory in radio communications. In an article in *Science* magazine in 1927, Terman cited data on the origins of new discoveries in the science of electricity, and argued that, compared to the capabilities of business firms, American engineering schools were distinctly inferior. That did not mean that institutions of higher learning were useless, but only that they needed to reassess their proper social role. "The laboratories of the big electrical companies make progress assured even without any university research, but the country's supply of technically trained young men can come only from the university."[5]

During the next several decades, Terman worked diligently to build Stanford into a center of engineering education and to foster strong links between the academy and the business world. He envisioned what he called "a community of technical scholars." Such a community, he wrote, "is composed of industries using highly sophisticated technologies, together with a strong university that is sensitive to the creative activities of the surrounding industry. This pattern appears to be the wave of the future."[6]

As dean of Stanford's School of Engineering and later as provost and vice-president of the university, Terman not only allowed science and engineering faculty members to work in industry, but actively encouraged them to do so. By the early 1950s, this policy was working well enough to enable the university to give it a permanent material embodiment in the new Stanford Industrial Park. Today the site, fashionably renamed Stanford Research Park, occupies 655 acres of land on the Stanford campus and leases space to some seventy technology-oriented firms. Its explicit purpose is to give corporations convenient access to the university's personnel and research findings and, in turn, to offer faculty members a chance to try out their ideas in the "real world" of business.

The success of this link between academic and corporate institutions, between the life of the mind and the lure of wealth, eventually attracted some of the world's best scientists, engineers, and managers to Palo Alto and its surrounding communities. What they found were not merely the interesting jobs, high incomes, and stock options that success can purchase anywhere, but also gracious California living in patio-style homes and the cultural environment provided by a major university. Most of all they found each other—a homogeneous community of high-achieving professionals in a wide range of fields, available at the workplace and at social events, a community composed almost entirely of former "gifted children" of the sort Terman's father studied decades earlier. The stimulating intellectual atmosphere and the many laboratories, think tanks, art galleries, and concert halls in northern Santa Clara County both symbolized and helped foster the region's economic boom.

Emblematic of Terman's influence upon the region's business was the success of two of his earliest students, William Hewlett and David Packard. In 1938, still the era of vacuum-tube electronics, they followed their mentor's advice and, in a garage behind the boarding house where they lived, founded a company to manufacture an audio oscillator. Walt Disney became their first customer, using eight audio oscillators in making the soundtrack for an ambitious full-length cartoon musical.[7] Thus Silicon Valley literally began with *Fantasia*. What Disney Studios spotted early on was the potential realized many decades later in sophisticated computer games, graphics, and sound synthesis: the power of electronics to create new realities, virtual realities, out of thin air. In the film, Leopold Stokowski shakes hands with Mickey Mouse: an old master joins forces with a fictitious creature—and a new tradition begins.

But Hollywood did not remain Hewlett-Packard's primary market for long. During World War II, the firm supplied electronic instruments to the United States military, and at war's end it continued to grow, selling its products to both the Pentagon and industrial firms. Today it is one of the major electronics firms in the region, employing some eighteen thousand people in the Bay Area.

If Stanford is a university modeled on a business firm, Hewlett-Packard is a business firm modeled on a university. It pioneered the campus-style architecture widely emulated by Silicon Valley firms, with well-appointed offices and laboratories placed in large and beautifully landscaped gardens. The company also perfected a quasi-academic managerial style—"management by walking around"—that gives employees considerable autonomy, with managers looking in only now and again, much like avuncular deans at liberal-arts colleges, to give advice and evaluate performance. This low-key method of motivation and control works well in organizations whose highly educated employees must display more than mere competence. Since fast-paced technological innovation is the essence of the electronics business, firms must find ways to stimulate and sustain the flow of new ideas. To keep its high-level employees happy and productive, Hewlett-Packard supplied a pleasant work environment, generous benefits, profit-sharing, paid sabbaticals, job security, and a lovely vacation park in the Santa Cruz Mountains.[8]

The Hewlett-Packard package of amenities was later adopted by other Silicon Valley firms, and sometimes carried to absurd extremes. By the late 1970s, high-tech firms had become notorious for lavishing the trappings of the good life on their employees. Afternoon beer busts, extravagant Christmas parties, and other ritual celebrations of collective well-being kept the workers happy. To accommodate the California mania for health and physical fitness, several firms built in-house exercise rooms equipped with chrome-plated Nautilus machines so that personnel could make optimum use of flextime. Some corporate leaders, most notably those at Apple and Tandem, embraced the techniques and therapies of humanistic psychology, looking to maximize profits through fostering personal growth. Widely popular philosophies of New Age business stressed "the pursuit of excellence," the felicities of "one-minute management," and the role of the corporation as a warm, nurturing, unifying force. "All people are good," proclaimed Tandem's founder James Treybig. "People, workers, management, and company are all the same thing."[9] Where the skills of scientists and engineers are the most sought-after commodities, this emphasis on "high-tech humanism" is an important bargaining chip in the competition for talent. Blending rationality with hedonism, work with play, business with pleasure, the culture of Silicon Valley offers a paradoxical utopia: a paradise for engineers.

From a purely technical standpoint, the crucial moment in the valley's rise as the center of discovery and invention came in 1956 when William Shockley, coinventor of the transistor at Bell Laboratories, decided to move to Palo Alto and begin his own company. He gathered eight of the most talented young engineers he could find and set about developing a new line of transistors. Shockley's brilliance as an inventor, however, was matched by his equally remarkable deficiencies as a manager. Soon he had alienated the core of his group of young engineers, who left to form their own company, Fairchild Semiconductor. One defector was Robert Noyce, who soon invented the integrated circuit—many transistors on a single, tiny silicon chip—which was the breakthrough that made microminiaturization feasible.[10]

Over the next fifteen years Fairchild was the source of a continuing series of inventions and spin-off companies—National Semiconductor, Intel, Advanced Micro Devices, and dozens of others—that now comprise the heart of the valley's economy. From the days of Shockley's "traitorous eight" to the present, the practice of engineers leaving their home companies to start new ventures has been the prevalent means through which the industry has expanded. In fact, growth through spin-off is the characteristic pattern of Silicon Valley development, a kind of urban mitosis in which mature cells divide to form new organisms roughly similar in form and function.

Although successful on the south shores of San Francisco Bay, this pattern has proved difficult to transplant to other parts of the country. As news of the technical and economic dynamism of Santa Clara County businesses spread during the 1960s and 1970s, a number of universities around the country sought to emulate Terman's Midas touch, building lavish industrial parks with large factory and office buildings on land next to their campuses and planting conspicuous TO SUIT TENANT signs on the front lawn. Such parks were thought to be a sure-fire method to attract vast sums of research-and-development money from the private sector, which could be used to enlarge university revenues and supplement the salaries of restless science and engineering faculty. While the strategy brought modest success in some instances, it was disappointing overall. High-tech firms felt little need to flock to the new academic-industrial theme parks. If corporations needed expertise or intellectual stimulation in a particular field, they could easily import well-qualified consultants. Why relocate just because an ambitious university president had gone into real estate?

Yet to fully understand why these hopes were frustrated, why it proved difficult to duplicate a formula so successful for Terman, Stanford, and Santa Clara County, one must take into account the factor most responsible for creating and sustaining Silicon Valley: the financial backing of the United States military.

The Electronics Race

The conflict in the Pacific during World War II brought a number of aircraft producers to the West Coast. California's sunny climate seemed particularly attractive, since it allowed year-round manufacture and testing of products. With the onset of the Cold War and the Korean War, California became the nation's busiest producer of jet fighters, guided missiles, and other sophisticated weapons systems. Los Angeles and San Diego, among the most conspicuous beneficiaries of increasing defense budgets, grew at phenomenal rates to meet the needs of a growing war machine.

Gradually, Santa Clara County too became an important focus for federal spending. Several features of the area attracted military contractors—Sunnyvale's Moffet Field naval air station, the ready availability of land, access to shipping facilities at the ports of San Francisco and Oakland, and the proximity of both Stanford and Berkeley as sources of well-trained scientists and engineers.[11] During the two decades after World War II, Sylvania, Fairchild, General Electric, Westinghouse, Philco-Ford, Kaiser, and other established firms all built plants in the region and began production under military contracts. Proving that it is always more profitable to beat plowshares into swords, the Food Machinery and Chemical Corporation (FMC) of San Jose, formerly a manufacturer of farm tractors, continued to make the Army tanks it had first produced in World War II. The most important piece of the growing defense ensemble arrived in 1956 when Lockheed Aircraft established a branch in the county. Today Lockheed Missiles and Space Corporation is the valley's largest employer, with some twenty-five thousand people on its payroll.

The permanent war economy provided fertile ground for the development of semiconductor technology. As a result of the increasing speed and complexity of modern weaponry, as well as the ever more subtle demands of command, control, communications, and military intelligence, the arms race became, to a great extent, an electronics race. The need for miniaturization, the fundamental contribution of microelectronics that would eventually transform modern society, was first felt in the realm of advanced weaponry. It would be hard to make "smart bombs" and the other machines of modern warfare with old-fashioned vacuum tubes and copper wires. The Department of Defense was prepared to spend whatever was required to produce miniature solid-state electronic components.[12]

A substantial portion of Defense money went to research and development. Between 1958 and 1974 the government spent nearly $1 billion in semiconductor R&D—nearly as much as all private firms together. Eager to push new electronic devices into production, the military offered lucrative cost-plus contracts, tacitly subsidizing the construction of manufacturing plants. During the Kennedy, Johnson, and Nixon presidencies, at the height of the arms and space races with the Russians, money was no object for the military, NASA, or their legislative overseers. Hence the early generations of electronic components could be developed virtually without regard to cost. And once a useful item was perfected, the Pentagon was a highly reliable, long-term, sometimes exclusive market. In 1965 the military purchased 70 percent of the nation's output of integrated circuits.

Without the military's enormous subsidies throughout the 1950s and 1960s, the microelectronics industry would certainly have developed more slowly, for there was no socially pressing need for its semiconductors, no significant domestic market. The government in effect absorbed the burden of risk of a number of highly uncertain enterprises—a point usually ignored in media and industry folklore. As silicon chips began to enter video games, microwave ovens, personal computers, and other consumer goods in the late 1970s, credit for the industry's success was showered on entrepreneurs like Robert Noyce, Jerry Sanders, Steven Jobs, Nolan Bushnell, Sandra Kurtzig, and their venture-capitalist counterparts Fred Adler, Arthur Rock, William "Pitch" Johnson, and other high-rolling risk-takers. They were praised as the contemporary equiv-

alents of the California prospectors of 1849, searching for the lode-
stone, assembling a grubstake, following their instincts for
adventure, gambling everything, and striking gold. Although their
story echoed a cherished American myth, the new entrepreneurs
and venture capitalists had merely skimmed the cream off the top,
bottled it, and made a killing. The true long-term risk-takers, over-
looked by *Fortune* and *Business Week*, were ordinary American
taxpayers.

Public investments in microelectronics spawned countless opportunities for private gain. For once it was in place, the complex
of plants and personnel assembled to produce weapons could turn
out a broad variety of other goods. In much the same way that
automobile production in Detroit depends upon thousands of shops
that supply parts, pieces, and services for the auto industry, microelectronics in Santa Clara County depends on an array of smaller
companies—perhaps eight thousand—ready to provide everything
from complex circuit boards to packing boxes. This diverse, flexible
collection of suppliers, subcontractors, and services makes it relatively easy for any company, new or old, to move into a new
product line. Several of the earliest personal computers—the original Apple, for example—were low-cost machines built from off-
the-shelf components. In retrospect, the only puzzle is why it took
so long for personal computers to emerge from this well-developed
industrial landscape.

Silicon Valley's flair for speed and adaptability is expressed in
a fascinating new architectural specimen: the tilt-up building.
Reinforced-concrete walls, one or two stories high, are poured on
site and then tilted up to join with other parts of the structure.
Used as assembly plants, warehouses, and even offices, these win-
dowless shells provide makeshift quarters for established firms as
well as new enterprises. Along the Central Expressway in south
Sunnyvale, blocks of tilt-ups that house the latest dreams of
inventor-entrepreneurs form a kind of start-up ghetto. The periodic
appearance of FOR LEASE signs in the place of corporate logos is one
indicator of the industry's cycles of boom and recession.

The combination of such flexible facilities, a highly talented,
mobile pool of engineering talent, and extensive support services
makes the region an enduring power in an extremely mercurial
business. In recent years Silicon Valley has, in fact, lost its domi-
nance in worldwide sales of semiconductors—the very product that

gave the place its name—to its competitors in the Far East. Much
of the problem can be traced to the decline and fall of the U.S.
consumer-electronics industry, a market that might have sustained
heavy demand for chips.[13] The weakening of the microelectronics
industry has caused much anguish among American businessmen
and politicians; in the mid-1980s an advisory panel of leading
scientists and engineers warned that national security would be
jeopardized if the United States were forced to rely on foreign
suppliers for crucial military electronic components. Bowing to such
pressures, the Reagan administration defied its own gospel of free
trade and endorsed flagrantly protectionist measures to bolster the
chipmakers' flagging fortunes. But this wave of panic was largely
unfounded. In fact, the region has the economic resiliency needed
to weather, for many years to come, the industry's inevitable cycles.

Envious of Silicon Valley's wealth and vitality, many declining
American cities have tried desperately to persuade an electronics
firm or two to move to town, convinced that the industry was the
key to the valley's success. A more faithful replication, however,
would be to anticipate the next boom in government spending and
to position the local economy to be at the receiving end of new
military contracts and grants. In fact, even as Silicon Valley began
to shift emphasis toward broader markets from the mid-1960s
onward, it nevertheless maintained its economic foundations in the
federal budget. When the period of phenomenal growth for microelectronics entered a long slump in the middle 1980s, some
observers worried that the shift from consumer goods, such as video
games and personal computers, to military contracts in excess of
$4 billion a year represented a new and dangerous development
for the industry. But such concerns reflected only the naïve humanism of Silicon Valley's social ideology—the belief that microelectronics is an inherently humane, democratizing force in
contemporary life—rather than anything substantial in the region's
economic history, one intimately tied to Pentagon largesse.

A Divided Culture

During this period of serious decline in American farming and heavy
industry, the success of Silicon Valley raises hopes that a new way
of life, a new variety of social organization is taking shape. Behold,
its prophets say, the dawning of the Computer Age, the Information

Society, the Service Economy! Whether or not these grand expectations are valid, the valley does present one working model of a plausible future. If one studies this future not only for the technological and financial wealth it promises, but also as an emerging set of social and cultural possibilities, which features stand out?

Most notable, of course, are the valley's tens of thousands of scientists, engineers, and managers responsible for high-level research, development, and corporate management. This well-educated and well-paid elite is, for the most part, male and white; relatively few women or minorities are included among the privileged. Working in well-equipped laboratories and office buildings in the northern part of the county (as near to Stanford University as possible), they own homes in the wealthy hillside communities of Los Altos, Portola Valley, Saratoga, and Los Gatos.

To gain entrance to this exclusive community a person must hold a bachelor's degree or better in electrical engineering, computer science, or physics, preferably from one of the nation's better universities. Even want ads in such nonscientific fields as personnel management often specify that applicants must have a strong technical background; the club is closed to most others. Initiates are welcomed into a strenuous, fast-paced life of long hours and intense pressure. For many, work becomes an all-consuming passion, leaving little time for family, friends, or any activities not directly connected to the project at hand. Many, to be fair, were work-obsessed even before they took their first jobs. The same young men who denied themselves any time off as they "tooled" away to earn their degrees at MIT, Cal Tech, and Berkeley feel no regrets about putting in prodigious amounts of overtime for computer firms. T-shirts worn by the development team of the first Apple Macintosh proudly announced WORKING 90 HOURS A WEEK AND LOVING IT. This is a world in which, contrary to the expectations of Thorstein Veblen, wealth no longer generates a leisure class. Silicon Valley's professionals simply do not have much spare time, nor do they appear to want any. It is exactly what one might expect of a paradise built by and for engineers: a place where hard work has become life's ultimate pleasure.

The flexibility of the valley's system of material facilities is matched by a plasticity of social roles and relationships. Encouraged by plentiful employment opportunities and the industry's norms of career advancement, people change jobs frequently. Each year, an estimated 30 percent of Silicon Valley employees switch companies. In recognition of this fact, the benefits packages of many companies exclude a pension plan; after all, who is going to stay around long enough to collect? This willingness to abandon the pretext to long-term institutional relationships is reflected in other social statistics as well. During the early 1980s there were more divorces in Santa Clara County than marriages. To help relieve the psychological stresses attendant on such instability—and to profit from the abundance of disposable income—a wide range of therapies, dating services, and "personal growth" seminars have sprung up. Werner Erhardt's est and its successor the Forum, for example, remained popular. One enterprising organization marketed itself as a reliable matchmaker for persons who knew only one fact about a potential date: his or her automobile license number.

The cultural ideal for this community of workaholics is the heroic inventor-entrepreneur. According to the model, to succeed one must emulate the industry's early movers and shakers—conceive a new product idea, gather a skilled team, convince venture capitalists to invest, abandon one's present employer, and found a new corporation. Everyone understands that the valley's greatest rewards come from being the owner of a successful new enterprise. The payoff comes when a fledgling outfit "goes public," selling its shares for the first time on one of the public stock exchanges. The founders of such an outfit may then become wealthy virtually overnight. The little county of Santa Clara contains some two thousand millionaires.

At popular gathering places like Walker's Wagon Wheel Restaurant and Lounge in Mountain View, engineers and managers "network" and discuss ideas for new corporate ventures with inexhaustible delight. For established firms, of course, the tendency of high-level employees to split off and form new enterprises can become a serious problem. Far-sighted firms have begun to support what is called "intrapreneurship," allowing employees to experiment with risky inventions and product ideas within the existing organizational setting. It remains to be seen how effective such a policy will be in apportioning the profits reaped from new innovative technologies.

The characteristic aphorisms of Silicon Valley businessmen reflect both pride and cynicism. "Money is life's report card." "He who dies with the most toys, wins." "Cash is more important than your mother." But within this fast-paced, upwardly mobile social stratum it is often difficult to display just how well you're doing. One's colleagues are often too busy to notice subtle signs of success. Hence the tribe has evolved a system of easily discernible public symbols—the display of luxury automobiles, for example—to mark exactly who stands where. More than posh hillside homes, more than expensive California sportswear, the vehicles on the roads and in the corporate parking lots narrate prosperity. Newly hired young engineers drive Porsches or BMWs; older, more established professionals with families generally prefer Mercedes or Jaguar sedans; the most extravagant movers and shakers like to be seen in Lamborghinis and other custom-built sports cars. American and Japanese automobiles, even the most expensive models, are excluded from the sacramental code, thought to lack the styling and technical refinement that engineers value.

The wealth, daring, and flamboyance of Silicon Valley notables was tragically dramatized in the story of computer executive Dennis Barnhart. On the day in June 1983 that Eagle Computer of Los Gatos went public, Barnhart, forty, its president, became an instant multimillionaire. To celebrate his triumph he joined friends for a few drinks and then invited a female companion for a spin in his new Ferrari. A short while later the speeding car blasted through a highway railing and rolled down an embankment, killing Barnhart and his passenger.

The region, however, is not peopled exclusively by flashy entrepreneurs and work-obsessed technical professionals. In stark contrast stands the valley's second world—its hundred thousand manufacturing and assembly workers. They are, for the most part, female, poorly educated, unskilled, and badly paid. They are also predominantly nonwhite—Hispanic, Asian, and black. Although their work is based primarily in the production facilities of the north of the county, they live in modest apartments and houses south of there, mainly San Jose and adjacent Campbell. Far from the creative centers of planning, imagining, moving and shaking, the working life involves routinized production processes—making semiconductors, handling noxious chemicals, stuffing chips in circuit boards, assembling computers and communications equipment, putting it all in boxes.[14]

While production work of this sort is quite plentiful, it is also highly precarious. Layoffs and plant closings are common even in good times, as the industry shifts investment priorities. Efforts to unionize the microelectronics workers have made little progress. Firms let their production employees know that if unions are established and wage rates rise too high, workers in the valley will not be able to compete with low-cost, nonunionized labor in other parts of the country and in foreign lands. Employees discovered to be union organizers have been fired. The last official move to establish a union came at Atari in November 1983, and failed—29 in favor, 143 opposed.[15] Silicon Valley companies are therefore able to continue their operations unencumbered by collective-bargaining agreements covering wages, hours, benefits, and work rules.

In place of a negotiated relationship between labor and management, the corporation offers itself as a warm, sustaining, encouraging environment, of the very sort cherished by technical professionals and praised in valley lore. But at the lower levels, the much-heralded opportunities for participation and self-actualization often look more like paternalism and the denial of autonomy. Invited to ritual beer busts where they rub shoulders with those earning six-figure salaries and listen to speeches outlining the company's latest marketing initiatives, factory workers participate in the uplifting unity of purpose that is somehow meant to dignify their $4.50 to $8.00 hourly wage. Clearly, it would be impolite for employees to question the policies, much less the motives, of such enlightened, generous firms. Journalist Robert Howard reports that one woman was given stern warnings when she skipped the obligatory coffee breaks at Hewlett-Packard. A supervisor explained that "Bill and Dave," the founders of the organization, "give you this ten minutes and you really ought to take advantage of it."[16]

Workers with steady employment at an hourly wage in normal factory settings are comparatively lucky, however. The less fortunate, usually recent immigrants from Third World countries, often have little choice but to take jobs in Silicon Valley sweatshops, garages, and warehouses where they are paid by the piece to assemble electronic subcomponents. Some do low-paid assembly work in their home, a repeat of the putting-out system of the early industrial revolution. For those who live in this part of the "post-industrial" world, the most common aspiration is certainly not to float a stock issue for a new computer or software firm. Their hopes center on sheer survival.

It is an ingenious feature of capitalism to shift the social costs of production away from those reaping the profits. In Santa Clara County, this means that the heaviest burdens of social services—schools, police, fire departments, welfare agencies, and the like—fall upon the less affluent communities of the "south county," those with the greatest needs for public services and the smallest tax base. The average income of the thousands of production workers living in San Jose, Campbell, and Milpitas is about one-fifth of the incomes earned by the professional-managerial personnel of the "north county." Yet these municipalities are left to deal with problems of crime, drug use, illiteracy, and other social ills that afflict low-income and minority residents—to provide, in effect, the institutions of social repair that support the economic gains enjoyed elsewhere.[17]

Drastic inequalities are apparent in the north as well. Just across Highway 101 from Frederick Terman's university-industrial complex, easily visible from atop Stanford's Hoover Tower, is East Palo Alto, a ghetto in which chronic poverty and unemployment among its black residents seem beyond remedy. East Palo Alto is a forgotten land, the neighborhood next door, territory excluded from and seldom acknowledged by "the community of technical scholars." The unprecedented concentration of wealth, talent, and problem-solving ability in the area has somehow left the problems of its poor and minority members unaddressed and unsolved. School-children in East Palo Alto have test scores in the lowest tenth of the nation's youth, while children in Palo Alto routinely test in the top one percent. But for those in the white, self-actualizing utopia of Silicon Valley the poor and black are of little concern. Creative energy is reserved for integrating computer software, not integrating society.

The income gap between rich and poor in the region is growing steadily wider. For those at the lower end of the scale, the American Dream offers its traditional solace of upward mobility. Indeed, the minority communities of the south county show a certain cultural and economic vitality, filled with locally owned markets, ethnic restaurants, and shops catering to Hispanic and Asian residents. To all appearances, those doing well are the ones who have gathered enough resources to escape the assembly lines altogether and start businesses outside microelectronics. But the industry itself contains no ladder of upward movement for those on its bottom rungs. Even lower-level administrative jobs typically require a engineering bachelor's degree or better. The Yankee ideal that one can work hard, demonstrate talent, and thereby ascend through the ranks is simply not a tenable life strategy; the industry's rigidly stratified social structure contains no middle levels to which one can aspire. For technical professionals, rapid turnover in work opportunities usually means better pay and enhanced responsibility; for factory workers, however, it requires moving from one dead-end job to another in a never-ending cycle of sideward mobility.

Beyond this state of tedium and insecurity lies the prospect that the routine jobs upon which thousands depend will simply be elim- inated. A common ideal shared by engineers and businessmen en- visages totally automated factories—workplaces without workers. In computer-integrated manufacturing, or CIM, the goal is to co- ordinate the activities of design, testing, materials handling, fab- rication, assembly, and inspection within completely computerized plants while keeping human presence to a minimum. Thus, de- velopers of the Apple Macintosh factory prided themselves on hav- ing cut labor's share of production costs to less than two percent. As the hardware and programming techniques of the field become ever more sophisticated, the ancient dream of living with perfect automata seems within reach.

Although the valley's two primary social strata are separate in many respects, they do find common ground twice each day—on the roadways. Because thousands of production workers must travel from their homes in the south county to factories in the north, and because public transportation is woefully inadequate, the highways and side streets of the valley experience severe congestion in the morning, afternoon, and early evening. The industry's staggered work hours seem only to compound the problem. In Sunnyvale, the "evening" traffic jam on Highway 280 begins as early as 3:00 P.M. Thus, the handsome, speedy luxury cars owned by engineers and managers inch along bumper to bumper with the hordes of old Chevies and Toyotas driven by the production workers. There is an ironic but uniformly unpleasant justice here.

Monumental congestion is merely one of the failings of Silicon

Valley as an urban environment. Over the past three decades the rapid growth in jobs has not been matched by adequate housing construction. Land-use policies strongly favored industrial expansion, creating a permanent jobs-housing imbalance throughout the region. When the influential Santa Clara County Manufacturing Group joined city and county planners in sounding the alarm, little was done to rezone the land for residential building. During the late 1970s the price of houses and rentals skyrocketed, making Silicon Valley one of the most expensive housing markets in the country. The continuing inflation in housing costs has become so severe that many companies now have difficulty attracting talented professionals to the area; on seeing how little house a handsome paycheck can buy, prospective employees think twice before moving.

The shortage of housing is matched by a paucity of public spaces. There is no civic center with the kinds of theaters, museums, well-stocked libraries, or sports stadiums that up-and-coming cities usually boast. Neither are there parks or recreational areas of any significance. With the exception of the upscale Stanford Shopping Center, Eastridge, Valley Fair, and other malls that dot the landscape, the valley offers no public gathering places attractive to local residents or visitors. What Gertrude Stein once observed about Oakland could more aptly be said of Silicon Valley: "There is no there there."

To some extent, this dearth of public space can be attributed to the almost total lack of civic concern among Silicon Valley business leaders. With few exceptions, the nouveau riche of Santa Clara County have not given generously of their personal or corporate fortunes. Unlike the earlier generations of industrialists and financiers who proudly donated libraries, parks, and concert halls, the new microelectronics moguls show little philanthropic impulse. As a *San Jose Mercury News* editorial observed: "To all outward appearances, Silicon Valley corporations inhabit the twenty-first century, with the sleekest offices, the smartest computers, and the slickest managerial talent. But when it comes to supporting charities or the arts, the attitude is more what one would expect to find in the executive suite of Ebenezer Scrooge Enterprises, Ltd."[18]

If there is a fatal flaw that threatens the sustainability of Silicon Valley's economic miracle, the handling of toxic chemicals could well be the one. It turns out that the celebrated "clean rooms" and "clean industry" are pure at the surface only. Production processes employ hydrochloric and hydrofluoric acids to etch and harden microelectronic components. Toxic solvents—dichloroethane, trichloroethane, methylene chloride, carbon tetrachloride, chloroform, and others—are used to clean the chips and other computer components. Such chemicals now pose serious problems not only to the health of production workers who handle them, but to the environment of the region as well. For years the industry stored its chemical wastes in underground tanks that proved susceptible to spills and seepage. Eventually these substances entered the soil and groundwater, where they now threaten the wells and whole aquifers that supply sixty percent of water used by local communities. Silicon Valley now has more hazardous waste sites on the U.S. government's Superfund cleanup list than any region of similar size in the country.[19]

For those who have made it in Silicon Valley's microelectronics and computer industry, such troubles still seem little cause for concern. After all, much of their enjoyment of the good life does not take place in the local setting, but in such affluent and fashionable hot spots as Malibu, Lake Tahoe, Palm Springs, Aspen, Telluride, or the Caribbean. High status comes from owning a house or condominium in one of these high-priced retreats and commuting on weekends in one's private plane. Undoubtedly, the access to beautiful residences elsewhere contributes to the notorious lack of concern on the part of the industry's leaders in the valley's chronic problems of congestion, housing, pollution, and environmental decay. Since personal and monetary commitments are focused on the workplace, not in the community at large, evidence of serious social and environmental ills does not incite action. For there are enough good jobs, nice homes, fine restaurants, convenient golf courses, yacht harbors, airports, and, of course, California sunshine to make the place seem, although somewhat tarnished, still almost ideal.

Technopolis or the Digital City?

The peculiar mixture of triumphs and failures that constitute Silicon Valley presents an ambiguous legacy. What can one conclude about the significance of the place for the shape of urban life? We have already seen that there are many who would like to copy its techniques and institutional forms wholesale, hoping to revitalize older cities or even to create whole new ones. Japanese social planners, for example, believe they have found the exact formula, one they express in a masterplan called "Technopolis." As part of its multifaceted "take-lead" strategy for the twenty-first century, the Ministry of International Trade and Industry (MITI) has begun to develop as many as nineteen science-and-technology centers along the Japanese archipelago. Each Technopolis is to be built around an existing "mother city." Each will include an integrated mix of industrial firms, academic institutions, and housing, along with a state-of-the-art digital information network, proximity to an airport or bullet-train station, and "a pleasant living environment conducive to creative research and thinking."[20] Each would become a dynamic center of scientific discovery, technological innovation, and industrial productivity. In the Japanese tradition of taking good ideas from abroad, refining them, and mass-producing them as high-quality products, the attempt here is to clone Silicon Valley many times over. Hence a series of New Towns are being created, not in response to the intrinsic needs of contemporary urban life, but through an effort to mass-produce the cultural magic of high technology.

First announced in MITI position papers of the early 1980s, the development plan is now being rapidly implemented through the close cooperation of national and local governments, business firms, and universities. The estimated $1 billion cost of each Technopolis will be financed by a combination of local taxes and contributions from business. By 1990, more than $10 billion had been spent building the basic infrastructure of industrial parks and university complexes at Nagaoka, Toyama, Hamamatsu, Okayama, and other cities. Ironically, both Hiroshima and Nagasaki have been selected as prime sites for such development. The Japanese believe that the Technopolis plan will enable them to vanquish other high-technology competitors, including Silicon Valley itself—for unlike their California forebears, they are armed with both the comprehensive strategy and the firm social consensus needed to carry it off.[21]

One has to admire the Japanese for the audacity of this project. In its Asian metamorphosis, Frederick Terman's modest proposal to revitalize Stanford University has at last become a grand scheme for the reconstruction of an entire society. But although the purposes and methods seem plausible, it remains to be seen whether or not Japan Inc. has correctly understood the true thrust of post-industrial development. For the idea of the Japanese Technopolis is marred by what may well be a lethal anachronism, an exaggerated commitment to a single nation-state.

As the twenty-first century draws near, an astonishing change becomes evident: the logic of economic and technical development in the microelectronics industry and other high-technology fields tends to eliminate the importance of spatially defined communities. The microcosm of microelectronic chips makes possible a macrocosm of worldwide communications and corporate operations. For those able to take advantage of this situation, the important horizons become global ones. Operations take place where there is the greatest competitive advantage. Locating a factory, office, shopping center, or even company headquarters in a particular place becomes an expediency of the moment, much like plugging a portable computer into an available outlet. The industrial age, with its cumbersome equipment and communications, tended to create productive enterprises in more or less permanent locations—the textile mill, the steel plant, the automobile factory. Very little in the material conditions of an information society requires any such anchor.

The most obvious feature of this new globalism—the movement of microelectronics production plants "offshore," to Asia and Latin America—has already been felt in Silicon Valley. Wages in Taiwan, Singapore, Korea, Mexico, Brazil, and other favored countries are typically a tenth of what is paid in the valley. The repressive political regimes that often govern such societies are able to provide their corporate suitors with lucrative tax advantages, a stable social order, and a compliant, nonunion factory workforce, made up mainly of young women. This does not mean that less-developed countries will be long-term beneficiaries of this economic activity. Often the plants and offices built have very narrow functions—stuffing circuit boards or keypunching data, for example—with few local economic spin-offs; hopes that a full-blown Silicon Valley will take root are unrealistic. Indeed, if the work is a sort that can be profitably automated, it is likely that operations will move yet again to locations favorable to the maintenance of robots—back to North America and Europe.

The transnational mobility of the industry is also apparent in patterns of corporate ownership and management. During the late

1970s and 1980s, favorable conditions in currency markets and
international finance contributed to an influx of foreign capital to
the United States, especially from Japan and Europe. Intel, one of
the bulwarks of semiconductor production in Silicon Valley, was
purchased by the Swiss corporation Schlumberger. Japanese investors became significant shareholders in a number of electronics
firms. To an increasing extent, microelectronics firms are now only
nominally "American" concerns. Capital has finally become thoroughly transnational.

Looking for ways to enhance technical innovation while min-
imizing its costs, a number of firms have formed multinational
consortia for research and development, sharing both facilities and
staff. Production and personnel managers are easily transferred
across national boundaries in order to improve worldwide operations. Some Silicon Valley spokesmen still worry about maintaining
America's lead in microelectronics for "national security reasons,"
and they lobby for protectionist legislation to prevent foreign take-
over of the microelectronics markets. But such talk is by now largely
hollow. The leading corporations in the field are quickly becoming
global combinations with no particular national allegiance.

The tendency to dissolve existing spatial boundaries is evident
not only in production and finance but also in the very form of the
organizations that rely upon computers and satellite communications. More and more, the space that matters is an electronic space
that requires no bodily human presence or physical movement.
What are in effect whole rooms, buildings, streets, highways, and
cities can be formed by computer programs linked by telecommunications signals. Conversations and meetings take place within
the architecture of teleconferencing software. Complex decisions
are made through the intersection of streams of computerized data.
World-shaking events unfold through the confluence of digital messages. Silicon Valley, Route 128 in Massachusetts, and similar centers of high technology in the United States, Japan, and elsewhere
are, in effect, launching pads which propel into orbit an expansive,
powerful, but increasingly disembodied form of social organization.

A convenient metaphor for these digital electronic entities can
be found in the representational signs used in office automation.
The goal of such systems is to do away with such material encum-
brances as rooms, desks, file cabinets, file folders, documents, and,
ultimately, people, and to make the information formerly contained

in such office paraphernalia available instantaneously on the screen. Operations on a computer display replace the physical and social movement of the workplace. In ergonomically well-designed programs, physical apparatus is represented by icons—nostalgic little pictures of file cabinets, folders, and documents. When a person wants a particular piece of information, she directs an electronic arrow to the relevant icon and the task is done. No longer is there any need to move through a world of people and material things; one does not, for example, get up from a desk, walk to a file cabinet, get a piece of paper, go back to one's desk, and sit down. Everything is done with a few simple motions on a keyboard or with a mouse. Computerized information systems of this kind replace bodily movement with actions that take place within a universe of symbols.

An iconography of a similar sort can now be employed to map the relationships, organizations, and events of high-speed digital communications. Within computer based networks linked by satellites and fiber-optic cables, separate nodes communicate easily over vast distances. Those who have access to the network's hardware and software enter a vast structure of offices, meeting rooms, mailboxes, bulletin boards, gateways, corridors, command centers, storage areas, repair shops, banks, police stations, even coffee houses, all composed of electronically produced images available instantaneously to the eye.

Consider, for example, the electronically embodied currency markets that now operate nonstop, twenty-four hours a day, worldwide. Within this intense, fast-paced, ethereal environment, banks and investment firms speculate on fluctuations of the yen, dollar, mark, pound, and franc, making millions on the slightest change in a currency's value. The traders who participate in the market stare intently at computer terminals that supply information on second-to-second changes in price, and signal their sales and purchases through brief messages over telephones. In this way the wealth of nations ebbs and flows in a setting totally detached from the traditional spatially centered arrangements that formerly produced and controlled economic value. Things ultimately achieve their worth as blips on a display terminal; all else is an illusion. To believe that this rapidly evolving complex is committed to preserving the values or power of any particular locality is, to an increasing extent, fantasy. Those who dwell on the land rather than in digital networks are frequently shocked to discover that the farms, factories, and offices that once seemed so crucial have been judged obsolete by the electronic city. It is likely that a similar surprise awaits those who suppose, as the Japanese Technopolis strategists evidently do, that the energy of high-tech development can be confined to designated geographical areas. As long as new institutions and practices rely upon advanced computing and tele-communications, it is foolish to suppose they will remain rooted in place.

To enter the digital city one must first be granted access. Having "logged on," one's quality of participation is determined by the architecture of the network and its map of rules, roles, and rela-tionships. Technical professionals are usually greeted by a com-puterized version of the social matrix, an organizational form in which there is at least superficial equality, and ready access to information and one's coworkers. They experience computer net-works as spheres of democratic or even anarchic activity. Especially for those ill at ease in the physical presence of others (a feeling not uncommon among male engineers), the phenomenon of disembod-ied space seems to offer comfort and fulfillment. Here are new opportunities for self-expression, creativity, and a sense of mastery! Some begin to feel they are most alive, most free when wandering through the networks; they often "disappear" into them for days on end.

Ordinary workers, on the other hand, typically face a much different set of possibilities. As they enter an electronic office or factory, they become the objects of top-down managerial control, required to take orders, complete finite tasks, and perform ac-cording to a set of standard productivity measures. Facing them is a structure that incorporates the authoritarianism of the industrial workplace and augments its power in ingenious ways. No longer are the Taylorite time-and-motion measurements limited by an awkward stopwatch carried from place to place by a wandering manager. Now workers' motions can be ubiquitously monitored in units calculable to the nearest microsecond. For telephone operators handling calls, insurance clerks processing claims, and keypunch operators doing data entry, rates of performance are recorded by a centralized computer and continuously compared to established norms. Failure to meet one's quota of phone calls, insurance claims, or keystrokes is grounds for managerial reprimand or, eventually, dismissal. A report issued by the Office of Technology Assessment revealed that by the late 1980s, four to six million American office workers were already subject to such forms of computer-based surveillance.[22] Such systems do not, as utopian dreams of automation prophesied, "eliminate toil and liberate people for higher forms of work." While the old-fashioned secretary was expected to perform perhaps 30,000 keystrokes an hour, the norm for modern keypunch operators now is closer to 80,000.

For those who manage the systems of computerized work, the structures and processes offer a wonderfully effective means of control. Here is an electronic equivalent of Jeremy Bentham's Panopticon, the ingenious circular design that allowed the guardians of a prison, hospital, or school to observe every inmate while totally isolating the inmates from each other. For today's workers under panoptic scrutiny, the system is, of course, totally opaque. They are allowed to see only what the program allows. Closely watched and clocked, workers within the city of icons may find even fewer chances to express their individuality or participate in decisions than they did in the old-fashioned office or factory. When space is intangible, where do workers organize?

The ideologies that have arisen to describe and justify the new social patterns of the Information Age typically recognize only their positive aspects. "Information wants to be free," exclaims Stewart Brand, proponent of liberation through personal computing.[23] "When a system runs on information, there is an endless supply for everyone," argues an otherwise solid study of the microelectronics industry.[24] What such dewy-eyed conclusions overlook are the strong tools of institutional control made conveniently available to those who will shape the rules, roles, and relationships of the age of electronic information. To build an electronic space based upon democratic, egalitarian principles would require deliberate effort, not merely the cheerful assertion that liberation has already occurred. If the organizations now responsible for designing and building the channels of an emerging information society—banks, business firms, the military, government bureaucracies, security agencies, and the like—are simply to replicate their present structures (by no means an unlikely prospect), then chances for the widely proclaimed renaissance of direct democracy seem bleak.

Place and Hyperspace

In sum, perhaps the most significant, enduring accomplishment of Silicon Valley is to have transcended itself, and fostered the creation of an ethereal reality, which exercises increasing influence over embodied, spatially bound varieties of social life. Here decisions are made and actions taken in ways that eliminate the need for physical presence in any particular place. Knowing where a person, building, neighborhood, town, or city is located no longer provides a reliable guide to understanding human relationships and institutions. For within the digital city, key organizational entities have been reconstituted to resemble motherships floating in electronic hyperspace. Occasionally they descend, landing on Earth long enough to invest capital, deposit a high-rise building, fund a university research project, close a factory, or launch a clever public-relations campaign. Then, just as quickly, they beam up, disappearing into the vapor.

Confronted with this potent force, it is difficult for traditional land-based peoples, communities, and even nations to identify exactly where and how the crucial choices are being made. Because power is most effective when least seen, this may be the most insidious political capacity yet devised, one that threatens to turn all the world into a colony. But the colonized are not, as in earlier times, subjects of a particular country or regional economic empire. What governs now has neither boundaries nor surfaces nor mass. It is a phenomenon about which standard social theories and familiar categories of everyday experience have little to say. Indeed, we may soon have to discard place-oriented theories and sensibilities altogether because they have become obsolete.

In its dazzling complexity, the digital-electronic edifice is something Sarah Winchester could easily admire, a rapidly expanding structure generating new branches, chambers, and passageways in a never-ending process of self-elaboration. Outsiders who seek to penetrate its mysteries are greeted with a maze that is at once formidable and incorporeal, an architecture of countless baffling features—dummy institutions, glossy advertising surfaces, mass-media spectacles, channels of participation leading nowhere—forms that mask the true order of things and prevent anyone from discovering the locus of control. While the structure also includes concrete, material features, its central core exists only as a pattern of signals mirroring the ebb and flow of capital.

Surely old Mrs. Winchester would also have understood the motive force behind this rapidly evolving hyperspace. Just as she renovated her mansion night and day in a frantic attempt to escape the vengeful ghosts of ill-gotten gain, so too the expansion of the digital electronic city is driven by fear, in this case the fear of declining profits. Building offices here, production plants there, hotels, shopping centers, and satellite hookups in a wild metastasis, computer-based organizations scour the globe in search of fleeting increments of economic advantage. That very little of the advantage has any direct connection to the pressing needs of local populations is of scant concern to those engaged in assembling this magnificent entity. In fact, no one knows whether all the frenzied activity will produce a humanly desirable world or even one that is remotely livable. Not to worry. Our destiny looms ahead, beyond the old mansion, beyond the Valley of the Heart's Delight, beyond the worried nations, beyond even our planet itself. Sarah Winchester could well be proud to see her vision so faithfully and superstitiously implemented: the secret is to keep on building.

N E I L   S M I T H

New City, New Frontier: The Lower East Side as Wild, Wild West

On the evening of August 6, 1988, a riot erupted along the edges of Tompkins Square Park, a small green in New York City's Lower East Side. It raged through the night, with the police on one side and a diverse mix of antigentrification protesters, punks, housing activists, park inhabitants, artists, Saturday-night revelers, and Lower East Side residents on the other. The battle followed the city's attempt to enforce a 1:00 A.M. curfew in the park, on the pretext of "cleaning out" the growing numbers of homeless people living or sleeping there, kids playing boom-boxes in the early hours, buyers and sellers of drugs using it for business. But many local residents and park users saw the action differently. The city was seeking to tame and domesticate the park to facilitate the already rampant gentrification of the Lower East Side. GENTRIFICATION = CLASS WAR! read leaflets and banners at the Saturday-night demonstration aimed at keeping the park open. "Die, yuppie scum!" went the chant. "Yuppies and real-estate magnates have declared war on the people of Tompkins Square Park," announced one speaker. "Whose fucking park? It's our fucking park," became the recurrent slogan. "CLASS WAR ERUPTS ALONG AVENUE B," explained the *New York Times*.[1]

In fact it was a police riot that ignited the park on the night of August 6. Clad in space-alien riot gear and concealing their badges, the police forcibly evicted everyone from the park before midnight, then mounted a series of "cossacklike" baton charges against demonstrators and locals assembled along the park's edge. "The cops seemed bizarrely out of control," recounted one eyewitness. They were "levitating with some hatred I didn't understand. They'd taken a relatively small protest and fanned it out over the neighborhood, inflaming hundreds of people who'd never gone near the park to begin with." Four hundred and fifty officers were eventually deployed, and they were "radiating hysteria," according to another witness. There were "cavalry charges down East Village streets, a chopper circling overhead, people out for a Sunday paper running in terror down First Avenue." Finally, a little after 4:00 A.M., the cops withdrew in "ignominious retreat," and jubilant demonstrators reentered the Park, dancing, shouting, and celebrating their victory. Several protesters used a police barricade to ram the glass-and-brass doors of the Christodora condominium, which abuts the park and which had become a hated symbol of the neighborhood's gentrification.[2]

In the days following the riot, Mayor Edward Koch described Tompkins Square Park as a "cesspool" and blamed the riot on "anarchists." The head of the Patrolmen's Benevolent Association enthusiastically agreed: "social parasites, druggies, skinheads, and communists"—an "insipid conglomeration of human misfits"—were the cause of the riot. The Civilian Complaint Review Board received 121 complaints of police brutality, and on the basis of a four-hour videotape made by local artist Clayton Patterson, seventeen officers were cited for "misconduct." Six were eventually indicted but none were ever convicted.[3] The police commissioner conceded that a few officers may have become a little "overenthusiastic" due to "inexperience," but he clung to the official policy of blaming the victims.

In the next months, the loosely organized antigentrification and squatters' movements grew quickly and connected with other local housing groups. Now a "liberated space," Tompkins Square quickly attracted more homeless people, some of whom also began to organize. But the city also regrouped. Citywide park curfews (abandoned after the riot) were gradually reinstated; new regulations governing the use of Tompkins Square were slowly implemented; several Lower East Side buildings occupied by squatters were demolished; and in July 1989, periodic police raids destroyed the tents, shanties, and belongings of park residents. By now there was an average of some two hundred people in the park on a given night, perhaps three-quarters men, the majority African-American or white, but also Latino, Native Americans, Caribbeans. On December 14, the coldest day of winter, the park's entire homeless population of more than three hundred people was evicted, their belongings carted away in a queue of garbage trucks. It would be "irresponsible to allow the homeless to sleep outdoors" in such cold weather, explained the parks commissioner, Henry J. Stern. In fact, the city's provision for the evicted ran only to a "help center" that, by one account, "proved to be little more than a dispensary for baloney sandwiches."[4] Many evictees from the park were taken in by local squats. In January 1990, with the supposedly progressive mayor David Dinkins newly installed, the city felt so confident in its recapture of the park that it announced a "reconstruction plan." Throughout the summer, the basketball courts were dismantled and rebuilt with tighter control over access; wire fences closed off newly constructed playgrounds designated for children or specific sports; and park regulations were more strictly enforced. In an effort to evict them, city agencies also heightened their harassment of neighborhood squatters, who now spearheaded the antigentrification movement. As the next winter closed in, though, more and more of the city's evictees filtered back to the park and began again to construct semipermanent structures.

In May 1991, the park hosted a Memorial Day concert organized under the slogan "Housing Is a Human Right," producing a further clash between police and park users. With as many as seventy shanties now constructed, the Dinkins administration finally closed the park at 5:00 A.M. on June 3, evicting more than two hundred park dwellers. Alleging that Tompkins Square had been stolen from the community by the homeless, Mayor Dinkins declared, "The park is a park. It is not a place to live." An eight-foot-high chain-link fence was erected, a posse of more than fifty uniformed and plainclothes police were delegated to guard the park, and a $2.3 million reconstruction was begun almost immediately. In fact, three park entrances were kept open and guarded by police: one opposite the Christodora condominium on Avenue B provided access to a dog run; the others accessed a children's playground and basketball courts. According to *Village Voice* reporter Sarah Ferguson, the closure of the park marked "the death knell" of an occupation that "had come to symbolize the failure of the city to cope with its homeless population."[5] No alternative housing was offered evictees from the park; people again moved into local squats, or filtered out into the city, but sporadic demonstrations and the instant burgeoning of a new shantytown—dubbed Dinkinsville—on a vacant lot only a block away suggest that the closure of Tompkins Square Park has in no way defused the struggle by homeless people.

As the site of the first major antigentrification struggle, ten-acre Tompkins Square Park has become a trenchant symbol of the new urbanism that threatens to reconstruct not just the Lower East Side but neighborhoods in cities throughout the developed capitalist world. Relinquished to the working class, abandoned to the poor and unemployed amid postwar suburban expansion, reconfigured as reservations for racial and ethnic minorities, the terrain of the inner city is suddenly valuable again, perversely profitable. Gentrification represents a geographical, economic, and cultural reversal of postwar urban decline and abandonment. Conceptualized by apologists in the spuriously neutral language of "neighborhood recycling" or the more celebratory "revitalization," gentrification has already remade SoHo and the Upper West Side and even affected such unlikely Manhattan neighborhoods as Harlem and Hell's Kitchen. From Amsterdam to Sydney, whole swaths of inner-city working-class neighborhoods have been transformed into middle-class and upper-middle-class havens devoted to boutique retailing, elite consumption, and upscale housing. Gritty industrial metropolises such as Baltimore and Pittsburgh have completely transformed their images; even Glasgow, known for its shipbuilding, its steel and textile industries, its militant working class, and more recently for its chronic deindustrialization, celebrated 1990 as European Capital of Culture, an honor previously bestowed on Paris, Amsterdam, Florence, and Berlin.

Gentrification is widely scripted in the media as a struggle to conquer and civilize the urban frontier. As the real-estate industry pushes new development and rehabilitation into existing neighborhoods, threatened areas mount a militant defense of home and community. In London's Notting Hill, for example—the scene of an annual Caribbean carnival that regularly pits police against local celebrants—there is a clear "front line" between a gentrified zone on the one side and a diverse working-class community on the other. But the new urbanism also expresses larger global shifts. Although systematic gentrification first began to convert neighborhoods to middle-class use in the 1960s and 1970s, a series of wider transformations—global economic expansion in the 1980s, the restructuring of national and urban economies toward services, recreation, and consumption, and the emergence of a global hierarchy of world, national, and regional cities—have propelled gentrification from a marginal preoccupation of the real-estate industry to the cutting edge of urban change.

Nowhere are these forces more evident than in the Lower East Side (*Loisaida* in the vernacular Spanglish; the East Village in art and real-estate lingo), a dense tenement neighborhood squeezed between the Wall Street financial district, Chinatown, Greenwich Village, 14th Street, and the East River. Described by local writers as a "frontier where the urban fabric is wearing thin and splitting open," and as "Indian country, the land of murder and cocaine,"[6] the Lower East Side began to experience sustained gentrification in the late 1970s. Not just supporters but antagonists of gentrification have found the frontier motif irresistible. "As the neighborhood slowly, inexorably gentrifies," wrote one reporter in the wake of the 1988 riot, "the park is a holdout, the place for one last metaphorical stand."[7] Several weeks later, *Saturday Night Live* made this Custer image explicit in a skit staged in a frontier fort. Custer (presumably Mayor Koch) welcomes the belligerent warrior Chief Soaring Eagle into his office and inquires: "So how are things down on the Lower East Side?"

The social, political, and economic polarization of "Indian country" is drastic and fast becoming more so, reflecting trends in the rest of the country. Apartment rents soared throughout the 1980s and with them the number of homeless people; record levels of luxury condo construction were matched by a retrenchment in public housing provision; a Wall Street boom generated seven- and eight-figure salaries while unemployment trapped the unskilled; women account for an increasing percentage of the homeless and poor while social services are axed; and the conservatism of recent years spews a recrudescent racism. With the emergence of deep recession in the early 1990s, rents have stabilized even declined, but unemployment has soared, and the polarization of the 1980s has only magnified. The Lower East Side lies at the vortex of such global and local forces. Though the details are local, they bring into sharp relief the general contours of a new urbanism.

Tompkins Square lies deep in the heart of the Lower East Side. On its southern edge along 7th Street a long slab of residential

buildings overlooks the park, mostly late-nineteenth-century five-
and six-story walk-up tenements adorned with precariously affixed
fire escapes, but also including a larger apartment building with a
dreary, modern, off-white facade. To the west the tenements along
Avenue A are barely more interesting, but the many cross-streets
and the mix of smoke shops, ethnic and upscale restaurants, bars,
candy stores, newsagents, groceries, and nightclubs make this the
liveliest side of the park. Along 10th Street on the northern edge
stands a stately group of Civil War–era townhouses gentrified, for
the most part, in the 1970s. To the east Avenue B presents a more
broken frontage of tenements, St. Brigid's Church, and the infamous Christodora apartment house—a sixteen-story brick mono-
lith built in the 1920s that dominates the local skyline.

The park itself is unexceptional. An oval rosette of curving,
criss-cross walkways, it is shaded by large plane trees and a few
surviving elms. The walkways are lined by long rows of cement
benches with green painted wooden slats, and some of the wide
grassy patches are badly in need of reseeding. At the south end,
before the park's closure, the bandshell hosted music performances,
plays, and other entertainment events, and offered shelter and a
place for park residents to store bedding. At the north end is an
enclosed, empty garden bounded by handball and basketball
courts. By day the park was filled with Ukrainian men on benches
playing chess, young guys selling drugs, yuppies walking to and
from work, a few remaining punks with boom-boxes, students reading, Puerto Rican women strolling babies, residents walking dogs,
kids in the daycare playground. Since the riot there were also cops
in cruisers and photographers, and of course a growing population
of homeless people attracted to this "liberated" if still-contested
space. Park residents constructed very diverse encampments using
tents, cardboard, wood, bright blue tarpaulins, any scavenged material to provide shelter. Hard-drug users traditionally congregated
in "crack alley" on the southern edge; a group of mostly working
people clustered on the east side; Jamaican Rastafarians hung out
by the temperance fountain closer to Avenue A; political activists
closer to the bandshell.

Variously scruffy and relaxing, free-flowing and energetic, but
rarely if ever threatening unless the police are on maneuvers, Tompkins Square exemplifies the kind of neighborhood park that Jane
Jacobs adopted as a *cause célèbre* in her famous antimodernist

tract, *The Death and Life of Great American Cities*. If it hardly has the physical features of a frontier, neither class conflict nor police riots nor the frontier iconography are new to Tompkins Square. The area was originally a swampy wilderness; its earliest displacees may have been the Manhattoes who "sold" the island to Peter Minuit in 1626 for some rags and beads. Donated to the city by the fur trader and capitalist John Jacob Astor, the swamp was drained, a park was constructed in 1834, and ever since it has been a traditional venue for mass meetings of workers and the unemployed. The financial collapse of 1873 threw unprecedented numbers of workers and families out of job and home; the city's charitable institutions were overwhelmed, and at the urging of the business classes the city government refused to provide relief. "There was in any case a strong ideological objection to the concept of relief itself and a belief that the rigors of unemployment were a necessary and salutary discipline for the working classes." A protest march on January 13, 1874 was turned into what a young Samuel Gompers remembered as "an orgy of brutality":

> By the time the first marchers entered the Square, New Yorkers were witnessing the largest labor demonstration ever held in the city. The Mayor, who was expected to address the demonstration, changed his mind and, at the last minute, the police prohibited the meeting. No warning, however, had been given to the workers, and the men, women and children marched to Tompkins Square expecting to hear Mayor Havemeyer present a program for the relief of the unemployed. When the demonstrators had filled the Square, they were attacked by the police. "Police clubs," went one account, "rose and fell. Women and children went screaming in all directions. Many of them were trampled underfoot in the stampede for the gates. In the street bystanders were ridden down and mercilessly clubbed by mounted officers."[8]

Within an hour of the first baton charges, a special edition of the *New York Graphic* appeared in the streets with the headline: "A Riot Is Now in Progress in Tompkins Square." Following the 1874 police riot, the New York press provided a script that would have gratified the 1988 mayor. Decrying the marchers as "communists," and evoking the "red specter of the commune," the *New York World* consistently built an analogy between the repression of the urban hordes in Tompkins Square and Custer's "heroic" expedition against the savage Sioux in the Black Hills of what is now South Dakota.[9]

The immigration of hundreds of thousands of European workers and peasants in the following decades only intensified the political struggles in the Lower East Side and its depiction in the press as a depraved environment. By 1910, some 540,000 people were crammed into the area's tenements, all competing for work and homes: garment workers, dockers, printers, laborers, craftsmen, shopkeepers, servants, public workers, writers, and a vital ferment of socialists, communists, anarchists, and activist intellectuals devoted to working-class politics and struggle. Successive economic recessions forced many into periodic unemployment; tyrannical bosses, dangerous work conditions, and a lack of workers' rights elicited large-scale union organizing efforts; and landlords proved ever-adept at rent-gouging. The Triangle Waist fire of 1911 engulfed 146 Lower East Side women, imprisoned behind locked sweatshop doors, forcing them to jump from windows to their deaths on the pavement below. Still the bosses resisted unionization. The decade ended with the Palmer Raids of 1919, which visited state-sponsored political repression especially against the now-notorious Lower East Side. In the 1920s as the suburbs burgeoned, landlords throughout the neighborhood let their buildings fall into dilapidation, and those residents who could were moving to the suburbs.

Like other parks, Tompkins Square came to be viewed by middle-class social reformers as a necessary "escape valve" for this dense settlement and volatile social environment. Following the 1874 riot, it was redesigned explicitly to create a more easily controllable space, and in the last decades of the century the reform and temperance movements constructed a playground and a fountain. The contest for the park continued, and when in 1938 Robert Moses proposed building a baseball diamond on most of its sixteen acres, local demonstrations forced a more modest reconstruction. A hangout for Beat poets in the 1950s and the so-called counter-culture in the 1960s, the park and its surroundings were again the scene of violence in 1968 when police attacked hippies sprawling in defiance of KEEP OFF THE GRASS signs.

The explosive history of the park belies its unremarkable form and makes it a fitting locale for a "last stand" against gentrification and the new urbanism.

Building the Frontier Myth

Roland Barthes once proposed that "myth is constituted by the loss of the historical quality of things." Richard Slotkin elaborates that in addition to wrenching meaning from its temporal context, myth has a reciprocal effect on history: "history becomes a cliché."[10] We might add the corollary that meaning must also be made transportable over space: the loss of the geographical quality of things is equally central to the making of myth. The greater the separation of events from their constitutive geography, the more powerful the mythology and the more clichéd the geographical landscapes expressing and expressed through the mythology.

The social meaning of gentrification is increasingly constructed through the vocabulary of the frontier myth. This appropriation of language and landscape—the new city as new frontier—seems at first playfully innocent, and in any case so common as to be wholly unremarkable. Newspapers habitually extol the courage of urban homesteaders, the adventurous spirit and rugged individualism of the new settlers, brave pioneers, presumably going where no (white) man has ever gone before. "We find a place on the Lower East Side," confesses one suburban couple in the genteel pages of the *New Yorker*,

> Ludlow Street. No one we know would think of living here. No one we know has ever heard of Ludlow Street. Maybe someday this neighborhood will be the way the Village was before we knew anything about New York. . . . We explain that moving down here is a kind of urban pioneering, and tell [Mother] she should be proud. We liken our crossing Houston Street to pioneers' crossing of the Rockies.[11]

In its Real Estate section, the *New York Times* announces "The Taming of the Wild Wild West" with the construction of the Armory Condominium two blocks west of Times Square: "The trailblazers have done their work: West 42nd Street has been tamed, domesticated, and polished into the most exciting, freshest, most energetic new neighborhood in all of New York."[12] The real-estate industry hires "urban scouts," the vanguard of gentrification, whose job it is to seek out neighborhoods ripe for reinvestment and to check out whether the natives are friendly. Realtors and developers are

praised for their selfless commitment to civic revitalization, regardless of the real-estate profits resulting from their putative
altruism.

As a new frontier, the city bursts with optimism. Hostile landscapes are regenerated, cleansed, reinfused with middle-class sensibility; real-estate values soar; the new urbanites are upwardly
mobile; elite gentility is democratized as mass-produced distinction.
The contradictions of the actual frontier are not entirely eradicated
in this imagery, but they are smoothed into an acceptable paradox.
As with the old West, the frontier is idyllic but dangerous, romantic
but ruthless. From *Crocodile Dundee* to *Bright Lights, Big City*,
there is an entire cinematic genre that makes of urban life a cowboy
fable replete with dangerous environment, hostile natives, and self-
discovery at the margins of civilization. In taming the urban wilderness, the cowboy gets the girl but also finds and tames his inner
self for the first time. In the final scene Paul Hogan accepts New
York—and New York him—as he clambers like an Aussie stock-
man over the heads and shoulders of a subway crowd. Michael J.
Fox can hardly end his fable by riding off into a reassuring western
sunset since today the bright lights are everywhere, but his own
salvation is crowned by a glorious sunrise over the Hudson River
and Manhattan's reconstructed financial district—Battery Park
and Wall Street. The manifest destiny of the earlier frontier visits
a reciprocal Valhalla on the big city.

This depiction of the new city is so entrenched, so apparently
natural, the geographical and historical quality of things is so lost,
that the blend of myth and landscape is difficult to discern. But
the myth was not always so powerful. The original analogy between
1874 Tompkins Square marchers and the Sioux Nation was tentative and oblique, the mythology too young to bear the full ideological weight of uniting such obviously disparate worlds. But the
conceptual distance between New York and the wild west has continually eroded. Perhaps the most iconoclastic evocation of a frontier in the early city came only a few years after Custer's Black
Hills campaign, when a stark, elegant, but isolated residential
building rose in the wilds of Central Park West and was named
the Dakota Apartments. By contrast, in the condomania that a
century later engulfed Manhattan—an environment in which any
social, physical, or geographical connection with an earlier frontier
is obliterated—the Montana, Colorado, Savannah, and New West

have been shoehorned into already overbuilt sites with never a comment about any iconographic inconsistency. As history and geography went west, the myth settled east, though it took time for the myth itself to be domesticated into the urban environment.

Today the frontier motif encodes not only the physical transformation of the built environment and the reinscription of the urban landscape in terms of class and race, but also the larger semiotics of the new city. Frontier is a style as much as a place. Hence the rash of Tex-Mex restaurants, the ubiquitous desert décor, the rage for cowboy chic. A *Sunday Times Magazine* ad gives the full effect: "For urban cowboys a little frontier goes a long way. From bandannas to boots, flourishes are what counts. . . . The Western imprint on fashion is now much like a cattle brand," the ad advises,

> —not too striking, but obvious enough to catch the eye. For city dudes, that means accents: a fringed jacket with black leggings; a shearling coat with a pin-stripe suit; a pair of lizard boots with almost anything. When in doubt about the mix, stride up to the mirror. If you're inclined to say "Yup," you've gone too far.[13]

New York's upmarket boutiques dispensing fashionable frontier kitsch are concentrated in SoHo, an area of artists' lofts and effete galleries, gentrified in the late 1960s and 1970s and bordering the Lower East Side to the southwest. Here, "frontier" aspires on occasion to a philosophy. Zona, on Greene Street, sells Navaho rugs, "Otomi Indian natural bark notepaper," Santa Fe jewelry, terracotta pottery, "Lombak baskets in rich harvest colors," bola ties. Zona oozes authenticity. All the "pieces" are numbered and a catalogue of the "collection" is being readied. On a small, plain, deliberately understated sign, with writing embossed on gold paper, the store offers its "personal" philosophy of craft-friendliness suffused with a whiff of New Age spiritualism:

> At a time when the ever-expanding presence of electronic tools and high technology is so pervasive the need to balance our lives with products that celebrate the textural and sensorial becomes essential. We think of our customers as resources and not simply

as consumers. We are guided by the belief that information is
energy and change is the constant.

Thank you for visiting our space.

Americana West, on Wooster Street, strives for a purer desert
look. On the sidewalk outside the front door, a noble Indian chief
complete with tomahawk and feathered headgear stands guard.
The window display features a bleached buffalo skull for $500
while inside the store are sofas and chairs made from longhorns
and cattle skin. A gallery as much as a store, Americana West
purveys diverse images of noble savages, desert scenes à la Georgia
O'Keeffe, petroglyphs and pictographs, whips and spurs. Cacti and
coyotes are everywhere (none real); a neon prickly pear is available
for $350. In lettering on the front window, Americana West an-
nounces its own theme, a crossover cultural geography between
city and desert: THE EVOLVING LOOK OF THE SOUTHWEST. DESIGNERS
WELCOME. . . . NOT FOR CITY SLICKERS ONLY.

The frontier is not always American nor indeed male. At La
Rue des Rêves the theme is "jungle eclectic." Leopard coats (faux
of course), antelope-leather skirts, and chamois blouses seem still
alive, slinking off their hangers toward the cash register. Fashion
accessories dangle like lianas from the jungle canopy. A stuffed
gorilla and several live parrots round out the ambience. At the
Banana Republic chain, customers have their safari purchases
packed in brown-paper bags sporting a rhinoceros. On the screen,
meanwhile, movies like *Out of Africa* and *Gorillas in the Mist*
reinforce the vision of pioneering whites in darkest Africa, but with
heroines for heroes. As middle-class white women are seen to play
an unprecedented role in contemporary gentrification, their prom-
inence on earlier frontiers is rediscovered and reinvented. Thus
designer Ralph Lauren centers a 1990 collection on "the Safari
woman," and explains the romantic nostalgia he intends to evoke:
"I believe that a lot of wonderful things are disappearing from the
present, and we have to take care of them." Mahogany furniture,
mosquito nets, jodhpurs, faux ivory, and a "Zanzibar" bedroom
set patterned with zebra stripes surround Lauren's Safari woman,
herself presumably an endangered species. Originally from the
Bronx but now ensconced on a Colorado ranch half the size of that
borough, Lauren has never been to Africa—"sometimes it's better
if you haven't been there"—but feels well able to represent it in

and for our fantasies. "I'm trying to evoke a world in which there was this graciousness we could touch. Don't look at yesterday. We can have it. Do you want to make the movie you saw a reality? Here it is."[14]

Even as Africa is underdeveloped by international capital, engulfed by famine and wars, it is remarketed in western consumer fantasies—but as the preserve of privileged and endangered whites. As one reviewer put it, the Safari collection "smacks of bwana style, of Rhodesia rather than Zimbabwe."[15] Lauren's Africa is a country retreat from and for the gentrified city. It provides the simulacra according to which the city is reclaimed from wilderness and remapped by the white upper-class settlers.

Nature too is rescripted in the new city. The frontier myth—originally engendered as an historicization of nature—is now reapplied as a naturalization of urban history. Even as rapacious economic expansion destroys deserts and rainforests, the new city—with its "harvest" colors and textured fabrics, authentic materials, and green sensibility—presents itself as nature-friendly: "All woods used in [Lauren's Safari] collection are grown in the Philippines and are not endangered."[16] The Nature Company, a store in "historic" South Street Seaport, is the apotheosis of this naturalized urban history, selling maps and globes, whaling anthologies and telescopes, books on the world's most dangerous reptiles, stories of exploration and conquest. The store's unabashed nature idolatry and studied avoidance of anything urban are the perfect disappearing mirror in which contested urban histories are refracted. In affirming the connection with nature, the new city denies its social history, the struggles that made it.

The nineteenth-century frontier myth and associated ideology were "generated by the social conflicts that attended the 'modernization' of the Western nations," according to Slotkin. They were "founded on the desire to avoid recognition of the perilous consequences of capitalist development in the New World, and they represent a displacement or deflection of social conflict into the world of myth."[17] The frontier was conceived as a social safety valve for urban class warfare brewing in such events as the 1863 New York draft riot, the 1877 railway strike, and indeed the Tompkins Square Park riot of 1874. "Spectacular violence" on the frontier, Slotkin concludes, had a redemptive effect on the city; it was "the alternative to some form of civil class war which, if allowed to break out within the Metropolis, would bring about a secular *Götterdämmerung.*"[18] Projected in the press as an extreme version of events in the city, a magnifying mirror to the most ungodly depravity of the urban masses, the frontier posited eastern cities as a paradigm of unity and social harmony in the face of external threat. Urban conflict was not so much denied as externalized, and whosoever disrupted this reigning urban harmony invited comparison with the external enemy, the "Other."

Frederick Jackson Turner's declaration of the end of frontier in 1893 only reinforced the myth. Omitting all ambiguities, he defined the frontier as "the outer edge of the wave—the meeting point between savagery and civilization."[19] Turner's frontier expressed a powerful amalgam of themes. It was simultaneously a distinct geographical place, the leading edge of economic expansion where fortunes were made and lost, and the focus of historical destiny for many Europeans in the New World. The supposed passing of the frontier therefore transformed the motif but did not diminish its efficacy. Rather the mythology was strengthened as the idea of the frontier was progressively removed from the specific historical and geographical qualities that generated it.

Today, too, the frontier ideology displaces social conflict into the realm of myth. If the nineteenth-century "urban frontier" first emerged to explain the social upheavals associated with industrialization, the present recycling of the imagery also occurs amid a new wave of urban restructuring. Following decades of disinvestment capped by the urban uprisings of the 1960s and the destruction wrought by urban renewal, the economics of inner urban redevelopment were propitious, and Americans were encouraged in the 1970s to rediscover the city. The frontier iconography stood ready to rationalize, even glorify, this abrupt reversal in cultural geography. Insofar as the declining postwar city was already seen by the white suburban middle class as an "urban wilderness" or "urban jungle," the naturalization of urban history did not prove particularly troublesome. As one respected academic proposed, unwittingly replicating Turner's vision (to not a murmur of dissent), gentrifying neighborhoods should be seen as combining a "civil class" and an "uncivil class," and such neighborhoods might be classified "by the extent to which civil or uncivil behavior dominates."[20] The class-based and race-based normative politics of the frontier ideology could hardly be clearer.

The frontier imagery is neither merely decorative nor innocent, but carries considerable ideological weight. The frontier motif makes the new city explicable in terms of old ideologies. Insofar as gentrification obliterates working-class communities, displaces poor households, and converts whole neighborhoods into bourgeois enclaves, the frontier ideology rationalizes social differentiation and exclusion as natural and inevitable. Defining the poor and working class as "uncivil," on the wrong side of a heroic dividing line, as savages and communists, the frontier ideology justifies monstrous incivility in the heart of the city. Disparaged in words, the working class is banished in practice to the urban edges or even deeper into the wilderness. The substance and consequence of the frontier imagery is to tame the wild city.

Selling Loisaida

The frontier takes different forms in different places; it adapts to place as it makes place. On the Lower East Side two industries defined the new urban frontier of the 1980s. Essential, of course, was the real-estate industry, which promoted the northern part of the Lower East Side, above Houston Street—the East Village—in order to capitalize on its geographical proximity to the respectability and aura, security and nightlife, culture and high rents of Greenwich Village. For its part, the culture industry—art dealers and patrons, gallery owners and artists, designers and critics, writers and performers—converted urban destruction into ultra chic. Together in the 1980s, the culture and real-estate industries invaded this rump of Manhattan from the west, "slouching toward Avenue D," as the critics Robinson and McCormick enthused. Building by building, block by block, the area was increasingly transformed from a dilapidated nineteenth-century tenement neighborhood into the new city where glamour and chic are spiced with just a hint of danger. The rawness of the neighborhood is part of the appeal. "As for ambience," continue the critics, "the East Village has it: a unique blend of poverty, punk rock, drugs, and arson, Hell's Angels, winos, prostitutes, and dilapidated housing that adds up to an adventurous avant-garde setting of considerable cachet."[21]

Enthusiastically endorsed as the new artistic Bohemia, effusively compared with the Left Bank in Paris or London's Soho, the

Lower East Side came to epitomize New York's fashion edge. Art galleries, stylish clubs, dance studios, and gritty hole-in-the-wall bars were the shock troops of economic reinvestment. And restaurants. A *Wall Street Journal* reporter describes dining possibilities in Indian Country: "For dining, a new restaurant on Avenue C called 'Bernard' offers 'organic French cuisine.' Frosted-glass windows protect diners from the sight of the burned-out tenements across the street as they nibble their $18 loins of veal."[22] The poor, abandoned, and homeless of the neighborhood were already invisible, of course, even without the frosted window; only the building shells from which they had been evicted threaten to intrude.

In the 1980s the Lower East Side moved to the forefront of the New York art world, surpassing in popularity the staid uptown galleries of Madison Avenue and 57th Street and the "alternative" art scene of neighboring SoHo, once itself the frontier of avant-garde, now corporate. There had always been artists in the area, but a new influx began in the late 1970s. With much fanfare, the first galleries opened in late 1981, and within four years there were as many as seventy in the neighborhood. It became the favored venue for dozens of novels and the setting as well as subject for numerous movies, including Spielberg's depiction of gentrification—*Batteries Not Included*—in which it takes benign space-aliens to rescue beleaguered tenants from gentrification-induced displacement.

The culture industry endows the Lower East Side with all the unabashed romanticism of the original frontier. "One must realize," observed one local art critic, "that the East Village or the Lower East Side is more than a geographical location—it is a state of mind." Only in the Lower East Side do art critics celebrate "minifestivals of the slum arts"; only here do artists cherish "a basic ghetto material—the ubiquitous brick"; and only here would the art entourage admit to being "captivated by the liveliness of ghetto culture." Frontier danger, of course, is the counterpoint of romance. Alongside the gallery called Fun, the knick-knack boutique named Love Saves the Day, and the bar called Beulah Land (Bunyan's land of rest and quiet), came Civilian Warfare and Virtual Garrison (both galleries), and Downtown Beirut (a bar that proved so popular that Downtown Beirut II has since opened). Frontier danger permeates the very art itself. As one apologist gushed, the scene is ruled by the "law of the jungle" and the new art exudes "savage energy"; neo-primitivist art, depicting black-figured urban natives running wild in the streets, presumably expressed this savage energy.[23]

Such urban warfare imagery might prompt us to acknowledge social conflict, especially in the context of intense media emphasis on crime and drugs in the area, but the artistic invocation of danger is usually too oblique to highlight the sharp conflicts over gentrification. First Avenue is manifestly not downtown Beirut, and at best the iconography conveys truth (pervasive urban conflict) in untrue form (the name of a bar). The art world's cooptation of violent urban imagery generally trivializes real struggles and projects a sense of danger that is difficult to take seriously. Social conflict is recast as artistic spectacle, danger as ambience. With the rapidity of openings and closings, movings and renamings, gentrification and decay, a landscape of happy violence becomes the stage for a dynamic and breathless new form of geographical performance art.

In "The Fine Art of Gentrification," Rosalyn Deutsche and Cara Ryan argue that the complicity of the art world with gentrification is not accidental, that indeed, gentrification "has been constructed with the aid of the entire apparatus of the art establishment."[24] Linking the rise of the "East Village" with the triumph of neo-expressionism, they argue that however countercultural the pose, the abstention from political self-reflection and from criticism of the larger social forces reshaping the neighborhood prevented many Lower East Side artists from seriously challenging the money and mores of the art establishment, and with it the dominant culture. The unprecedented commodification of art in the 1980s engendered an equally ubiquitous aestheticization of culture and politics: graffiti came off the trains and into the galleries, while the most outrageous punk and new-wave styles moved rapidly from the streets to full-page fashion ads in the *New York Times*. The press began sporting stories about the opulence of the new art scene: Don't let the poverty of the neighborhood fool you, was the message; this generation of young artists gets by with American Express Gold-cards.

The simultaneous disavowal of social and political context and dependence on the cultural establishment placed successful avant-garde artists in a sharply contradictory position. They came to function as broker between the cultural establishment and the majority of still-aspiring artists. Lower East Side galleries played the

pivotal role; they provided the meeting place for grassroots ambition and establishment money.[25] Representing and patronizing
the neighborhood as a cultural mecca, the culture industry attracted
tourists, consumers, and potential immigrants, thereby fueling the
process of gentrification. Not all artists so readily attached themselves to the cultural establishment, of course, and a significant
artists' opposition survived the commodification and price esca-
lation that boosted the neighborhood's real-estate and art industries
in the 1980s.[26] Following the Tompkins Square riot, in fact, there
was a flourishing of political art aimed squarely at gentrification,
the police, and the art industry. Many artists were also squatters
and housing activists, and a lot of subversive art was displayed as
posters, sculpture, and graffiti on the streets or in the most marginal
gallery spaces.

For the real-estate industry, art tamed the neighborhood, tout-
ing images of exotic but benign danger. It depicted an "East
Village" risen from lowlife to highbrow, donated a salable neighborhood "personality," packaged the area as a real-estate commodity, and established demand. Indeed "the story of the East
Village's newest bohemian efflorescence," it has been suggested,
"can also be read as an episode in New York's real estate history
—that is, as the deployment of a force of gentrifying artists in lower
Manhattan's last slum."[27] By 1987, though, the marriage of convenience between art and real estate had soured, and a wave of
gallery closures was precipitated by massive rent increases demanded by commercial landlords unconstrained by rent control. It
is widely speculated that these "landlords"—mostly anonymous
management companies operating out of post-office boxes—offered
artificially low rents in the early 1980s in order to attract galleries
and artists whose presence would hype the area and hike the rents.
Handsomely successful, they demanded large rent increases as the
first five-year leases came due. The neighborhood was now satu-
rated with galleries, artistic and economic competition was cut-
throat, and a financial shakeout ensued in which many galleries
closed while the more successful ones decamped to SoHo—but not
before they had spearheaded a fundamental shift in the neighborhood's image and property market.

That some artists became victims of the very gentrification process they precipitated has touched off a debate in the art press.[28]
However wittingly or otherwise, the culture and real-estate indus-

tries worked together to transform the Lower East Side into a new place—different, unique, a phenomenon, the pinnacle of avant-garde fashion. Culture and place became synonymous. Fashion and faddishness created cultural scarcity much as the real-estate industry's demarcation of the "East Village" established a scarcity of privileged residential addresses. Good art and good location became fused. And good location means money.

Pioneering for Profit

The Lower East Side has experienced several phases of rapid building associated with larger economic cycles, and the present-day built environment results from this history. A few early buildings remain from the 1830s and 1840s, but rectangular "railroad" tenements are more common, built in the 1850s or just after the Civil War to house the largely immigrant working class. In the decade and a half after 1877, with the economy expanding and immigration growing, the area experienced its most intense building boom. Virtually all vacant land was developed with "dumbbell" tenements, so named because unlike their strictly rectangular predecessors they narrowed at the middle to provide a token airshaft between neighboring buildings, mandated by an 1879 housing law. By the 1893 economic crash, which effectively ended this building cycle, almost 60 percent of all New York City housing comprised dumbbell tenements.[29] The next building boom, beginning in 1898, was concentrated at the urban edge, now miles away in the outer boroughs and New Jersey. There was a modicum of new construction in the Lower East Side, but many landlords had already begun disinvesting, neglecting maintenance and repairs on their grossly overcrowded buildings.

New York's ruling class has long been interested in taming and reclaiming the Lower East Side from the unruly working-class hordes. In 1929, the Rockefeller-sponsored Regional Plan Association offered an extraordinary vision for the Lower East Side. Their plan explicitly envisaged the removal of the existing population, the construction of "high class residences," modern shops, a yacht marina on the East River, and the redevelopment of the Lower East Side highway system in such a way as to strengthen the connection with neighboring Wall Street:

The moment an operation of this magnitude and character was started in a district, no matter how squalid it was, an improvement in quality would immediately begin in adjacent property and would spread in all directions. New stores would start up prepared to cater to a new class of customers. The streets thereabouts would be made cleaner. Property values would rise. . . . After a while, other apartment units would appear and in the course of time the character of the East Side would be entirely changed.[30]

The stock-market crash of 1929, the ensuing Depression, World War II, and the unprecedented wave of postwar suburban expansion all militated against the planned reconstruction of the Lower East Side as a high-class haven. Between the late 1930s and 1960s efforts were made to clear slums and build public housing, but many of these government policies, combined with withdrawal of private investment, intensified the long-term economic and social forces laying waste to the Lower East Side and countless similar neighborhoods. In the postwar period, disinvestment and abandonment, demolition and public warehousing were the major tactics of a virulent anti-urbanism that left neighborhoods like the Lower East Side free-fire zones. Especially hard hit were the area south of Houston Street and the eastern rump of the island north of Houston, known as Alphabet City for its Avenues A through D, east of First Avenue. The uprisings of the 1960s merely reinforced the panicked retreat of capital and the middle class from the wild city. The urban-renewal projects of this period amounted to little more than a forced ghettoization of the locals left among the debris. But in the late 1970s these were superseded by a wholly different kind of "renewal" through gentrification that, in effect, implemented much of the 1929 vision.

Even as yuppies and artists began to pick over the wreckage in the late 1970s, anyone who could was still moving out. From a 1910 peak population of over half a million, the Lower East Side has lost almost 400,000 inhabitants, giving it a 1980 population of 149,000. In the heart of Alphabet City, the population declined by an extraordinary 67.3 percent in the 1970s. The median household income of $8,783 was only 63 percent of the 1980 citywide figure, and twenty-three of twenty-nine census tracts throughout the area experienced an increase in the number of families living below the poverty level. It was the poor who were left behind; 59

percent of the remaining Alphabet City population survived below the poverty level. The neighborhood so sought after by yuppies and artists was the poorest in Manhattan outside Harlem. The polarization of wealth and poverty increased in the 1980s as destitute homeless men and women shared the shadows of Lower East Side streets with club-bound stretch limos.

Declining property values accompanied declining populations. Consider the case of 270 East 10th Street, a run-down but occupied five-story dumbbell tenement between 1st Avenue and Avenue A, half a block west of Tompkins Square Park. In 1976, at the time of peak disinvestment, it was sold by a landlord who simply wanted out; the price was a mere $5,706 plus the assumption of unpaid property taxes. By the beginning of 1980, it was resold for $40,000. Eighteen months later it went for $130,000. In September 1981 the building was sold again, this time to a New Jersey real-estate concern, for $202,600. In less than two years, the building's price multiplied five times—without any renovation.[31]

This is not an unusual case. On Tompkins Square Park the 16-story Christodora Building, now a symbol of the antigentrification struggle, experienced a similar cycle of disinvestment and reinvestment. Built in 1928 as a settlement house, the Christodora was sold to the City of New York in 1947 for $1.3 million. It was used for various city functions and eventually as a community center and hostel housing, among others, the Black Panthers. Run down and dilapidated by the late 1960s, the building attracted no bids at a 1975 public auction. It was later sold for $62,500 to a Brooklyn real-estate developer, George Jaffee. The doors of the deserted building had been welded shut and remained that way for five years while Jaffee unsuccessfully sought federal funds for rehabilitation as low-income housing. In 1980 Jaffee began to get inquiries about the building. The welder was called to provide entry, the building was inspected, and offers of $200,000 to $800,000 began to materialize. Jaffee eventually sold the building in 1983 to another developer, Harry Skydell, for $1.3 million, who "flipped" it a year later for $3 million, only to recoup it later in a joint venture with developer Samuel Glasser. Skydell and Glasser renovated the Christodora and in 1986 marketed its eighty-six condominium apartments. The quadruplex penthouse, with private elevator, three terraces, and two fireplaces, was offered a year later for $1.2 million.[32]

In both cases—the Christodora and 270 East 10th—it is real-
estate profits rather than the neighborhood that are revitalized. As
measured by the rate of property-tax delinquency, disinvestment
from residential buildings peaked in 1976 then again in 1980, but
fell continuously throughout the 1980s, marking a sustained
decade-long reinvestment. While an upturn in disinvestment has
accompanied the recession of the early 1990s, it nowhere approaches the levels of the early 1980s. Median sales prices for Lower
East Side apartments rose only 43.8 percent between 1968 and
1979, while the inflation rate neared 90 percent, but in the suc-
ceeding five years to 1984 the relationship reversed: sales prices
rose 146.4 percent, almost four times the inflation rate.[33] Even
after the 1987 stock-market meltdown, apartments in the neighborhood were selling for $250 to $300 per square foot. The Tompkins Court, a 1988 rehabilitation of two tenements at the southeast
corner of Tompkins Square Park, offered one-bedroom units for
$139,000 to $209,000, two bedrooms for $239,000 to $329,000.
For the least expensive of these, an estimated annual household
income of $65,000 was required; for the most expensive an income
of $160,000. Even the small studios were inaccessible to those
earning less than $40,000. Several blocks away at another tenement
rehab, seventeen co-ops were sold, with two-bedroom units ranging
from $235,000 to $497,800.[34] Mortgage and maintenance costs
on the latter amounted to close to $5,000 a month. Two months'
payment on this apartment easily exceeded the neighborhood's
median annual income. Only by the early 1990s did sale prices
begin to drop appreciably—as much as 15 percent at the top end
of the market.

Commercial rents and sales rose even faster. Long-time small
businesses were forced out as landlords indiscriminately raised
rents. Maria Pidhorodecky's Italian-Ukrainian restaurant, the Or-
chidia, a fixture on Second Avenue since 1957, closed in 1984
when, in the absence of any commercial rent control, the landlord
raised the monthly rent for the 700-square-foot space from $950
to $5,000.[35]

The key force in gentrification is the real-estate market. When
alternative investments promise higher returns, private-market
competition makes it rational for property owners to disinvest—to
draw capital systematically out of buildings for investment elsewhere. Repairs and maintenance are skimped on or cut altogether

as the building is "milked." When the building becomes physically dilapidated, its economic devaluation brings about an attendant devaluation of the land it sits on. Land rent—the price of land—follows building value in a downward spiral. But while *actual* land value decreases as the neighborhood deteriorates physically, its *potential* value (the price land could command if the area were redeveloped or the neighborhood gentrified) increases with further urban development of the city around it. It is the gap between this actual land rent under current deteriorated conditions and potential land rent under a new land use—the "rent gap"—that prompts rehabilitation and redevelopment.[36]

In his investigation of the workings of Lower East Side real estate, journalist Martin Gottlieb witnessed the results of the rent gap first hand. Take the building at 270 East 10th Street. While the combined sale price (land and building) soared from $5,706 to $202,600 in five and a half years, the value of the building alone, according to city property-tax assessors, actually fell from $26,000 to $18,000. And this is a typical result. The land is more valuable than the building. The perverse rationality of real-estate capitalism thus allows building owners and developers to garner a double reward for milking properties and destroying buildings. First, they pocket the money that should have gone to repairs and upkeep; but second, having effectively destroyed the building and established a rent gap, they have thereby created for themselves the conditions and opportunity for a whole new round of capital reinvestment. Having produced a scarcity of capital in the name of profit, they now flood the neighborhood with capital for the same purpose, portraying themselves as civic-minded heroes—brave, risk-taking builders of the new city for a grateful populace. But in Gottlieb's words, this self-induced reversal in the market means that "a Lower East Side landlord can drink his milk and have it too."[37]

The economic geography of gentrification is not random; developers don't just plunge into the heart of slum opportunity, but tend to take it piece by piece. Rugged pioneering is tempered by financial caution. "The main point is that you want to be out on the frontier of gentrification," explains one building manager. "You try to be far enough out on the 'line' that you can make a killing —not too far, where you can't offload the building, but far enough that the building is cheap and you can make money turning it over."[38] Developers tend to move in from the outskirts, building "a few strategically placed outposts of luxury."[39] They pioneer first on the "gold coast" between safe neighborhoods where property values are high and disinvested slums where opportunity is higher. Successive beachheads and defensible boundaries are established on the frontier. Thus economic geography defines the strategy of urban pioneering. Whereas the myth of the urban frontier is an invention that justifies the violence of gentrification and displacement, the everyday frontier on which the myth is hung is the stark product of entrepreneurial exploitation and economic reality. In the Lower East Side as elsewhere, the frontier is before anything else a frontier of profitability. It is the profit rate that is "revitalized"; cultural revitalization is an optional extra, and indeed many working-class neighborhoods experience a dramatic "devitalization" as the immigrant middle class put bars on their doors and windows, disavow the streets for parlor living, fence off their stoops, and evict undesirables from "their" parks.

In some places developers' strategies can smack of a military as well as an economic geography. "What we have to do is tackle Harlem from the edges," says Donald Cogsville, president of the Harlem Urban Development Corporation, a public body devoted to enticing investment into the neighborhood. "The private market is beginning to move in the west; we have to help it, especially in the south where the northern end of Central Park at 110th Street is a real attraction," says Cogsville. "First we establish a beachhead on 112th Street and invest in some anchor rehabs in that area. When these blocks are secured, we move north and establish a second beachhead on 116th Street."[40]

The Lower East Side exhibits a classic gentrification frontier. The first signs of sustained real-estate reinvestment came between 1977 and 1979 on the western border of the area, immediately adjacent to Greenwich Village in the north and close to Wall Street and Chinatown in the south. After 1980, gentrification spread out from the safety of its western borders and in two years, despite a national recession and depressed housing market, coursed eastward through the "East Village" from Third Avenue to Second, from First to Avenue A—the western edge of Tompkins Square Park. The park became a test for the conquest of the Lower East Side; on the other side lay Alphabet City, the core of abandonment and disinvestment. But the speculative fever that surrounded the Christodora in 1983 convinced developers that the derelict landscapes to the east represented more opportunity than risk. As the real-estate section of the Sunday *New York Times* enthused, "Gentrification continued its inexorable march across 'Alphabet City' "— from Avenue A to Avenue B, then C and D. By 1985 disinvestment had been reversed all the way to the East River, leaving only city-owned buildings unaffected by reinvestment: racing, not slouching, toward Avenue D.[41]

If the real-estate cowboys invading the Lower East Side in the 1980s used art to paint their economic quest in romantic hues, they also enlisted the cavalry of city government for more prosaic tasks—reclaiming the land and quelling the natives. In its housing policy, drug crackdowns, and especially in its parks strategy, the city devoted its efforts not toward providing basic services and living opportunities for existing residents but toward routing the locals and subsidizing opportunities for real-estate development. In the words of a consultants' report, entitled *An Analysis of Investment Opportunities in the East Village,* "The city has now given clear signals that it is prepared to aid the return of the middle class by auctioning city-owned properties and sponsoring projects in gentrifying areas to bolster its tax base and aid the revitalization process."[42]

The city's major resource in the Lower East Side was its stock of over two hundred properties foreclosed from private landlords for nonpayment of property taxes. In 1981 the city administration made its first significant foray into the real-estate frenzy of gentrification. Artists were to be the vehicle. The Department of Housing Preservation and Development (HPD) solicited proposals for an Artist Homeownership Program (AHOP), and in 1982 announced a renovation project that would yield 120 housing units in sixteen buildings, each costing an estimated $50,000, aimed at artists earning at least $24,000. The purpose of the renovation, Mayor Koch proclaimed, was "to renew the strength and vitality of the community," and five artists' groups and two developers were selected to execute the $7 million program.

But many in the community vigorously opposed the plan. The Joint Planning Council, a coalition of more than thirty Lower East Side housing and community organizations, demanded that so valuable a resource as abandoned buildings should be renovated for indigenous use. City Councilwoman Miriam Friedlander denounced the plan as "just a front for gentrification" and claimed that "the real people who will profit from this housing are the developers who renovate it." In contrast to the artists who supported the AHOP plan and portrayed themselves as victims of gentrification deserving housing as much as anyone else, another coalition—Artists for Social Responsibility—opposed the use of artists to gentrify the neighborhood. HPD, the mayor, and AHOP were ultimately defeated by the City Board of Estimate, which refused to provide the initial $2.4 million of public funds.[43]

But in fact, AHOP was a warm-up for a larger auction program, in which HPD encouraged gentrification citywide by selling abandoned properties and vacant lots to private developers. Ignoring community proposals, the city presented a "cross-subsidy" program, whereby developers would purchase land, build or renovate housing, and in return for a battery of public subsidies agree to sell at least 20 percent of the new apartments to tenants unable to afford market prices. Initially some community groups gave the program tentative support, while others sought to adjust the ratio of subsidized to market-rate units to 50–50.

But opposition mounted as the program's intent became clearer: In 1988, the city contracted with the Lefrak Organization—a major national developer—to build on the Lower East Side's Seward Park site where, in 1967, eighteen hundred poor people, mostly black and Latino, had been displaced and their homes demolished. The people had been promised apartments in a new complex scheduled for the site, but twenty-one years later, they remained unbuilt. Lefrak paid $1 for the land, would pay a further $1 per year for the ninety-nine year lease, and received a thirty-two-year tax abatement. Under the plan, Lefrak would build 1200 apartments, of which 400 would be market-rate condominiums, 640 would be rented at $800 to $1200 to "middle-income" households earning $37,000 to $53,000; and the remaining 160 units would go as "moderate-income" units to those earning $19,000 to $37,000. Significantly, no apartments were earmarked for low-income or homeless people; indeed, after twenty years, all units would revert to Lefrak as luxury apartments. "Yupper-income housing in low-income neighborhoods" is how one housing activist described the plan; "the purpose is creating hot new real estate markets."[44]

In addition to its housing strategy, the city in January 1984 launched a drug crackdown—Operation Pressure Point—that was widely seen as part of a larger pro-gentrification strategy. An estimated 14,000 drug busts were made in eighteen months throughout the Lower East Side, and the *New York Times* gloated that "thanks to Operation Pressure Point, art galleries are replacing shooting galleries."[45] But the petty offenders were quickly released, the kingpins never apprehended. When the pressure eased the sellers returned.

A mural at St. Mark's Place and First Avenue exposes the relationship between the drug crackdown and gentrification. Painted in 1987 by Geoff, a local artist, it is part of a series adorning the St. Mark's Bar and Grill. A poignant commentary on the gentrification of the neighborhood, it is constantly revised by anyone who chooses, and periodically too by Geoff. In stark neo-expressionist style it depicts a dark street lined by tenements with stick figures scurrying to and fro, imparting an overwhelming sense of imminent danger. In the background a huddle of helmeted police officers glowers down on the street, surveying its activity. In the foreground, a yuppie couple in a ritzy cafe is being served by a punk waiter with mohawk; two kids are staring in from the street. But the most ominous presence is an arm stretched onto the street from between two tenements; the hand holds a dripping heroin needle; the sleeve is pin-striped. The meaning of the mural is clear: the police drug crackdown is a deliberate reinforcement of gentrification, which protects the class interests of the real drug profiteers, if not the runners and street sellers.

Along with Operation Pressure Point came the City's assault on the parks. As developer William Zeckendorf secured massive tax abatements and zoning variations for his twenty-eight-story luxury towers on Union Square, north of 14th Street—a "fortress" development intended to anchor future pioneering efforts—the city had already weighed in with tactical support. Under the new plan, the homeless and others deemed socially undesirable were evicted from Union Square Park, which then underwent a two-year, $3.6 million renovation. Inaugurating the renovation in the spring of 1984, Mayor Koch excoriated the poor and homeless who occupied the park: "First the thugs took over, then the muggers took over, then the drug people took over, and now we are driving them out."[46] With its initial sparkle, the new park complemented the facade of the Zeckendorf condo. Trees were thinned out, paths were widened, and an open plaza was constructed at the south end, all essen-

"Operation Pressure Point"
Loisada Mural by Geoff

tially to provide long-range visibility for surveillance and control. Sharp-edged, bright new stone replaced slabs worn by weather and footsteps, the farmers' market was spruced up, and the park's monuments cleaned and polished in a nostalgic "restoration" of an idealized past. The same strokes that restored the park's green statues to their gleaming bronze splendor attempted to wipe away the city's history of homelessness and poverty.

The gentrification of Union Square Park hardly lived up to expectations, though, as patrolling cops and returning evictees restored the park to the frontier. Nonetheless, the city continued its strategy, moving south to Washington Square Park in the Village. Here too, boundary fences were erected, a curfew imposed, police patrols increased. Then in 1988 it was the turn of Tompkins Square Park, deep in the Lower East Side. Here the city's traditional park-gentrification strategy of curfews and closures followed by "restoration" was defeated—for a time—by the August riot.

"Another Wave More Savage than the First": The New (Global) Indian Wars?

"A sort of wartime mentality seems to be settling onto New Yorkers affected by the housing squeeze," commented *New York* magazine as the gentrification boom got under way in the early eighties.[47] Especially in the Lower East Side, the geography of recent urban change reveals the future gentrified city, a city sparkling with the neon of elite consumption and at the same time anxiously cordoned off from homeless deprivation. The gentrification frontier courses through neighborhood after neighborhood, advancing rapidly during periods of economic expansion, more sluggishly during recessions. Former working-class and poor sections of the old city are dragged into the circuits of international capital as Lower East Side art is shown in London and Paris, and its fanciest condos are advertised in the *Times* and *Le Monde*.

Gentrification portends class conquest of the new city. Urban pioneers seek to scrub the city clean of its working-class geography and history. By remaking the geography of the city they rewrite its social history as a justification for its future. Slum tenements become historic brownstones, and exterior facades are sandblasted to reveal a future past. Likewise with interior renovation. "Inner-worldly asceticism becomes public display" as "bare brick walls and exposed timbers come to signify cultural discernment, not the poverty of slums without plaster."[48] Stripping later additions from the original structure effaces social history. If the past is not entirely demolished, it is at least reinvented—its class contours rubbed smooth—in the refurbishment of a palatable heritage, oozing fake authenticity.

Where the militance or persistence of working-class communities or the extent of disinvestment and dilapidation render such genteel reconstruction a Sisyphean task, the classes can be juxtaposed by other means. Squalor, poverty, and the violence of eviction are called an exquisite ambience—the Lower East Side becomes an "avant-garde setting of considerable cachet." Rapid reformulation and polarization along class lines is glorified for its excitement rather than condemned for its violence or understood for the rage it provokes.

The effort to recolonize the city involves a strategy of systematic eviction. New York City now has at least 70,000 homeless people—fully one percent of its population. In its various task-force reports for gentrifying the urban frontier, New York City government has never proposed a plan for relocating evictees. Denying any connection between gentrification and homelessness, city officials do not admit even the possibility of displacement. Public policy is geared to let us "see no homeless," to quote the words of Lower East Side graffiti. The 1929 Regional Plan for the Lower East side was more honest:

> Each replacement will mean the disappearance of many of the old tenants and the coming in of other people who can afford the higher rentals required by modern construction on high-priced land. Thus in time economic forces alone will bring about a change in the character of much of the East Side population.[49]

An East Village developer is blunt about future prospects for evictees as gentrification closes in on Avenue D: "They'll all be forced out. They'll be pushed east to the river and given life preservers." Another developer justifies the violence of the new frontier: "To hold us accountable for it is like blaming the developer of a high-rise building in Houston for the displacement of the Indians a hundred years before."[50]

Some have gone further, hoping to illegalize homelessness. "If it is illegal to litter the streets," proclaims George Will, "frankly it ought to be illegal . . . to sleep in the streets. Therefore, there is a simple matter of public order and hygiene in getting these people somewhere else. Not arrest them, but move them off somewhere where they are simply out of sight."[51] A Burlington, Vermont, restaurateur takes seriously the mission to get "these people" out of sight. The owner of Leunig's Old World Cafe, in the gentrified, cobblestone, boutique-filled Church Street Marketplace, became incensed at the homeless people who, he said, were "terrorizing" his restaurant's clients. Funded by donations from the town's restaurateurs and others, he began an organization called "Westward Ho!" to provide the homeless with one-way tickets out of town, as far away as Portland, Oregon.

Media representations of homeless people generally blame the victim—explaining homelessness as a result of drug abuse, alcoholism, mental illness, or some other individual tragedy rather than the result of an exclusionary housing market with prohibitive rent levels. At best, the media chooses sympathy and charity toward homeless individuals, each with a personal story, rather than an investigation of causes, and this too reinforces the public perception that personal rather than social realities cause homelessness. Public appeals for sympathy, paradoxically, inure us to the possibility of effective action. "The homeless" are more accurately described as "the evicted," since people don't simply fall out of the housing market—they are usually pushed. Friedrich Engels's admonition of more than a century ago seems the best predictor of the urban future: "The bourgeoisie has only one method of settling the housing question. . . . The breeding places of disease, the infamous holes and cellars in which the capitalist mode of production confines our workers night after night are not abolished; they are merely *shifted elsewhere.*"[52]

The dramatic shifts affecting gentrifying neighborhoods are experienced as intensely local. The Lower East Side is a world away from the upper-crust noblesse of the East Side three miles north, and within the neighborhood, Avenue C is still a very different economic, social, and cultural place from First Avenue. Yet the processes and forces reshaping the new city are global as much as local. Gentrification and homelessness in the new city are a microcosm of a new global order etched by the rapacity of capital. Not only are broadly similar processes remaking cities around the world, but the world itself impinges dramatically on these localities. The gentrification frontier is also an "imperial frontier," according to Kristin Koptiuch.[53] Not only does international capital flood the real-estate markets of New York, but international migration provides a workforce for the new service jobs associated with the new urban economy. In New York, the greengrocers are now mainly Korean; the plumbers fitting gentrified buildings are often Italian and the carpenters Polish, while the domestics and nannies looking after the houses and offspring of gentrifiers come from El Salvador or the Bahamas.

Immigrants come to New York from every country where American capital has opened markets, extracted resources, removed people from the land, or sent marines as a "peacekeeping force." This global dislocation comes home to roost in the "third-worlding" of the American city—which, combined with increasing crime and repressive policing of the streets, invites visions of a predaceous new city threatening gentrification. In her research on the disruption of the ways in which children are socialized, Cindi Katz finds a clear parallel between the streets of New York City and rural Sudan.[54] The primitive conditions of the periphery, from the Brazilian Amazon to Hong Kong sweatshops, are reestablished at the core. "As if straight out of some sci-fi plot," writes Koptiuch, "the wild frontiers dramatized in early travel accounts have been moved so far out and away that, to our unprepared astonishment, they have imploded right back in our midst."[55] It is not just the Indian wars of the Old West that have come home to the cities of the east, but the global wars of the New American World Order.

As the rent gap is eagerly filled by spasms of capital reinvestment in the new world city, the gentrification frontier will spread outward toward the city-suburban edge, where disinvestment is already severe. Evicted from the emerging bourgeois playground of the urban core, many minorities, unemployed, and poor among the working class are displaced even further out, to newer districts on the outskirts. Indeed, "if the evolving spatial pattern of black residential development is not significantly altered," suggests geographer Harold Rose, the next generation of "ghetto centers will essentially be confined to a selected set of suburban ring communities" in metropolitan areas that already have a large black central-city population. There "appears to be little concern regarding the social and economic implications associated with the present spatial reorganization upon the future of urban blacks," Rose concludes, "or for that matter upon the future of the city."[56]

A new social geography is being born, but it will not be a peaceful process. The attempt to reclaim Washington, D.C. (probably the most segregated city in the country) through white gentrification is known by the African-American majority as "the Plan." In London's gentrifying Docklands and the East End, an anarchist gang of unemployed working-class kids justify mugging as their "yuppie tax," giving a British twist to the Tompkins Square slogan, "Mug a yuppie." As homes and communities are converted into economic frontiers, people defend themselves, with violence if necessary. Frontier violence comes with cavalry charges down city streets, rising crime rates, police racism, and assaults on the natives. It comes with the murder of Bruce Bailey, a Manhattan tenant activist, in 1989 (his dismembered body was found in garbage bags in the Bronx, and although the police openly suspected angry landlords of the crime, no one has been charged). And it comes with the torching of several homeless New Yorkers as they slept, presumably to get them "out of sight."

But it also comes with frontier organization. Before 1862, when the Homesteading Act was passed, the majority of rugged frontier heroes were illegal squatters. They simply took the land they needed, organized community clubs to defend their land claims against large speculators, established basic welfare circles, and encouraged other squatters to settle because strength lay in numbers. The whole force of the frontier myth has been to dull this central threat to authority in a romantic cloak of individualism, when of course the original pioneers were *highly* organized among themselves. It was widespread squatting, in fact, that forced the passage of the Homestead Act. If we are to embrace the city as new urban frontier today, the first act in pioneering, if historical accuracy is to be observed, will be squatting. That the city has become a new Wild West is perhaps beyond contest; but the character of this Wild West is precisely what's at stake.

EDWARD W. SOJA

Inside Exopolis:
Scenes from Orange County

Scene 1: "Toto, I've Got a Feeling
We're Not in Kansas Anymore"

It's a theme park—a seven-hundred-and-eighty-six-square-mile
theme park—and the theme is "you can have anything you want."
    It's the most California-looking of all the Californias: the most
like the movies, the most like the stories, the most like the dream.
    Orange County is Tomorrowland and Frontierland, merged
and inseparable. 18th century mission. 1930s art colony. 1980s
corporate headquarters.
    There's history everywhere: navigators, conquistadors, pa-
dres, rancheros, prospectors, wildcatters. But there's so much
Now, the Then is hard to find. The houses are new. The cars are
new. The stores, the streets, the schools, the city halls—even the
land and the ocean themselves look new.
    The temperature today will be in the low 80's. There's a slight
offshore breeze. Another just-like-yesterday day in paradise.
    Come to Orange County. It's no place like home.[1]

    The first theme is explicit: You can have *anything* you want in
Orange County, where every day seems just like yesterday but
where the ever-present *Now*-ness of tomorrow makes the *Then* hard
to find; where every place is off-center, breathlessly on the edge,
but always right in the middle of things, smack on the frontier,
nowhere yet now/here like home. To its avid promoters, Orange
County is a park-themed paradise, the American Dream repetitively

renewed and infinitely available, as much like the movies as reel life can get. It is a resplendent bazaar of repackaged times and spaces that allows all that is contemporary (including histories and geographies) to be encountered and consumed with an almost edemic simultaneity.

Orange County presents itself as a foretaste of the future, a genuine re-creation of everyday life in a brilliantly recombinant postmodern world, beyond Oz, beyond even the utopic late-Modernisms of Disney. It claims to have taken the lead in the new competition for the Happiest Place on Earth, and if anyplace else is still in the running, it is purely through faithful simulation of the original. Every day, more simulations of Orange County spring up—around Boston, New York, San Francisco, Chicago, Washington, Dallas–Fort Worth, Miami, Atlanta—propelling the most spectacular transformation of urban landscapes, and of the language we use to describe them, since the industrial city first took shape in the nineteenth century. It is almost as if the urban is being reinvented to celebrate the millennium. And *you* are *there* whether you like it or not, looking at the coming attractions being screened beyond modernity's urban fringe.

Some have called these amorphous replacements of suburbia outer cities or edge cities; others dub them technopoles, technoburbs, silicon landscapes, postsuburbia, metroplex. I will name them collectively *exopolis*, the city without, to stress their oxymoronic ambiguity, their city-full non-city-ness. Perched beyond the vortex of the old agglomerative nodes, the exopolis spins new whorls of its own, turning the city inside-out and outside-in at the same time. The metropolitan forms that have become so familiar to us—with dominating downtowns, concentric rings of land uses spreading out from the tightly packed inner city to sprawling dormitory suburbs, density gradients declining neatly from core to periphery—are now undergoing radical deconstruction and reconstitution, exploding and coalescing today in multitudes of experimental communities of tomorrow, in improbable cities where centrality is virtually ubiquitous and the solid familiarity of the urban melts into air. We're certainly not in Kansas anymore, but neither are we in old New York or Chicago—or even Los Angeles, the centrifugal ur-exopolis that is now being left behind in the wake of its endlessly repetitive contemporary simulations.

Phel Steinme

Orange County, California

Scene 2: The Origins of Exopolis

Orange County epitomizes the industrial and urban geography of the Sunbelt with its transaction-intensive economy, deeply segmented local labor markets, regressive labor relations, and high-tech defense-related industries. Growth has been exponential. In the mid-fifties, Orange County was uncluttered—a little industry, a few residential communities in the north and along the coast. But its varied natural environment, copious recreational facilities, and (even then) archly conservative politics made it a mecca for the middle class and for business.

> Sometime in the 1960s . . . Orange County manufacturers began to draw together into a *complex* in the true sense, i.e., a congeries of interlinked industries sharing a common pool of labor and various infrastructural services. . . . By the early 1970s, the high-technology complex had become as tightly organized in geographical space as it apparently was in economic space. . . . [Today,] the loose subsystem of plants around Anaheim and Fullerton remains a strong element of the overall industrial pattern of the county. In addition, the subsystem in and around Irvine has developed into . . . the dominant focus of the county's proliferating electronic components, computer, and instrument industries.[2]

Allen J. Scott thus confidently depicts exopolis as industrial and industrious, a transactional web efficiently knotted into a series of flexible manufacturing and service complexes able to capture the new "scope" economies of post-Fordist technology. No longer bound by the rigid hierarchical demands of mass production and assembly lines, a new kind of industrialization is begetting a new kind of "peripheral" urbanization, an offset urban form, a manufactured landscape of flexible economic specialization that is the seedbed of exopolis, not only in Orange County but around nearly every major American metropolis.

Scott's mapping of the Orange County exopolis shows clusters of symbols representing high-technology plants multiplying like weeds over the siliconed landscape of this latest reflowering of the garden city. The densest and busiest of these industrial parklands is the Irvine "subsystem," the masterplanned field of operations of the Irvine Company, owner of one-sixth of Orange County and the packager of the largest New Towns in America. To the north, Anaheim and Fullerton anchor another, older, major whorl of participants, while several other clusters of industrial activity lie scattered about, each a pointillist focus in the urbanizing landscape.

To call this extraordinarily dense and tightly knit assemblage of manufacturers and their subcontracted servants "postindustrial" is surely to miss the point. And just as surely the area is no longer "sub" urban. Orange County may have no dominant city in the traditional sense, no easily identifiable center or skylined downtown to signify the Modernist urban citadel, but it is a metropolis nonetheless, a Standard Metropolitan Statistical Area of around two and a half million inhabitants, an industrial capitalist city of a new kind, a city whose "flexible accumulation" signifies a restructured political economy. Industrialization thus concretely sets the exopolitan scene.

Scott, attached to an older vision of urban dynamics, searches for rational order in this bubbling postmodern complexity. He calculates the geographical "center of gravity" for the Orange County industrial complex and imposes concentric patternings in the cartography of industrial production and employment. Some fuzzy sets of statistical concentricities emerge, but what is most revealing about this exercise is what it inadvertently reveals about the inner circle itself. The center of gravity is almost empty of high-technology industry, a curious doughnut-hole of maximum accessibility around which the subsystems pivot. How exquisitely exopolitan for the middle to be missing, for the center to be defined almost entirely by the weight of its productive periphery.

But contained within this inner circle are some of the peak population densities of Orange County and a large chunk of the Latino barrio of Santa Ana, the county's choice pool of cheap labor and stopover haven for the thousands of undocumented immigrants who pass through the border one county away. There is also, close to the intricate interchange of three freeways and the concrete cut of the Santa Ana River, a large shopping mall semaphorically named "The City." A small stuccoed prison and a vast new hospital complex line such streets as City Drive and Metropolitan Avenue, further signaling this citadellean ambition. And then, rearing up in all its translucent pomposity, is the Crystal Cathedral of Garden Grove, the Philip Johnson–designed white-steel-and-silver-glass extravaganza of televisual prayer, with its spiky tower soaring to 124 feet, to compete with Disneyland's Matterhorn for peak visibility on the lowflung Orange County skyline. Perhaps this is the center of centers, after all.

All the signs are here to begin a different mapping of exopolis. From the vantage point of this calculated center of gravity, we begin to see beyond the industrial base of Orange County and to visualize other defining spaces. We should never lose sight of that industrial base, for it undergirds every exopolis. But there is so much more to see as we move around to the softer cities of illusion and aspiration.

Scene 3: Iconic Emplacements

> When it comes to spiritual emotions nothing can equal what you feel at the Palace of Living Arts in Buena Park. . . . It doesn't confine itself—except for some statues—to presenting reasonably faithful copies. The Palace reproduces in wax, in three dimensions, life-size and, obviously, in full color, the great masterpieces of painting of all time. Over there you see Leonardo, painting the portrait of a lady seated facing him: She is Mona Lisa, complete with chair, feet, and back. Leonardo has an easel beside him, and on the easel there is a two-dimensional copy of *La Gioconda*: What else did you expect?[3]

I must interrupt critic and semiologist Umberto Eco's *Travels in Hyperreality* to point out that the Palace (today no longer in existence) was itself an imitation of a far more impressive and technologically advanced display of lively simulations, the Pageant of the Masters, still held each summer at Laguna Beach, on the other side of Orange County. There the masterpieces are painted —with acrylics to deflect the stage lighting and with shadows and form-fitting indentations—so that live models can slip in to pose immobile for the required one and a half minutes in "magical tableaux" that still attract over a hundred thousand visitors every year. The 1990 pageant, for example, featured twenty-three "live re-creations" of paintings (culminating, by tradition, with *The Last Supper*) and various "living versions"—of a gold ornament, a carved wooden altar piece, a butterfly brooch, Japanese dolls, and Jules Charet posters.[4]

The theme of Eco's trip is "the Absolute Fake"; he is interested only in cities that are absolutely fake, "cities that imitate a city, just as wax museums imitate painting." His first sample is the Knott's Berry Farm of Buena Park:

> Here the whole trick seems to be exposed; the surrounding city context and the iron fencing (as well as the admission ticket) warn us that we are entering not a real city but a toy city. But as we begin walking down the first streets, the studied illusion takes over.

Knott's Berry Farm bills itself as the oldest themed amusement park in the world, an entertainment enclosure that celebrates the "wholesome aspects of an idealized and simpler America." Its founding father's arch-conservatism also set the fundamentalist tone for "old" Orange County's right-wing political traditions and the entrepreneurial dreams that fed not only the theme-parking of exopolis but also its post-Fordist industrialization.

Although it is still popular, Knott's simpler America was eclipsed by its more subtly modern corporate neighbor, Disneyland. Our semiological journeyman describes this extraordinary site, this brightly encoded *semeion* (Greek for both sign and specific location in space) as a "degenerate utopia," an "ideology realized in the form of a myth . . . presented as at once absolutely realistic and absolutely fantastic." It is, he says, "a disguised supermarket, where you buy obsessively, believing that you are still playing," but at the same time it is "more hyperrealistic than the wax museum," which pretends to imitate reality absolutely, "whereas Disneyland makes it clear that within its magic enclosure it is fantasy that is being absolutely reproduced." However,

> once the "total fake" is admitted, in order to be enjoyed it must seem totally real. . . . Disneyland tells us that faked nature corresponds much more to our daydream demands . . . that technology can give us more reality than nature can. . . . Here we not only enjoy a perfect imitation, we also enjoy the conviction that imitation has reached its apex and afterwards reality will always be inferior to it.

Eco's tour unveils the symbolic birthplaces of first-wave hyper-reality. The visiting observer always stops here, in the county's cannily crystallized cathedrals of iconic reassurance, often going no further than these primal reference points and their screaming semiotics. This is a mistake, for there has been a second wave that has carried hyperreality out of the localized enclosures and tightly bounded rationality of the old theme parks and into the geographies and biographies of everyday life, into the very fabric and fabrication of exopolis. Today the simulations of Disneyland seem almost folk-loric, crusty incunabula of a passing era. The rest of Orange County is leaving these absolutely fake cities behind, creating new magical enclosures for the absolutely fantastic reproduction of the totally real.

Something new is being born here, something that slips free of our old categories and stereotypes, resists conventional modes of explanation, and befuddles long-established strategies for political reaction. The exopolis demands more serious attention, for it is fast becoming the nexus of contemporary life—the only remaining primitive society, Jean Baudrillard calls it: a primitive society of the future. It is a society increasingly regulated by absorbing sim-ulacra: exact copies of originals that no longer exist, or perhaps never existed in the first place. Now, however, in Orange County America, the original simulacra are being simulated again, to ever higher powers and lengthening chains, all over the map of its ter-ritory. And the map that appears is a strange one: completely filled with those little directive arrows that tell the onlooker YOU ARE HERE.

> There are engines and anchors in every country, and they change over time. When I was born in Yorba Linda, the area was an anchor—an agricultural region and something of a playland. It is now the engine of progress in America, an area where entre-preneurs are gathering to drive the American dream forward. Look at the educational infrastructure, the corporate infrastruc-ture, the political leadership, and you see America's future. It is a dynamic, forward-looking place. Its people and products are changing America. . . . [Its political leaders] are *responsible* for the peaceful revolution of the East Bloc. Some of my old friends . . . will remain stalwarts of freedom. We owe them a great deal of thanks for their patient support of a sound defense that helped bring about global change. Others are new, shining stars . . . among the most talented additions to the United States Congress

in the last twenty-five years. In time, with seniority's assist, they will become superstars. . . . Far from being out of step, all these leaders and others are actually playing the tune.[5]

Thus spake Richard Milhous Nixon in 1990. The same tune continued to be played at the grand opening of the Nixon Library and Birthplace in the first of his hometowns, Yorba Linda, once a Quaker settlement and now a large-lot, zoned-for-horses, almost lily-white municipality that advertises itself as the "Land of Gracious Living" tucked away in the northern reaches of Orange County. Public television had a sniggering segment covering the celebration. On the show, bicoastal Buck Henry hosted an essentially Eastern view of the spectacle, with its thousands of red, white, and blue balloons, Tom Brokaw interviewing Richard Milhous himself, and all kinds of Republican presidents present for a make-believe summit. Only Jimmy Carter, who was supposed to be in Ethiopia, was not there among the allegedly living American presidents.

From the peaceful garden court, filled with (transplanted) indigenous trees and bushes, Buck pointed to the difficult-to-find subterranean Library, which had earlier stirred some controversy over whether it would be opened to anyone who might find something in it critical of Nixon. No way, it was later decided. We also were shown around the Birthplace, a $400,000 copy of the original home built by Nixon's father from a $300 Sears Roebuck kit. Buck smiled as Nixon's deep voice piped in to reminisce about his first nine years in Yorba Linda amidst all kinds of reproduced memorabilia, including the humble family piano that Dick's mother often whipped him into playing, and the mnemonic sound of passing trains to re-create history. Could it all be real? You bet!

The biggest enclosure was the audiovisual museum sitting atop the Library, tracing some chosen episodes in the Nixon career. From the grand entranceway, lined with *Time* magazine covers, one could march through his packaged political biography in a series of magical tableaux filled with indicative mementos and simulated moments. Buck took us quickly past the early years, through Mrs. Nixon's Passage (filled mainly with old dresses) to the dimly lit Watergate Room. There we listened to snippets from the famous tapes and simultaneously read the matching transcripts, the correspondence of sight and sound somehow adding authenticity. After viewing a montage of Nixon's last day in the White House and a large picture of his emotional helicopter farewell, we entered the Presidential Forum. Here the spectator can have what the information sheets call a "conversation" or a "dramatic interaction" with the thirty-seventh president via a "touchscreen" video system. Buck buttoned in one of the more than four hundred questions and we watched another representation of a representation of a representation. . . .

By far the most fascinating sight was the World Leaders Sculpture Room, where Nixon, Reagan, Ford, and Bush arrayed themselves amid "bronze-tone" life-size figures of what were described as "ten of the century's greatest political leaders," posed "in characteristic wardrobe and stances." Information about these world leaders will, we are told, soon be available through a touch-sensitive video monitor presenting biographical sketches and quotations, along with stories of their relationships with Nixon.

The television segment ended with appropriate Eastern detachment, showing the Park Avenue building that rejected Nixon's attempt to find a new home in New York City. But what can we make of all this? Is snide detachment enough? Not completely satisfied with this long chain of representations, I went to Yorba Linda to see for myself. I can remember little of my visit, however, for the videosimulation dominated the real experience, closing off much more than it opened. I felt once more a need to explore "other spaces," to understand the exopolis, to move beyond its oldest and newest amusement parks.

Scene 4: A Campus by Design

Looking out over the empty hills of the Irvine Ranch almost thirty years ago, planner William Pereira searched his mind for a powerful metaphor to match the UC campus he envisioned.

Pereira's aim . . . was "to establish a heart and a sense of place" that would offer the first students a feeling for "the destiny of the campus."

The plan became . . . a series of concentric rings—the innermost containing undergraduate facilities, the outer one housing graduate and research buildings. This ring-within-a-ring metaphor was intended to express a student's progress, from the self-absorbed concentration of the first years of study to the wider circle of the world beyond the campus.

   While the late architect's masterplan was bold, the buildings he fleshed it out with in the 1960s and 1970s were, in the view of many observers, overscaled and boringly detailed. Campus wags dubbed the modernist concrete boxes that enclose UCI's inner ring mall "a bunch of giant cheese graters."

   Now all this is changing. . . .[6]

Prehistory all over again: the ring-within-a-ring representing progress and modernity, disenchantment flourishing when the outer limits are reached. Now modernity itself is being displaced by deliberately postmodern architectonics, by a new kind of *campus* (field, plain, level space), as the inner rings are left behind.

   The story begins with the Irvine Ranch-cum-Company, benefactor to the University of California branch-ranch that bears its name. Exemplary promoter of the manufactured landscapes of exopolis, the Irvine Company is hard at work filling in the missing middles, creating ex-centric bundles of urban identity. Orange County's sleepy second-rate suburban conglomerations are growing up into a whirled series of dreamily dispersed semi-urbane gatherings. The county abounds with these synthetic identities, with what Baudrillard called "artificial paradises" in which "space lends a sense of grandeur even to the insipidity of the suburbs."[7] The transformation is nowhere better signaled than in microcosmic UCI, which some say stands for "Under Construction Indefinitely."

   As the City of Irvine and surrounding Orange County have burgeoned from a disaggregation of suburbs into a set of nearly urban centers, UCI has also—in the words of campus architect David Neuman—changed from "a suburban college into an urbane campus with an ambition to be academically and architecturally first rate." Indeed, the campus has become a virtual architectural theme park, with a building each from a covey of the world's trendiest architects. Here, a colonnaded management school by Robert Venturi. To the south, quirky, raw-looking structures by Frank Gehry and Eric Owen Moss. On the west, a "Food Satellite Center" for the humanities faculty by Morphosis, featuring a row of free-standing columns meant to look like an instant architectural ruin. Across the mall, a pop-postmodern science library by James Stirling in banded stucco. To the north, a folksy, red-tiled, Fine

Arts Village by Robert Stern. And, on the eastern quadrant, Charles Moore's Italianate Alumni House and Extension Classroom, described by one critic as "a stage set for an opera by Puccini."

Actually the playfulness of Moore's Extension Building, located where UCI's spoke for the social sciences meets the outside world, is less operatic than televisual. Moore himself saw the place as the piazza of some imagined Italo-Spanish-Californian town, bounded by three Baroque church-fronts and a rancho-style verandah, into which, on some dark night, a sworded Zorro might ride and slash his Z in the dust. Sure enough, during the dedication ceremonies, a masked man dressed in black swooped out of the shadows, presented a plaque to establish his authenticity, bowed with a smile beneath his penciled mustache, and cut the air with three swipes of his sword. With this instant memory, fantastically faked, the reassuring reel-world connections were made.

Reactions to this orbital and exceptionally contemporary *Ringstrasse*, and to UCI's attendant search for identity, were mixed: From a student-user of Gehry's new facility: "Looks like a hardware store." Gehry's deconstructive response: "The engineers who occupy my building are interested in how things are put together. So I gave them an architectural metaphor that takes its clues from the assembly of components you might find in a machine." The UCI chancellor responds more coyly: "I don't have to like it, but it draws attention, and it's important that people come to see us." Conservative members of the County Board of Supervisors worry, however, that the new architecture might upstage the "unremarkable buildings" that dominate the neighboring City of Irvine and create too much traffic, with all those people coming to see UCI, Orange County's dizzy-kneed University of Californialand.

Scene 5: Spotting the Spotless in Irvin

Lying just outside, in the exocampus of UCI, the Irvine Company is busy manufacturing other centers and nodes, ceaselessly creating more absolutely real fakes in order to simulate the appearance of urbanity. Here we enter another but related scene.

> Throw out those visions of pool tables and dart boards. Forget about pickled eggs and older waitresses who call you "hon." The city of Irvine [now with around 100,000 inhabitants] just got its

very first bar, and none of the above are anywhere to be seen.

For the Trocadero—not surprisingly—is Irvine incarnate, a so-Southern California watering hole located across the street from UC Irvine and characterized by its owners as "an upscale, traditional Jamaican plantation."

. . . As the very first real bar in Irvine history, the Trocadero is as much a symbol as it is a saloon. The Trocadero's owners and site were both hand-picked by the Irvine Company, which controls 50 percent of the city's retail space and has spent decades carefully molding the retail mix in this spotless suburb. The scrupulous planning has been so successful that enterprises such as dive bars and massage parlors can only be found on the wrong side of the city's boundaries. . . .

As owners Mark and Cindy Holechek say of their latest endeavor, [it is] a bar where patrons can graze on appetizers including fresh oysters injected with Stolichnaya and topped with orange hollandaise.[8]

About a year and a half ago, the development company approached Mark Holechek to design and run this bar-to-be and its very trendy kitchen. Holechek, at the time, was co-owner, along with brother-in-law Chuck Norris of action-film fame, of a successful Newport Beach bar called Woody's Wharf.

Holechek was also engaged to the former Cindy Kerby, a modeling school owner who just happened to be Miss California/ USA 1981, third runner-up for Miss USA in the same year, and voted by her cohorts as Miss Congeniality and Most Photogenic.

What's a barkeep to do when faced with such an opportunity? Holechek sold the Wharf, married Kerby, and went on an extended honeymoon in the Caribbean . . . collecting ideas for the proposed pub . . . The product of all that honeymoon research was . . . a Honduran mahogany bar and back bar to suggest "manliness," Holechek said, marble-topped tables, ceiling fans, palm trees and primary colors for a "feminine touch."[8]

Why did it take so long for Irvine to get a bar like the Trocadero, the story asks. The answers are illuminating. They speak of the grand existential dilemmas facing the makers of exopolis. "First, there's the history problem. Irvine doesn't have one." This "history problem" exists everywhere in Orange County, where, as we have been told, even the land and the ocean themselves look new. As the mayor said, "One thing I've learned is that you cannot telescope the evolution of an urban community into a matter of years. These things take time. You talk about Venice or Los Angeles, it's a hundred years of history. Here, history in a municipal sense is twenty years old."

Then, there is the more immediate "Irvine Company problem." Company representatives explained the delay as "a question of place and time: 1988 and Campus Drive are the right ones; any earlier and anywhere else are the wrong ones." The mayor added: "When you own most of the developable real estate, you can pretty much proceed at your own pace and discretion." Obviously, the place and time were right. "When we went before the Planning Commission to tell them our idea," Cindy Holechek said, "they gave us a standing ovation, they were so pleased to finally have a bar here."

Scene 6: Roots and Wings

Swinging over to the west bank of the UCI campus, we find another gathering of masterplanned spaces of a different sort in a corridor running along the Newport Freeway from Santa Ana and Tustin to Costa Mesa and Newport Beach. This is the Grand Axis Mundi of exopolitan Orange County, a true Champs Élysées of commercial development. An appropriate tour guide is provided by an old (1984) copy of the *Airport Business Journal*, a thick monthly serving the huddled masses next to John Wayne International Airport, one of the MacArthur Corridor's chief *arcs de triomphe*.

> Not since 1849 have Californians witnessed anything quite like it: a massive stampede of fortune-seekers eagerly laying claim to any piece of land they can lay their hands on. . . .
> MacArthur Boulevard, once a two-lane asphalt path running through orange groves and tomato patches, has widened like a flooded river, its waters rich in development dollars and its banks giving root to towering office complexes.
> . . . All signs point to this section of the County . . . becoming *the* major financial center in the County, and perhaps California, and perhaps the United States.[9]

The showpieces of many of the mixed-use projects taking root in the rich floodwaters seeping outward from the MacArthur Cor-

ridor are fake lakes. A project manager bubbles over on these
veritable pools of urbanity:

> "People are attracted to water. . . . The people of Orange
> County like a sense of openness and they like the romance and
> the ambiance that water brings. We felt it was a good investment
> to have that water."

The article goes on to identify the "crème" of MacArthur Corridor's business parks. The billion-dollar Koll Centers (one North
and another South), along with the Jamboree Center and Mac-
Arthur Court (both developed by the Irvine Company), anchor the
still-growing Irvine Business Complex just east of John Wayne Airport. Just south of the airport cluster, almost overlooking Newport
Harbor, the Civic Plaza, Pacific Mutual Plaza, an art museum, and
a country club surround the massive Fashion Island shopping mall.
All together, they comprise the Newport Center business complex,
another circular site masterplanned by William Pereira and the
Irvine Company, and now experiencing reconstruction of its own.
Together, the overlapping Newport and Irvine complexes, should
they reach their maximum planned development, promise to contain over 100 million square feet of office space—surely the biggest
out-of-downtown office complex in the world (unless the exopolis
around Washington, D.C., catches up to it).

This loaded zone is fantastically reproduced in miniature in the
Irvine Exhibit, housed at the Jamboree Center. To get there, you
pass through a colonnade of transplanted palm trees and the revolving doors to an imposing security desk, where you are asked
to leave your cameras behind. Disarmed, you are led to the plush
seats of a small theater that vibrates with anticipatory technologies.
The whole front wall is a split-screen panorama upon which is
projected a dazzling array of scenes—of birds and babies, sunsets
and shorelines, family outings and businessmen's lunches, clouds
and lakes (always lakes) and cuddly animals—all set to stereo-
phonic music and soothing voices announcing the supraliminal
messages that are repeated in the brochure clutched in your hands:

> There are only two lasting things we can give our children. One
> is roots. The other is wings. . . . Roots and wings. . . . Both in the

community and the natural environment, a balance must be established if the integrity of the system is to remain secure. . . .
We have the dream. We have the place where we can put down
roots. Where our lives can take wing.

The air is almost drugged with an effort to make you believe,
to make you want to consume new promises. But suddenly the
flashing pictures stop and the screen-wall becomes transparent, a
shimmering gossamer film behind which a secret room appears.
Still in your seat, with the music still throbbing in your ears, you
realize that the whole floor of the secret room is moving, tilting up
before your eyes, coming at you slowly to fill up the wall with a
portentous overview of Irvine Earth, an exact model of the real
world of Roots and Wings. You gather your belongings and move
toward the alluring model as it slowly tilts back to receive you, to
embrace you in person. It is a fascinating site, detailed down to
lane markers on the freeways and the loose dust where new homes
and offices are being built.

But this totalizing "area model" is not enough. After a brief
lecture, a guide takes you through marbled halls and up steel cap-
sule lifts to another floor, where the model is itself reproduced in
progressively larger-scaled closeups. You are moved, room by room,
closer and closer to the ultimate one-to-one correspondence between representation and reality. The final stop is a space almost
entirely filled with a giant structure very much like the building
you are in, exact in nearly every detail, offices lit and filled with
miniature accoutrements, including little people and tiny framed
pictures on the walls (made by computers, you are proudly told).
You feel like peeking into the second floor to see if you too can be
seen there, peeking into the second floor . . .

The experience is finally capped when the proud guide pushes
a button and an apparently solid outside wall disappears, revealing
a huge window onto the palm-colonnaded entranceway and the
surrounding buildings and grounds of the Irvine Business Complex.
It is a beautiful sight, so much bigger than its replica behind you,
so much more beautiful than your actual memories of having seen
it on the ground just an hour ago. You thank the guides, walk back
to the security desk, retrieve your camera, and exit, noting how
disappointing and dull the real columns of palm trees look in comparison to their artful imitations.

I could not help but think of Jean Baudrillard's reflections on California when he too stepped off at Irvine:

> Still, there is a violent contrast here . . . between the growing abstractness of a nuclear universe and a primary, visceral, unbounded vitality, but from the lack of roots, a metabolic vitality . . . in work and in buying and selling. Deep down, the U.S., with its space, its technological refinement, its bluff good conscience, even in those spaces which it opens up for simulation, is the *only remaining primitive society*. The fascinating thing is to travel through it as though it were the primitive society of the future, a society of complexity, hybridity, and the greatest intermingling, of a ritualism that is ferocious but whose superficial diversity lends it beauty . . . whose immanence is breathtaking, yet lacking a past through which to reflect on this.[10]

Scene 7: It's a Mall World After All

On the other side of John Wayne Airport, mainly in the city of Costa Mesa, the Irvine empire has its chief competitor, an offside supercenter with ferocious intimations of becoming the true upscale downtown simulacrum of Orange County. Here one finds the rest of the business parks: South Coast Metro Center, Center Tower, Home Ranch, Town Center—the names virtually reek with anticipatory pretensions. And there is more here—in what is collectively called "South Coast Metro . . . the shape of the future"—than merely intimations of urbanity. Its immanence, too, is breathtaking and transcendent.

> When America gets around to culture, the pioneers used to say, America will make culture hum. Except for places like Texas, there's nowhere the frontier spirit hums better than in affluent Orange County, which finally has symphony, opera, ballet, Broadway musicals, you name it, in a $73-million Orange County Performing Arts Center, known by its awful acronym OCPAC. Victory over any barbarian past is signified by a mighty triumphal arch.
>
> But this isn't imperial Rome. . . . The arch doesn't command intense life at the Forum, but at South Coast Plaza, the vast shopping mall and high-rise office development owned by Henry T. Segerstrom and his family, along the San Diego Freeway at Costa Mesa.

Never mind that the arch is a structural fake. Its reddish granite cladding is pure veneer, covering a trussed inner frame, all angles and squares, that has nothing to do with a rounded form. The great forward wall is nothing more than a free-standing screen, an enormous advertisement, cut open in the shape of an arch. . . .

Yet the superficial effect is grand. . . . The great symbolic portal—which turns out to be not a real entrance at all—swells majestically across the front of Segerstrom Hall, the three-thousand-seat auditorium that is OCPAC's pride and joy . . .

There could be no better emblem for Orange County, crashing through provincialism to the big-time world of music and art. . . . Despite many architectural flaws, Segerstrom Hall is, functionally, the finest multipurpose facility of its kind in the country.[11]

So too, one might say, is all of Orange County: a structural fake, an enormous advertisement, yet functionally the finest multipurpose facility of its kind in the country. How did it grow? The Swedish Segerstroms came to Orange County nearly a century ago to farm, and they claim to still be the world's largest lima-bean producers. But it is culture without the agri that the sons of Segerstrom dig today. Henry T., for one, is now "building a city" where anything you want can be found along the orange brick road that winds its way through the "phalanx of showy department stores" and "many-arched portals" of the "curiously insubstantial" South Coast Plaza, California's largest and most profitable shopping mall, with nearly three million square feet of space and almost ten thousand parking places, Nordstrom's, Mayco, Sears, Bullock's, Saks Fifth Avenue, Robinson's, the Broadway, over two hundred other stores and boutiques, and nearly half a billion dollars of taxable retail sales in 1986 . . . around and inside the C. J. Segerstrom and Sons office buildings and the tall South Coast Plaza Westin Hotel, bedecked with sculptures by Henry Moore, Alexander Calder, Joan Miró . . . edging next toward the intersection of Town Center and Park Center Drives not far from the Center Tower and Town Center office complexes (centers growing everywhere), from which "the charming little South Coast Repertory Theatre perks up to the right" . . . to a point where in front of you, "like the ascent to a shrine," the ceremonial ramp of OCPAC rises toward the brightly lit auto pavilion drop-off point and "lofty, glass-

enclosed lobby where [Richard Lippold's] 'Firebird' flies outward
above the broad terrace" of Segerstrom Hall itself, with its superb
view of the plazas and mesas of the coastal plain in the distance.

Just around the corner stands "the remarkable glass and steel
gates by Los Angeles artist Claire Falkenstein that lead to
Segerstrom's most exalted public gift to the environment," Isamu
Noguchi's "California Scenario," a spectacularly calm stone-and-
water garden nestled nonchalantly in an eerie scene that both mirrors and hides from the buildings around it, a piece-ful urban oasis
where civilized nature is preserved in stone and water.

I was once shown around it by a younger son of Segerstrom,
whose primary, visceral, unbounded vitality was indeed breathtaking. He had worked personally with Noguchi to shape the scenario, to seek that balance between the "human community" and
the "natural environment" that secures "the integrity of the system" and makes it soar to new heights—using much the same
words as the Irvine Exhibit. Dressed tightly in Italian silk, he coolly
spoke of family and farming in the blistering heat as he explained
to me the symbolism of the various sculpted forms. As we approached one of my favorite spots, a neat pile of large fairly
regularly-shaped stones turned orange by the late afternoon sun,
he recounted how each stone was carefully cut and shaped in a
particular Japanese village that specialized in making natural-look-
ing objects from Nature so that no one can tell the difference. He
watched Noguchi assemble these stony simulacra—exact copies of
non-existent originals—into a stimulating pile that would eventually be named in his family's honor: "Ode to the Lima Bean."

"I want to excentre myself," says Baudrillard, "to become ec-
centric, but I want to do so in a place that is the centre of the
world."[12] Perhaps here, in the illusive calm of the "California Scenario," one comes as close as possible to the center of the contemporary world, the "highest astral point," the "finest orbital space."
But I wonder if it is possible to find a single center in this terrain,
filled with what Peter Halley, the hyperreal artist and cultural critic,
calls

> cities that are doubles of themselves, cities that only exist as
> nostalgic references to the idea of city and to the ideas of com-
> munication and social intercourse. These simulated cities are
> placed around the globe more or less exactly where the old cities

were, but they no longer fulfill the function of the old cities. They are no longer centers; they only serve to simulate the phenomenon of the center.[13]

Scene 8: Cities That Are Doubles of Themselves

Thus far we have concentrated on the breathtaking industrial-cum-commercial-cum-cultural landscapes of exopolis, only hinting at the existence of residential populations. It is time now for another spin outward, to the sleeping margins of exopolis, the super-dormitories of the southern half of Orange County.

> Mission Viejo—swim capital of the world, mecca for medalists, home of the perfect-10 high dive, three competition swimming pools but only one public library—is nestled alongside a freeway in the rolling hills of south Orange County.
> Billed by its developer as "The California Promise," it has emerged as the epitome of the American Dream. . . .
> Swimmers and divers trained here before reaping a harvest of Olympic medals [in 1984], nine gold, two silver and one bronze —more medals than were won by France or Britain or, for that matter, 133 of the 140 nations taking part in the Games. . . .
> The world-famous Nadadores swim and diving teams train here, and are subsidized by the Mission Viejo Company, the developer. But there also are three wading pools, four hydrotherapy pools, a twenty-five-meter Olympic diving pool, nineteen lighted tennis courts, twelve handball and racquetball courts, five volleyball courts, two outdoor basketball courts, men's and women's saunas, two weight rooms, four outdoor playgrounds, a multi-purpose gym, nineteen improved parks, four recreation centers, a 125-acre man-made lake, two golf courses, and three competition pools (one a fifty-meter Olympic pool), and more—all built or donated, some still owned and operated, by the company.[14]

A local real-estate saleswoman and Municipal Advisory Council member summed it up: "It's a community that offers a great life style—a house in the suburbs, and your children kept busy." Another member of the council asks, "How can anybody from the East have anything but desire to move out here with us? I guess you'll just have to excuse us gloating about it. I couldn't speak too highly of the community—I'm in love with it." Some, however, are less sanguine. A forty-year-old housewife feels "out of step."

> "It's just a status thing here." she explained. "You must be happy, you must be well-rounded and must have children who do a lot of things. If you don't jog or walk or bike, people wonder if you have diabetes or some other disabling disease." . . .
>   She later asked a reporter not to identify her because her comments could create friction for her husband with his business and golfing friends, who, she said, "are *very Mission Viejo*."

Mission Viejo speaks for itself through the ventriloquy of the Mission Viejo Company, since the late 1970s part of the gargantuan empire of Philip Morris Inc., but with deeper roots going back to the large landholding families that continue to dominate the present-day political economy, even under new corporate umbrellas. The contemporary corporate connections, however, are worth contemplating, for they too deal in illusion.

With its purchases first of General Foods and then Kraft Foods, Philip Morris has become one of the largest conglomerates in America. Mission Viejo's stablemates now include not only the coughless Marlboro man and the tastes-good/less-filling Miller drinker but also the good-to-the-last-drop spouses of Maxwell House, the wish-I-were-an Oscar Meyer wiener kids, and the Kool-Aided and Tang-flaked babies—a cradle-to-grave conglomeration if there ever was one. And General Foods bolsters the list with even more mimetic products: Pop-Rocks, Dream Whip, Stove Top stuffing, Jell-O. Kraft's "foods" are still more specialized and further removed from the real things. Some years ago, they marketed an "engineered" cheese made with vegetable oil instead of butterfat. This cheese "analog." as it was officially classified—it was to be called Golden Image—caused some problems with the National Cheese Institute. Since processed cheese is an imitation cheese to begin with, what do you call an imitation of an imitation? The National Cheese Institute suggested that perhaps the category should be identified as "Golana," because "it is pleasant sounding . . . and is analog spelled backwards."[15] No one, it seems, suggested "Murcalumis."

Imitations and analogs of the corporate New Town of Mission Viejo (itself an imitation of the corporate New Town of Irvine) are filling up the frontierlands of south Orange County, lining the Saddleback Valley and other areas with a sprawl of coalescing urblets. Like the originals, they reach out for specialized residential niche markets and tightly package the local environment and life-style, to the point of prescribing the colors you may paint your house, whether you may hang an American (or other) flag outside your front door, and how best to keep up with the residential theme (Greek Island, Capri Villa, Uniquely American). Everything is spelled out in lengthy contracts with the developer, which venture too close to private-sector socialism for some tastes. Housing struggles focus around permissions and exceptions. May I construct a basketball hoop? May I line my pool with black tile? Do I dare to paint it peach?

Mission Viejo is now cloning toward the beach in the new development of Aliso Viejo, while just inland there is an even bigger, five-thousand-acre New Town Urban Village in the works, billing itself as Rancho Santa Margarita: "Where the West begins. Again." Just across the way, where the 1984 Olympic Pentathlon was held, Arvida Disney (along with Chevron and City Federal Savings and Loan) initiated the development of the upscale "resort and residential community" of Coto de Caza, building upon its preexisting facilities for riders of horses and for hunters of pheasant, quail, and clay pigeons. It continues growing today under new corporate wings.

Along the coast at Monarch Beach, Tokyo-based Nippon Shinpan Company, which owns Japan's largest credit-card service, recently purchased (from Quintex Australia Ltd.'s Laguna Niguel subsidiary) a 231-acre bite out of the last large undeveloped coastal property in Southern California. Here development is planned to revolve around a "world-class" golf course, a reminder (if any is needed) of the growing internationalization of exopolis, the local becoming global with blinding speed.

Orange County also has its Elderly New Towns, aging rather nicely. Leisure World, in the Laguna Hills, considered the largest retirement community in America, has given rise to a curious kind of ancillary development:

> The one-time bean fields outside Leisure World . . . have sprouted at least nine securities brokerage houses, five banks, twelve savings institutions, and numerous other money handlers. The institutions have turned a five block area outside Leisure World's main gate

off El Toro Road and Paseo de Valencia into a supermarket of
financial services. And many more brokers, bankers, and lenders
are a short distance away.

Retirement communities attracting brokers is not unusual.
. . . But Leisure World, which opened in September, 1964, is
different.[16]

The development is "the largest growth of upper wealth in the
country." The five bank branches outside the main gate reported
deposits totaling more than $343.1 million in 1985. Of the 21,000
residents, mostly retirees, many are former "captains of industry
—retired corporate executives, bank executives, publishing executives and successful doctors, dentists, and lawyers. At least three
retired Army generals and two Navy admirals, along with a retired
German U-boat captain," live in the targeted El(derly) Dorado of
Leisure World. The generals and admirals bring to mind another
fitful presence in the exopolis, a more secretive series of theme
parks being exposed as the outer spaces fill in.

Scene 9: On the Little Tactics of the Habitat

Marine Lt. Col. William J. Fox was still angry about the Japanese
attack on Pearl Harbor as he flew over the wide-open farmlands
of Orange County. It was 1942 and Fox was searching for "just
the right place" for a mainland airfield where Marine Corps avia-
tors could be trained for the campaign to regain the Pacific.

As he swept over a tiny railroad whistle-stop called El Toro,
Fox spotted a sprawling plot of land covered with bean fields and
orange groves.

It was perfect: few and far-away neighbors; close to the ocean
so pilots could practice carrier landings; within range of desert
bombing ranges, and near Camp Pendleton. . . .

"Orange County was an ideal place for military bases," Fox,
now ninety-two and a retired brigadier general, recalled. . . .
"There was hardly anyone living there."

Today, that Orange County airfield—the El Toro Marine
Corps Air Station—is under a siege Fox could not have imagined
forty-six years ago. Tightly packed housing tracts have brought
tens of thousands of neighbors creeping closer and closer to the
base fences. . . . With the advance of urban development have

come the volleys of complaints about the thunderous screams of low-flying Marine Corps jets.[17]

Around Boston, San Diego, Seattle, Jacksonville, Los Angeles, inside nearly every exopolis, the entrenchment of the military in the once-empty outer reaches is making its presence felt.[18] And once this presence is revealed, it triggers new insights into daily life on the exopolitan frontier, where the observant reporter finds several armies struggling for territorial security and recentered identity:

- The besieged military commanders and weapons-testers seeking protection from the peacetime assault on their once-pristine fortresses, deeply disturbed at being discovered but willing to enter into preliminary negotiations.
- The "well-organized community groups" and homeowners' associations fighting for their property rights and values against all encroachments upon the premises and promises they have so faithfully purchased.
- The "environmental activists" desperately searching for sanctuaries to protect the many endangered species of the exopolis.
- The "land-hungry developers" hunting for ever more room to accumulate and build their spectacular capitals of fiction.
- The "demanding local political leaders," seemingly stunned by it all, attempting impartially to turn every which way to serve their fractious constituencies.
- Finally, of course, the army represented by the reporter himself, the consultant media and imagineering specialists who selectively inform while performing as environmental spin doctors to it all, shaping the vantage points and defining the battlelines of nearly all the little exopolitan wars.

This six-sided contest for power (with its decided absence of foreign ethnicities and the well-barricaded alien poor) effectively describes the recentered local politics of the exopolis, where everything seems to revolve around emplacement and position, or what Michel Foucault once described as "the little tactics of the habitat." In the peculiar geometry of Orange County, where every point in space lays special claim to being a central place, the local wars over habitat and turf sometimes assume a grander, more global, scope.

If the neighbor is nuclear, for instance, what do you do? The people of San Clemente try not to think about it, reflecting the nation's complacency and only occasional concern about possible apocalypse. There are three reactors nearby at the largest nuclear power plant west of the Mississippi. Much of the population of the county lives in the Basic Emergency Planning Zone, "with its questionable promise that, in the event of something untoward, there will be a sure and hasty evacuation of everyone. The people hereabouts depend on that," says one local activist,

> even as they depend on assurances that it won't ever be needed. . . . What will it take to arouse them? . . . I have told some people that a single reactor meltdown . . . could cause 130,000 early deaths, 300,000 latent cancers, and the evacuation of 10 million people. . . . They listen, but they cannot allow themselves to consciously accept such grim processes. They choose not to live in fear.[19]

It can be harder to ignore military neighbors. Camp Pendleton produced a chain-reaction wreck on Interstate 5 when tank maneuvers raised a cloud of dust that reduced visibility on the highway to zero.

> Just to the north, Irvine community leaders became alarmed in 1986 over safety when a CH-53E Super Stallion transport helicopter based in Tustin came down for an emergency landing near a residential area. And earlier this year, an out-of-control Navy F-14 returning to Miramar Naval Air Station in San Diego crashed at a suburban airport near the base, killing one and injuring four others seriously.[20]

As a Marine spokesman explained, "The West Coast is right now in the lead as far as these encroachment problems go."

So the military tries at times to be a good neighbor. As development speeds forward throughout the county, 125,000-acre Camp Pendleton (in adjacent San Diego County) has become the last sanctuary for many endangered species. As a consequence, troops on field maneuvers "must be careful to avoid the nesting areas of the lightfooted clapper rail, the Belding's savannah sparrow, or the California least tern."

Occasionally even the future can be derailed by simple everyday reality, by inept Everyman, the worker left out of the hexagonal habitactics. A 1987 fire near San Juan Capistrano delayed crucial testing of the Alpha laser—designed to kill missiles, but capable of obliterating whole cities if necessary, a part of President Reagan's "Star Wars" defense system.

> The fire broke out . . . at the sprawling 2,700-acre TRW Inc. plant in southern Orange County when a worker opened a valve at the wrong time. . . . With the vacuum chamber contaminated by smoke and debris, officials said it is impossible to conduct experiments in which the laser beam would be produced and tested in spacelike conditions.[21]

Scene 10: Scamscape: On the Habitactics of Make-Believe

Under the conditions depicted in all the preceding scenes, it is no surprise that image and reality become spectacularly confused inside exopolis, that truth not only disappears but becomes totally and preternaturally irrelevant.

> Orange County holds the dubious title of "the fraud capital of the world," according to U.S. Postal Service inspectors. Five inspectors working out of the Santa Ana post office will handle mail-fraud complaints involving as many as 10,000 victims this year, said . . . the inspector who heads the team. [He] estimated that Orange County suffers losses of $250 million a year in fraud. . . . Orange County's affluence and the large number of retired people living here combine to make the area a favorite of con men. . . .
>
> Postal inspectors say the hottest current schemes involve precious-metal futures. Underground boiler-room operations typically convince investors they can reap huge profits and then spend their money on parties, drugs, and cars. . . . The operators usually disappear about the time the investors become suspicious.
>
> Another popular scam, envelope-stuffing, is difficult to trace

because victims who send in money to learn how to participate are usually too embarrassed to admit they've been had.[22]

The "seven-hundred-and-eighty-six-square-mile theme park," the place where "you can have anything you want," has become the most active and creative scamscape on earth. The boiler rooms may be densest in Newport Beach—"simply because it sounds classier over the phone than, say, Pomona," says one inspector—but frauds of every kind are being perpetrated all over Orange County in response to its seductive postmodern geography. And with instant communications, the frauds quickly reverberate outside the outer city.

The Defense Criminal Investigative Service office in Laguna Niguel is now the largest in the country. In just the past few years, the DCIS has filed nearly a hundred indictments and recovered more than $50 million in cases involving such imaginative practices as product substitution and the falsification of test results. Its most controversial case forced the bankruptcy and closure of a local firm that produced "fuzes" for the warheads of Phoenix air-to-air missiles—the weapons of choice for "Top Gun" Navy jet pilots. The fuze's frightening function is appropriately contrary: it both detonates the warhead and prevents it from detonating prematurely. Although local workers confidently boasted on an embossed metal sign that "THE BEST DAMNED FUZES IN THE WORLD ARE MANU-FACTURED BEHIND THIS DOOR," Pentagon procurers and DCIS officials apparently worried that the difference between the two functions of detonation and antidetonation was being insufficiently attended to on the factory floor. To this day, no one knows which viewpoint was correct.

Other leading categories of fraud take us back to the boiler rooms and their investment and bankruptcy schemes, crimes by computer, environmental crimes, real-estate fraud, insurance fraud (including a particularly serious problem with staged automobile accidents), Medicare and Medicaid fraud, and an amazing variety of other scams and cons that depend on the habitactics of make-believe. According to authorities, the average boiler-room victim (or "mooch") loses between $40,000 and $50,000. One was reported to have invested $400,000 based on a single telephone call, and another, a ninety-year-old widow, sent off $750,000 to a man who told her he was a "native Nebraska boy brought up with high morals." It is not uncommon for some of the boiler rooms to have a gross take of $3 million a month, certainly competitive with narcotics. During a police raid, a placard was found on a salesman's desk that effectively captures the sincerely duplicitous honesties of the boiler room, another of the magical enclosures of exopolis: "WE CHEAT THE OTHER GUY AND PASS THE SAVINGS ON TO YOU."

Most recently, the mythic peak of financial fraud was scaled by a "thrift" headquartered in Irvine but connected all over the country, and especially so to the junk-bond empires that rise and fall in Southern California. So costly were the unregulated scams of Charles H. Keating's unthrifty Lincoln Savings and Loan that its sincerely duplicitous failures will probably cost taxpayers billions of dollars to cover up and repair. Here the scamscape exceeds itself, transforming mere fraud into metafraud, wherein, to tap Baudrillard again, "it is no longer a question of false representation (ideology), but of concealing the fact that the real is no longer real." The exopolis reeks of metafrauds, "an ecstatic form of disappearance," an inability to tell the difference between pretense and reality because it no longer exists—whatever referent you pick for *it*.

Closing/Opening

It's not just Orange County where everything is possible and nothing is real. Creatively erosive postmodern geographies are being invented at a furious pace in every urban region in the country. Everyday life seems increasingly to have moved well beyond the simpler worlds of the artificial theme parks that you visit when you want to. The new theme parks now visit you, wherever you may be: the disappearance of the real is no longer revealingly concealed. This ecstatic disappearance is fast feeding a new mode of social regulation in the contemporary postmodern world, absorbing us unobtrusively into politically-numbed societies of hypersimulation where even everyday life is thematically spin-doctored and consciousness itself comes in prepackaged forms.

It is important to remember that the exopolis works—that it may be functionally the finest multi-purpose habitat to be found lying around the contemporary capitalist city. Its ecstatic inhabitants deeply believe in make-believing, and their shared fabrications are so diverting that they can carelessly laugh at those who so confidently tell them that they have been had. Is there no hope for successful resistance, no convincing alternative to the scam-scapes of exopolis?

For those of us who have the strength left to struggle against their alluring and illusive embrace, stubbornly Modernist modes of resistance and demystification will probably not be enough, for the terrain has shifted too much, the landmarks that anchored our old political maps have mostly disappeared, and the allure and illusion of the new geographies are filled with historically unexpected power. New postmodern modes of criticism and confrontation will be needed.

A beginning might be to understand that it is space, more than time, that now hides consequences from us, that these new geographies are what now push us away from the centers of power, and that this peripheralization is played out at many spatial scales, from those little tactics of the habitat to the strategic discourses of global geopolitics. If we can recapture our critical ability to see the "spatiality" of social life as inherently and instrumentally political, we may be able to take apart those deceptively embracing simulations and reconstruct a different cartography of power than the one now being mapped out inside exopolis.

TREVOR BODDY

Underground and Overhead: Building the Analogous City

Streets are as old as civilization, and more than any other human artifact, have come to symbolize public life, with all its human contact, conflict, and tolerance. One would not have thought, then, that they would be so vulnerable. Yet across North America, downtown streets are now subject to attack, a slow, quiet, but nonetheless effective onslaught underground and overhead, by glittering glass walkways above streets, or tiled tunnels beneath them.

Step from the wind and cold of the street outside into the new urban realm. At the entrance there is the logo for the building, the identi-kit for the isolated empire within, with reminders that what lies beyond is private property—emphatically both private and property. As the glass doors firmly close, the mental realm changes. We are inside, contained, separate, part of the system, a consumer, a peruser, a cruiser—membership has its privileges. Up the escalator, down the stair, along the bricked passageway, numbed by the incessant whirring and the mechanical breeze. Vaguely reassuring icons drift by like freeway signs: the information kiosk; the chain shoe store; the trickling fountain; the food fair garnished in neon. Like George Romero's ghouls in *Dawn of the Dead*, who return to the shopping mall "because that is what they knew in their former lives," the generations raised in suburbia feel at home among the familiar visual and environmental cues of this new downtown realm. Barely audible, snatches of conversation drift in the air—mortgages, promotions, kids, pictures. And the repertoire of body language is equally limited—never a clenched fist, a pas-

sionate kiss, a giddy wink, a fixed-shoulder stride. Pleasantly an-
esthetized, the new world underground and overhead doesn't seem
so new anymore, and its difference from the pace and rhythm of
real urban streets seems to matter less and less. Those other, older
streets, with their troubling smells and winds and unpredictability,
swirl into a distant and wispy memory, as vaporous as the smoke
and rain outside.

Over the past decade, new extensions to the city have appeared
in downtowns across the continent. In cities as various as Minneapolis, Dallas, Montreal, and Charlotte, raised pedestrian bridges
connect dispersed new towers into a linked system; mazes of tunnels
lead from public transit to workplace without recourse to conventional streets; people-mover transit systems glide above the scuffling
passions of streetbound cities. Grafted onto the living tissue of
existing downtowns, these new urban prosthetics seem benign at
first, artificial arms and plastic tubes needed to maintain essential
civic functions. Promoted as devices to beat the environmental
extremes of heat, cold, or humidity that make conventional streets
unbearable, they seem mere tools, value-free extensions of the existing urban realm.

They are anything but that. These pedestrian routes and their
attached towers, shopping centers, food fairs, and cultural complexes provide a filtered version of the experience of cities, a simulation of urbanity. By eliminating the most fundamental of urban
activities—people walking along streets—the new pedestrian systems underground and overhead are changing the nature of the
North American city.

There is ample reason to suppose the new downtowns of tunnels
and bridges have specific urban and social agendas. As we shall
see, they accelerate a stratification of race and class, and paradoxically degrade the very conditions they supposedly remedy—the
amenity, safety, and environmental conditions of the public realm.
The new pedestrian systems are the logical and necessary corollary
to the mounting investment in downtown shopping centers and
public infrastructure of the past two decades. As global capital has
recombined into increasingly monolithic structures, as real-estate
development has come to be dominated by fewer and larger concerns, as interaction between social classes has become more problematic in racially and economically segmented cities, it is inevitable

that architectural devices would have been found to render even the centers of the new corporate North American city sealed, separated, singular.

The particularly insidious quality of what William Whyte has called the "surrogate streets" of the new pedestrian systems is that they introduce a new scale and efficacy to the corporate retooling of the North American city.[1] Where development was once limited by the pattern of land assembly, with the largest unit being the block, the new bridges and tunnels allow the extension of the filtered corporate cities over entire sectors of downtown. Where once streets and sidewalks intervened between the islands of glass and spandrel panel, the new bridges and tunnels continue the same architectural order, and with them, the same socioeconomic order, between blocks. Heretofore streets functioned as periodic reminders and enforcers of the civic domain; the new patterns of city building remove even this remaining vestige of public life, replacing them with an analogue, a surrogate.

Precisely because downtown streets are the last preserve of something approaching a mixing of all sectors of society, their replacement by the sealed realm overhead and underground has enormous implications for all aspects of political life. Constitutional guarantees of free speech and of freedom of association and assembly mean much less if there is literally no peopled public place to serve as a forum in which to act out these rights. Only the myopic magnifying lens of the television camera maintains the demonstration, march, and picketing as a modality of political expression; they have otherwise faded into meaninglessness since the end of the Vietnam War with the shift of urban form and activity. These acts and activities have been displaced over the past decade from the square and main street to the windswept emptiness of City Hall Mall or Federal Building Plaza. To encounter a ragtag mob of protesters in such places today renders them even more pathetic, their marginality enforced by a physical displacement into so unimportant, uninhabited, and unloved a civic location.

The new pedestrian systems are only one manifestation of the principal mode of postmodern urbanism—the analogous city. It is one of the basic observations of postmodern cultural theory, linking Jean Baudrillard with Robert Venturi, that our age everywhere prefers simulation to reality. The postmodern analogous city begins with what Charles Moore has called the most influential piece of postwar American urbanism, Disneyland.[2] The three-fifths-scale recreation of Main Street America, situated between the technological utopia of Tomorrowland and the mythic past of Frontierland, has increasingly become the accepted model for city building and renovation in both the popular imagination and the professional mindset. It is impossible to imagine the success of the Rouse Corporation's "festival markets" (Faneuil Hall, South Street Seaport, etc.), the conflation of theme park with shopping center in the West Edmonton Mall, or the rustic nostalgia of new towns like Seaside, Florida, without this first and most resonant of the contemporary analogous cities. The controlled simulation of urban life extends to instant suburban "town centers," refashioned metropolitan civic centers, and the ersatz visuals and activities of far too many historic districts. In all these cases, the messy vitality of the metropolitan condition, with its unpredictable intermingling of classes, races, and social and cultural forms is rejected, to be replaced by a filtered, prettified, homogeneous substitute. The decline of metropolitanism as a civic ideal is one of the great underacknowledged cultural trends of the twentieth century in North America, and we are just beginning to glimpse the long-term impact of these less diverse cities. The new pedestrian systems represent only the latest development of the analogous city on one of its last frontiers, the streets of the downtown core.*

Seamlessly sutured into the downtown corpus, these reshaped pedestrian routes not only replace, they transform. Their status as

---

* A footnote to the rise of urban simulacra is the tale of one of the most respected critics of contemporary urbanism. Jane Jacobs left New York for Toronto in part because the ethnically diverse street life of the Lower East Side she remembered from childhood was disappearing, and in the 1970s Toronto seemed to maintain this street vitality. The situation in Canada's largest city has since deteriorated with the emergence of a nonwhite underclass, a declining infrastructure and school system, and the highest rents on the continent; Toronto has now gone far to repeat those same conditions that prompted her original flight. Sadly, the cornerstones of Jacobsian urbanism—picturesque ethnic shops piled high with imported goods, mustachioed hot-dog vendors in front of improvised streetcorner fountains, urban life considered as one enormous national-day festival—are cruelly mimicked in every Rouse market and historic district on the continent. Contemporary developers have found it eminently easy to furnish such obvious symbols of urbanism, while at the same time eliminating the racial, ethnic, and class diversity that interested Jacobs in the first place, and launched a widespread reconsideration of our cities a generation ago. Jacobsian urbanism has not failed, but succeeded too well—or more accurately a diorama of its most superficial ideas has preempted the public domain.

infrastructure makes their unspoken agendas—to make the city less public in the name of public amenity—all the more frightful. This is the quiet subterfuge of what is underground—immanent, unspoken, deeply insinuated—and overhead—above and beyond criticism, out of view and review, disengaged. In this final turn, the new tunnels and bridges can be seen as irksome metaphors for other processes transforming the North American city. Their conflation and reversal of private and public realms, their very artificiality, makes them an excellent entry to the broader anti-metropolitan forces at work in our cities.

A Short History of the Analogous City

Before there is the analogue, there is the thing itself. Broadly considered, in the Neolithic era there is an astonishing degree of convergence of form for human settlements. Widely separated peoples simultaneously invented not only streets—a vastly powerful cultural innovation—but hierarchical patterns of streets. With the increased concentrations of wealth and political power into imperial systems, the urban grid became the organizing framework in the Babylonian, Roman, Chinese, and Meso-American city. While there are important and fascinating variations, remarkably uniform street patterns had emerged worldwide by the Christian era.

The multilevel human settlement is just as old. The underground dwellings of China, the hillside burrows of Cappadocia, the stacked houses and lanes of the Pueblo cultures are all adaptations for purposes of defense or agricultural development. Yet all these multitiered urban forms use some variation of conventional streets; a two-level movement system—a doubling of streets—is surprisingly rare. The English market town of Chester developed a two-level street system in medieval times because of periodic flooding and the need for building sites within the walled town. Much of it is still intact, and Chester's combination of half-timbered bridges, wattle-and-daub walkways hung on buildings, and hand-hewn stairs to the street below make it disarmingly similar to contemporary raised-walkway systems.

The Italian Renaissance prompted new consideration of the multilevel city, notably in Leonardo da Vinci's 1490 sketches for a civic center. The most famous alternate pedestrian system grafted onto a living city was built in Florence in 1565. Designed by Vasari

for the Medici, the system of bridges and passageways ran nearly
a kilometer from the Palazzo Vecchio across the River Arno atop
the Ponte Vecchio, and on to the Palazzo Pitti. Presented by Fran-
cesco de Medici as a wedding gift to his bride, Johanna of Austria,
the *corridoio vasariano* was first intended as a defensive system
permitting the family to flee from the center of the city and government to their new Palazzo Pitti when street-fighting broke out
between the Guelphs and the Ghibellines.

This system was such a success that the noble families and their
hangers-on began to spend time there even when there was no
urban insurrection in sight. The *corridoio* was soon handsomely
furnished and decorated, and the views from its windows permitted
a refined analogue of the urban experience, the sense of being in
the city without the clash of classes, the randomness, the smells
and confusions of the actual Florentine streets below. To further
enhance the atmosphere, paintings were hung on the walls—nearly
the first time art was used to permanently embellish a large non-
religious interior space. The paintings lining the *corridoio* offered
nostalgia, romance, piety, and grandeur as modes of survival—and
strategies of evasion—in an urban realm rent by conflict.

For five centuries Paris has been the preeminent urban laboratory, and some of its experiments shed light on the notion of the
analogous city. The continuous arcades of the rue de Rivoli created
a type of urban space new to France. Providing shelter from the
rain in an intermediate realm between shops and street, the many
blocks of arcades helped foster the development of the urban
bourgeoisie by providing a venue for the conspicuous rituals of
consumption and display which are their essential folkways. Today
the arcades host a vibrant mix of races and classes, but this was
not always the case. At their peak in the eighteenth century, these
promenades of fashion and society were as guarded and socially
demarcated as any golf resort today. For Zola and Balzac, the view
to the arcades, or from them, became a central emblem of the
separation of classes. But their openness to the weather and their
interruption by city streets proved less than ideal; footmen had to
carry ladies of station from corner to corner across the threatening
and messy streets.

The next development of the analogous city was the covered
shopping arcades built in the early nineteenth century in every

Ponte Vecchio
Florence, Italy

major European city. This refined the idea of a pedestrian system
lined with exclusive shops, completely eliminating exposure to the
public street and the natural elements. By the 1860s a plan called
the Crystal Way was proposed for London, which would bring
together the underground railway, a pedestrian passageway, shops,
offices, and residences, all under a continuous glass arcade. Never
completed, it prefigures the modernist schemes of a century later.
In his novel *Palais Royal*, Richard Sennett explores a theme that
has been central to his writing, the social segregation of urban
space, accomplished in this case by the new covered arcades in
Paris and London:

> The arcades have spread their tentacles throughout modern Paris,
> radiating from the Palais-Royal to the north, east and west. The
> Passage des Panoramas, the Galerie Vivienne, the Galerie d'Or-
> léans: these have become glass capillaries of the city. London has
> its Burlington Arcade, its Royal Opera Arcade; more primitive in
> construction than many of the iron and glass creations in Paris,
> yet also triumphs over water and cold. The fabricator of arcades
> may . . . point with pride to his glass roofs which keep out smut
> and smoke. He invokes fashion: a lady in the Galerie d'Orléans
> promenades without fear that her dress will be grimed. He invokes
> more serious advantages: an infant in his perambulator breathes
> easily in an arcade, without choking on coal dust. Man, far from
> suffering at the hands of blind Nature, laughs at its terrors. The
> arcade nullifies cold, its brilliant lighting erases night; man admits
> into this architecture of control only that what is pleasing—trop-
> ical plants, for example, to decorate the corridors of his life under
> glass. [The arcade's] light and airy canopy suggests only peace,
> its aisles only the most refined intercourse, the precincts enclosed
> here containing objects made with the most devoted care.[3]

When Baron von Haussmann built the great boulevards of Paris,
it was one of the largest physical upheavals in any European capital
short of war. In fact, much of the impetus, rationale, and managerial wherewithal for their construction was military. Though
Haussmann and his sponsors certainly had other motives—the improvement of traffic, the connection of monuments and key streets,
the need for relief from the squalor and overcrowding of inner
Paris—military concerns were paramount. A mounting series of
urban insurrections, climaxing with the events of 1848, led to pro-

posals for new boulevards as a practical means to deploy armies rapidly throughout the city. The new boulevards would have the additional benefit of slicing problematic inner-city neighborhoods into more manageable units, and would create a plethora of desirable new building sites. By the 1870s, an increasingly wealthy Paris presented, along its bold new boulevards, a continuous face of middle-class jollity and frivolity. Haussmann's work can be seen as the first class-driven "theme-parking" of a major metropolis— a key precedent for new techniques of scenographic reassembly of urban components.

Throughout all these stages, the city remained tied firmly to the single ground level. Curiously, the construction of underground and elevated railways in the major European and American cities in the late nineteenth century, though it led to increased housing and commercial densities, did not at first create interest in the multilevel city. The existing ground-based streets continued to serve, superbly, as the horizontal pedestrian system. None of the elevated transit systems—whether the El in Chicago, the urban railways of Berlin, or elevated sections of subway systems in London, Paris, and New York—sparked extensive new retail levels or an alternate pedestrian system in the air. Except for certain major stations, the same is true of underground rail systems. Until well into this century, extended tunnel or bridge systems for purely pedestrian movement were surprisingly rare. There are simple but powerful reasons for this: the investment in street infrastructure (lighting, buses, fountains, businesses, signs) and the enduring cultural attraction of street-oriented activity was such that the separation of walker from traffic seemed foolish and wasteful.

With new building technologies and skyrocketing values of urban land, ever-larger buildings appeared throughout the late nineteenth and early twentieth centuries. And it is in these buildings that the multilevel arcade made its appearance. One example is Moscow's immense GUM department store, covering an area of several city blocks. Inspired by Milan's Galleria Vittorio Immanuele III, GUM surpasses the model, with numerous bridges connecting continuous walkways at various levels under a glass canopy, rather than Milan's single retail level integrated with surrounding streets. GUM, in turn, anticipated and inspired other multilevel downtown shopping precincts, such as Toronto's Eaton Centre.

Another influential multilevel construction was Rockefeller Center, designed and built in the late 1920s and early 1930s. While it incorporates the Manhattan urban grid, and its public spaces are exemplars of civic tolerance and amenity, in many ways it broke with the city that surrounds it. The subterranean shopping concourse served to link the various buildings to each other and to the subway below, but also rendered the complex more islandlike. Early accounts of Rockefeller Center announce the possibility of spending a day there working, shopping, and dancing without once venturing outdoors; half a century later, this notion of spending a day in a downtown mixed-use complex without once encountering a real urban street is finally banal. The undeniable success of Rockefeller Center's sunken plaza and the spaces off Fifth Avenue must not obscure the reality that it served as the prototype for the corporate makeover of North American downtowns, a makeover that relies heavily upon isolated multifunctional islands linked by pathways underground and overhead.

Not until well into the twentieth century did an urban theory evolve that actively promoted separating pedestrian movement from conventional streets. By this point the motorcar was having a deleterious effect on even the historic centers of European cities, and, in the spirit of the antihistoricism of the era, entirely new ways were sought to move about the city. Previously, the Garden City and City Beautiful movements in urban planning had advocated separating pedestrian zones from other traffic, but stratification of uses was seldom proposed or needed, given the densities involved. The multilevel city turned up more often in popular fiction and art than in professional literature. Visionary illustrations showed sweeping roadways connecting the tops of skyscrapers, with imagined aircraft clotting the sky above; the set designs of Fritz Lang's *Metropolis* and Alexander and Vincent Korda's *Things to Come* created multilevel dystopias on film. Emerging reality was only a bit less spectacular: Grand Central Station (under construction from 1903 to 1919) drew Park Avenue up a ramp from the south and across 42nd Street, swung it on raised roadways around the windows high above the station's main concourse, and projected it to the north, built on piers over the New York Central's split-level trainyards; it funneled pedestrians through its tunnels, ramps, stairways, balconies, and two levels of concourses from subway or sidewalk to train or taxi, shop or bar, ticket window or waiting room, or to one of the three major hotels that rose over its wings —a massive, autonomous early exemplar of that numerously replicated gray elephant of the analogous city, the megastructure.

By the late 1920s, this separation of pedestrian movement from motorized traffic on streets had become a cornerstone of the urbanism promoted by the Congrès Internationale d'Architecture Moderne (CIAM), and most notably by Le Corbusier. In *Towards a New Architecture*, Le Corbusier recommends removing pedestrian movement—and much else—from the ground plane. "Short passageways in the shape of bridges above the ordinary streets," he proposed, "would enable foot traffic to get about among these newly gained quarters consecrated to leisure amidst flowers and foliage."[4] Le Corbusier's dislike of the hurly burly of streets is well known, and formulating a more rationalized alternative became the generative idea of his urbanism, pursued in books such as *La Ville Radieuse* (1935) and projects ranging up to and including the Unité d'Habitation.

His Ville Contemporaine of 1922, for example, promoted a rigid vertical zoning of vehicular, pedestrian, and even airplane movement. The unlikely juxtaposition of soaring office and apartment towers, biplane landing strip, multilaned freeway, idyllic cafés, and pedestrian bridges in the same utopian landscape went surprisingly unquestioned, no doubt in part because of the machine-gun polemic of Le Corbusier's text, which simultaneously describes the inevitability and the desirability of such a new urban realm. Crucial to these urban schemes is their rigid vertical zoning, which goes hand in hand with the rigid separation of land uses on the urban plane proposed by the architect. This link between horizontal and vertical zoning is, as we shall see, essential.

With CIAM and Le Corbusier proselytizing for them, alternate pedestrian systems became central to postwar reconstruction efforts in Europe. Traffic was banned in all-new pedestrian districts in Rotterdam, while bridge and tunnel linkages saw limited application in Germany and Britain. But given the urgency of postwar rebuilding and the capital cost of constructing an alternative movement system, these efforts remained tentative; the rationalized, complete systems envisioned by the CIAM planners were never implemented in the centers of war-ravaged European cities. Or more accurately, in *Western* European cities, because the later rebuilding of Eastern Europe would be carried out almost entirely in a simplified-to-the-point-of-parody version of CIAM urban ideals, including notions of pedestrian-grade separation. Only with the rise of the British New Town movement of the 1960s did heavy public investment in pedestrian infrastructure merge with a modernist urbanism in the Corbusian mode. At Cumbernauld, Thamesmead, and elsewhere it became standard practice to include a wholly or largely pedestrian core, linked by bridges and walkways to the surrounding housing estates, with traffic and service and support functions woven in between the areas.

Meanwhile on this continent, architects and planners had been infected with Euro-envy.[5] Dormant for half a generation, Euro-envy exploded during the late 1940s and early 1950s, with the publication in popular and architectural magazines of gleaming modernist shopping precincts and ribbed phalanxes of housing projects in the recently bombed-out centers of Western European cities. Just as the destruction of cities by natural disaster exerts a powerful attraction for visionary architects and planners, the bombed districts of European capitals promised them commissions and the freedom to rewrite the past—both of which excited Euro-envy in the postwar generation.

With the heady gas of modernity everywhere, North Americans spoke loudly and lustfully of the shining new potential for European and Japanese cities, and longed for a strategy that would allow them, too, to build massive, boxy projects at the very center of town. This hyper-modern desire, when coupled with the Dickensian virtues of slum clearance, resulted in a similar transformation of cities on this continent. Present, too, was a scarcely disguised racism among planners and politicians, who sought to eradicate the most vocal—and visible—pockets of nonwhite inner-city life (which had grown enormously as blacks migrated from the South to the defense plants in the North and on the West Coast). All of these factors came together under the rubric of urban renewal, and its wide-spread application produced the first large-scale alternate pedestrian systems in North America.

That the practice of urban renewal never measured up to its theory hardly mattered; virtually every major city on the continent was to see a large inner-city neighborhood razed. This profession-ally and academically legitimated destruction of living sectors of the city was inevitably accompanied by a gleaming modernist rendering of allées of towers and plazas promoted in a whirl of civic boosterism. This frenzy of critique, demolition, and proposition was almost everywhere followed by a long and increasingly nervous wait for the supposedly inevitable moment when the private land market would begin to fuel the transformation. In the name of urban renewal, the leveling and clearing continued unabated for decades, even extending into the 1970s in cities such as Calgary and Montreal. There as elsewhere, the magic fingers of the self-correcting urban land market never appeared, and hoped-for private development in the now-emptied blocks never materialized, except in a pathetically few special cases. Sensing an embarrassing void, politicians of every stripe promoted these desolate zones for public or nonprofit buildings. Since their tax-generating capacity had already been reduced to zero, these uses became a means of cutting losses.

The renderings of soaring towers now forgotten, city after city filled its urban-renewal zone with cast-concrete city halls, aluminum-ribbed school-board headquarters, monolithic convention centers, and YMCAs. The long queue for the unemployment office like as not formed beneath the offices of some grandly named but nonetheless doomed redevelopment agency. Because of the memory of the slums that once stood on these lands, because of the inevitable remnant of a threatening nonwhite neighborhood a few blocks away, and because of the suburban mindset of those now returning to the inner city, internal links to connect and protect these new citadels of civic virtue seemed increasingly desirable. Sometimes traffic was banned and a mall was created, a forlorn zone of skateboarders and nervous commuters. More often, though, tunnels and bridges joined the new buildings. Effectively set apart in a quasi-public zone, the freshly housed bureaucrats could proceed with the business of networking and careering without the messy sights and sounds of the city they had been hired to serve.

Without conscious will or plan, then, a new urban order had been established in an area that had long resisted it. By default, in response to the abject failure of urban renewal, the first larger-than-block-scale change in the fabric of Downtown Everywhere had been accomplished. It was now possible to circulate through whole sectors of downtown on quarry tile and indoor-outdoor carpet, never encountering the sobering realities of concrete and asphalt; to walk from office to agency to restaurant under silkscreened banners waving in the pale wind of climate-controlled regularity; to approximate shopping-mall and home-and-school life in the heart of even the darkest downtown.

Inside the Analogous City I:
The Skyways of Minneapolis

Minneapolis was the first major city to propose elevated walkways—locally called skyways—throughout the downtown, and to include them in urban-planning negotiations. They were first suggested in the 1959 Central Minneapolis Plan, which also proposed the construction of the Nicollet Mall and a variety of other downtown improvements. Climate was not a factor in these early discussions; rather the plan argued the modernist case for efficiency and circulation, seeing the elevated pathways as a means of improving the civic mechanisms of Minneapolis. But as the first bridges were built in the 1960s and plans for the system became more ambitious, the rationale for skyways shifted—the efficient movement of pedestrians, separated from vehicles, became less important than the avoidance of extremes of climate. This shift coincides with the construction of the first enclosed suburban shopping malls in the Twin Cities. While generations had managed to use the windswept streets of this city famous for some of the coldest winters on the continent, Minnesotans now flocked to the new malls. Until the arrival of the enclosed mall, the street had been the unquestioned locus of commercial activity. After it, Minneapolis and St. Paul, like so many other cities, began the unhappy process of attempting to recreate the environmental, social, and commercial character of the shopping mall in their formerly unchallenged downtowns.

As the bridges were built one by one, a true pedestrian network emerged among the key downtown projects. After some initial arm-twisting by civic officials to get things started, developers in Minneapolis were increasingly drawn to the skyway concept, with the enticement of the extra rents to be generated from two-level retail coverage throughout the downtown and the zoning bonus of increased office space above. While prosperous and corporate Minneapolis allowed the private sector to build most of its skyway system, smaller and poorer St. Paul, not wanting to be outdone, built its bridge and corridor links with civic funds. Architecturally, the imagery of the two systems is different: the bridges of Minneapolis extend the cladding, color, and design quirks of the adjacent buildings over the street; those in St. Paul repeat a standard design again and again. It is an open question whether the public monotony of St. Paul or the private-sector hodgepodge of Minneapolis is more visually offensive; in either case, the bridges block views and light, and have forever changed the quality of downtown streets in the Twin Cities. It was once possible to look up and down Nicollet Mall, writes Judith Martin of the University of Minnesota:

> Today, two skyways cross the mall; a third one is being built in connection with City Center. Placing these bridges overhead will radically change the Mall. The ability to gaze down a street, even an ordinary downtown street, is an important way of orienting ourselves. Increasingly, the skyway connections across the downtown streets are hindering us in this process. They also destroy street-level views of buildings.[6]

When Johnson and Burgee's Crystal Court opened in the IDS Center in 1973, Minneapolis gained what Calgary and many of its other subsequent imitators lack—a major indoor space that lends openness and grandeur to the skyway system. At noon in winter, at any rate, the Crystal Court is one of the few interior plazas of its era and type to combine visual variety with amenity. It is not a glorified lobby or mere extension to a shopping center, but the indispensable hub of the skyway system, and a pleasing alternative to more conventional outdoor urban places.

Throughout the 1970s the Minneapolis system was extended in fits and starts, with most major downtown towers eventually connected to the pattern of bridges and walkways. With few exceptions, the second-level retail spaces never achieved the rents of ground level, and no skyway-linked interior plaza constructed since has matched the elegance of the Crystal Court. The bridges of the late 1970s and early 1980s were narrower, darker, and less well-detailed than those of the first cycle. As with most urban-development prototypes, the skyway had attained the status of the formula, and the formula was reduced to its essentials. With the onset of the 1982 recession, expansion ground to a halt, leaving many of the bold predictions made for the skyway unfulfilled.

At the same time, back on terra firma, street culture was changing. Even a state as liberal and affluent as Minnesota saw huge shifts in the quality of life. The litany of changes in the 1980s is familiar: the virtual collapse of federal housing programs under President Reagan; the unforeseen side-effects of community-release programs for the insane and infirm; the gradual whittling away of the continuities of the welfare state during a recession. All these conspired to radically change the street culture of this Midwestern metropolis. Crime rates rose and a new generation of urban professionals started to fear the downtown streets. More and more often, they had to run the disquieting gauntlet of babbling people in cardboard shanties as they dashed for the skyway entrance.

In reaction to the worsening social climate, the skyway system became something it was never intended to be: a fortress, a filter, a refuge. While the skyways had previously been policed only informally, security firms now received increased contracts to post officers whose purpose was to subtly dissuade the poor, infirm, black, native Indian, or mentally ill from entering the skyway system without explicit and closely monitored business. More than ever, the skyway system became the preserve of the middle class, and the downtown streets outside were left to the walking wounded, the urban casualties of Reaganomics.

In any public discussion of skyway bridges and other manifestations of the analogous city, we are confronted with the metaphoric use of climate and the interior. Americans and Canadians are notoriously unable to talk publicly about race and class. Precisely because these realities contradict civics-class homilies in both countries, North Americans resort to quiet codes and comforting metaphors to mask those urban factors they most fear. Europeans from Tocqueville to Baudrillard have often remarked upon our inability to admit race and class as active issues in the public realm, and to mask them in rhetorical camouflage. The immense appeal of "climate protection," at both conscious and subconscious levels of public debate, is that it can serve as a convenient code word or marker for other factors—principally race in the United States and class in Canada. Today, when we talk of protecting our citizens from the extremes of climate with new downtown bridges and

tunnels, what is actually being promoted is more social than me-
teorological. People now say they're "never going shopping downtown in winter" in exactly the same tone they use to say they're
"never going into that neighborhood anymore." The proposition
that one is incapable of venturing into the climatic void is powered
by the same sensibility that locks car doors from the inside at certain
intersections—no doubt en route to the local ski hill. Crime, poverty, and the disquieting clash of race and life-style have become
environmental—they have extended to become the virtual ideas of
"climate" or "openness" themselves—and nothing less than an
environmental barrier will render things inhabitable. With the new
urban skyways and tunnels, fear has been rendered architectural.

Both climate as metaphor and interioricity as symbol extend
the antiurban bias of North American culture—outlined by Leo
Marx in *The Machine in the Garden*—to new frontiers. No longer
are just the seedy areas of downtown to be avoided; as crime and
urban problems spread to every part of the city, even the streets
around the commercial, office, and institutional core are threatening. In the current environment of drugs, crime, and festering
race relations, "being inside" becomes a powerful symbol for being
protected, buttressed, coddled, while "being outside" evokes exposure, isolation, and vulnerability. In an increasingly blighted
urban landscape these code words become loaded, bearing meanings far beyond their prosaic origins. The symbolic power of bridges
and tunnels in the discourse of public space is such that, though
their purpose and promotion are couched in seemingly neutral
terms, their very physical properties pander to some of our deepest
fears. It is an unspoken terror for many white middle-class Americans to be surrounded by hostile blacks in an open street, or in
the case of Canadians, to be accosted by abusive, panhandling
urban Indians. We will go to considerable lengths to avoid these
zones of potentially frightening friction outside, and the urban
passageways of the analogous city are the solutions proposed by
too many cities.

By the mid-1980s, increasing race and class stratification, in
combination with a revived economy, sparked a new boom in skyway construction. Like other cities in the heartland, Minneapolis
now confronted a largely benign but visually offensive street population that had previously only been obvious in cities on the coasts
and the Great Lakes. The people of the Twin Cities reacted by

retreating into their skyways as never before. Two forms of policing kept the skyway system a haven of middle-class propriety: formal, by police officers at key entrance stairs and security guards in lobbies, and informal, through the visual codes and cues indicating that anyone not dressed appropriately or behaving in an acceptable manner was unwelcome.

In Minneapolis there are still large and happy lunch-hour crowds outside on fair summer days, and there one is tempted to believe that the skyway system has had little impact on ground-plane street life. But by 2:30 P.M. these crowds have disappeared, the supposed safety in middle-class numbers having vanished, leaving the street plane as firmly in the hands of the underclass as on any January afternoon. Despite the evident changes both overhead and below, the Minneapolis skyway system is still almost exclusively defended along climatic lines—protection from the heat and cold, a quasipublic infrastructure for the sake of convenience and nothing more. But it is clear that it is a refuge not just from the elements, but from the social climate. With the symbolically resonant and convenient code language of climate and exposure, a new city has been quietly laminated onto the core areas of Minneapolis and St. Paul. Architect Jaquelin Robertson sees the skyways as needless and ill-designed continuations of the suburbanization and privatization of downtowns throughout the country:

> Ironically, for a city with skybridges, Minneapolis has missed all the joy of bridges. . . . Blind decisions [about urban infrastructure] will continue to create a dreadful, hopelessly inefficient sprawl. They will further the privatization of space, of which the Minneapolis skyways system is one example. The notion of the public realm in the American city has all but vanished. The moment that we abandon the street for an enclosed, controlled, second level, we have furthered that privatization and have removed the citizen farther from his city.[7]

The Minneapolis–St. Paul experiment has been emulated by many cities. Charlotte, North Carolina, is home to one of the most appalling applications of the skyway concept, the aptly named "Overstreet Mall." Even the usually pleasant urban analyst William H. Whyte is compelled to call down the Charlotte system; in *City* he notes that the Overstreet Mall has created a virtual spatial apartheid in the city, with middle-class whites above, and blacks and poor people below.[8] Perhaps missing the point, or at least dulling it, Whyte insists that these groups "get the best of it" with their isolated inhabitation of the ground plane.

This same spatial apartheid is apparent in Detroit and other cities that have applied the concept. Radiating from Renaissance Center are the spokes of protected glassed walkways, connecting to a monorail drifting emptily around the squalid remnants of a once-great metropolitan center. The discontinuity between the metallic separateness of the Renaissance Center and the city it was to save is all too apparent. Inside the hermetic bridges and atria of the New Detroit, one is struck by the very conservative and very expensive clothes worn by young black men, even those who are clerks, messengers, and trainees. One soon starts to wonder whether the overdressing is a survival strategy, the entrance ticket to the new fortified urban encampments. Even Miami, with its warmer climate, is increasingly opting for grade-separated bridges and a monorail in its downtown, to spare tourists and suburbanites any encounter with the Latino street life immediately below. And in San Francisco, where protection from climate is surely not a factor, the bridges and walkways of the Embarcadero Center have brought new customers and vitality, as Market Street increasingly becomes the refuge of the infirm and nonwhite. The skyways of this new generation make the quiet subterfuge of the Twin Cities system seem benign by comparison.

Inside the Analogous City II:
Calgary's Plus Fifteen

Modeled closely on the Minneapolis skyways, Calgary's Plus Fifteen has surpassed its predecessor to become the world's largest off-the-ground pedestrian network. The system is named for the height of its midblock passageways and bridges, fifteen feet above the ground.[9] First proposed in the late 1960s in a report by Montreal architect Ray Affleck, working with Calgary urban designer Harold Hanen, the system was inspired by theories and projects of Le Corbusier, a variety of Team Ten projects, and early reports on the Minneapolis skyways. The Plus Fifteen, like analogous pedestrian systems elsewhere, was first rationalized along climatic lines, a means of making it possible to avoid Calgary streets during the annual six months of Canadian winter.

Calgary's high water table and unstable soils meant that underground tunnels were never an option. The first bridges—almost entirely paid for with municipal funds—linked public buildings in an urban-renewal district. As in Minneapolis, these early bridges displayed remarkable architectural variety—covered or open, acrylic domes or brick walls, controlled climates or simple windscreens.

Under Hanen's direction as key planner for the City of Calgary, the Plus Fifteen was formally incorporated into downtown urban-planning policy. Unlike the Minneapolis skyway system, the Calgary system was publicly owned and open twenty-four hours a day from the start. The first objective was to link the two major downtown department stores, Eaton's and the Hudson's Bay Company. At first, office-density bonuses were approved for towers that included walkways and bridges. By the mid-1970s, private developers were required to build Plus Fifteen bridges in their projects, and to contribute to a fund to finance missing links in the system. By the early 1980s, this fund permitted the city to construct missing walkways and bridges, making for a much more continuous system, and Calgary surpassed Minneapolis as a city of bridges in the air.

A major lubricant for the rapid completion of Plus Fifteen was the 1970s oil boom. As the headquarters for the Canadian energy industry and as the site of branch headquarters for multinationals, Calgary grew faster than any other medium-sized city in North America in the late 1970s and early 1980s. In 1979 more square feet of office space were built in Calgary than in New York and Chicago combined. The Plus Fifteen's first bridges and passageways were located in the urban-renewal zone in Calgary's east end; the second wave went up in the western reaches of the core, and this area too was soon crowded to capacity. As new corporate headquarters, speculative office towers, and retail and hotel complexes filled in the remaining central zone, the entire system had become linked by the early 1980s. Today, virtually every major building is connected, and the square mile of downtown Calgary completely interlaced with bridges and passageways.

As with most metropolitan building schemes on this scale, there were some unintended consequences. The bridges blocked views west towards the Rocky Mountains, highly prized as a symbol of

the active outdoor life so cherished in Calgary, host to the 1988
Olympics. Moreover, the bridges have truncated the formerly continuous street space into a series of discrete and uncomfortable
half-block urban "rooms" and have reduced sunlight and increased
wind velocities at ground level, all of which further encourage
citizens to flee the streets for the Plus Fifteen, even in temperate
seasons when streets were previously abuzz with pedestrians. Once
begun, the Plus Fifteen took on a life of its own, creating the very
social and environmental effects it intended to mitigate.

Of course, here as elsewhere, the bridge system undermined the
vitality of the streets. It is a tribute to the "peace, order, and good
government" so beloved by Canadians that the entire Plus Fifteen
system remains open twenty-four hours per day, inconceivable in
most American cities. From arrival in a high rise parking structure
in the morning through the dash to the deli at coffee break, shopping
at lunch, and the afternoon doctor's appointment, the middle and
managerial classes are able to accomplish their daily rounds totally
within the hermetic seal of the Plus Fifteen: happy to avoid the
ground plane on all but the most irresistible summer days. Unbearable winter days, of course, make the Plus Fifteen even more
desirable; during the severe winter of 1980, Calgary's prostitutes
moved from the streets to the bridges and passageways near the
major hotels. Predictably, there was a public hue and cry, and the
local police were required to leave their beloved cruisers and go on
foot patrol for the first time in years, in order to restore propriety
inside the above-ground system.

By 1985, as a result of Plus Fifteen's success, the last major
outdoor pedestrian space in downtown Calgary, the historic Stephen Avenue Mall (Eighth Avenue), was in serious decline, its
businesses failing, its surviving denizens ever more haggard. When
a light rail-transit system opened along the adjacent Seventh Avenue, it drew the secretaries, students, elderly, and service workers
away from the Stephen Avenue Mall, further stratifying a formerly
integrated city. The mall was left to the urban none-of-the-aboves:
the unemployed and never-employed, the dopers, bikers, punks,
urban Indians, and drifters—which in turn has accelerated business
closings, transforming a once-vibrant street into a forlorn strip.
Predictably this, in turn, has sparked ever-more-desperate gestures:
a hulking new mirrored City Hall at the east end of the mall; a
saccharine New York–designed Olympic Plaza; sweetheart deals

with developers to despoil its western flanks with more ungraceful, sun-blocking towers.

Today, downtown Calgary is dominated by the Plus Fifteen system. The ground plane is given over to traffic movement as it never was before. There is little doubt that the modest success of the extensive Plus Fifteen–level retail areas has been at the expense of the quantity and quality of retail activity at ground level. At first, the glittering tubes and canopied bridges above promise a new urban realm, the newest of New World cities, but upon arrival at the top of the escalator or entry stair, its emptiness and antiseptic air disappoint. There are winter gardens, craft galleries, and an endless cycle of shops, but there is little cause to think the analogous realm overhead aspires to the state of streets, or the companion conditions of urbanity.

Because shopping and strolling have been siphoned onto this higher plane, the streets give little evidence, even at noon, that this is one of the densest downtown cores of any medium-sized city on the continent. On a winter day the social stratification is complete, except for the joggers of this fitness-obsessed city, their bright clothing giving their sorties past the glass barrier the appearance of the extra-vehicular activities of the Apollo program. The clean, air-conditioned, tasteful, managed, unsurprising corridors, bridges, and shopping complexes of the Plus Fifteen have a surfeit of what Jan Morris has identified as the most insidious and deadly Canadian vice—"niceness."[10]

Inside the Analogous City III:
Montreal's Underground

The underground city in North America evolved much the way the overhead one did, with Montreal assuming Minneapolis's role. The Montreal system began with a single project, and an architecturally enlightened one at that—Place Ville Marie (PVM). Conceived by developer William Zeckendorf and designed by Henry Cobb and I. M. Pei, Place Ville Marie and its underground shopping concourse had an enormous impact on Montreal, and on Canadian urbanism as a whole. Opened in 1962, the cruciform tower contained as much office space as had been built in Montreal since World War II. Zeckendorf's original concept for the Montreal project included 150 boutiques and restaurants, placed underground to make room for the large formal plaza above. The topography, the adjacent structures, and a former commuter rail line beneath the site lent even more rationale to the underground plan.

Mayor Jean Drapeau was keen to make Place Ville Marie the hub of downtown redevelopment, and helped negotiate tunnel connections to the Queen Elizabeth Hotel and to the major commuter train station. Shops would line this active pedestrian route from rail station to Place Ville Marie, and on to the major shopping axis, rue Ste. Catherine. Looking ahead towards a World's Fair and a rubber-wheeled subway system, Mayor Drapeau considered PVM the first of his *"grands projets,"* which included the 1976 Olympics and the wholesale transformation of central Montreal—in most cases for the worse. Working closely with the mayor, the planner and traffic engineer Vincent Ponte proposed an underground pedestrian network radiating from the Place Ville Marie. Once the Drapeau-Ponte plan was in place, projects then being planned, such as Place Bonaventure, were designed to include connections to the PVM concourse. The overall plan was aided by topography: downtown Montreal lies on a sloping plane between Mount Royal and the St. Lawrence River; the slope makes extensive excavations necessary for all projects, and makes some understreet connections easier. Ponte saw Montreal's underground city as "more than a pedestrian thoroughfare; it will be an environment that people may enjoy all day long."[11] The mayor, Ponte, Pei, and the associated architects found their precedent for Place Ville Marie in Rockefeller Center. As the concept of a complete and autonomous urban realm was promoted, the New York example was invoked time and time again.

Pei's designs for the PVM shopping concourse set a high standard. The generous pedestrian areas, the design-controlled signage and storefronts, the reflective interior materials, and the ingenious light wells contribute to an airy and open quality. The underground concourse at Place Ville Marie has been a continuous commercial success, with its high-end retailers, its captive population of commuters heading north from the train station, and, not least, the concentration of Quebec's largest corporations—and highest discretionary incomes—in the elegant tower above. The continued success for over twenty-five years of the shopping concourse at Place Ville Marie is a tribute to the forward-looking ideas of Zeckendorf and Drapeau, but even more to the architectural finesse of

Pei and his Montreal design associates. While many of the architect's concepts have been compromised in a recent renovation of
the public spaces and concourses, many more remain. Here, as in
Philip Johnson's Crystal Court in Minneapolis, it is clear that original and considered architectural design can be a beneficial investment, underground as overhead.

Because of a huge investment in the new subway system, each
new cycle of downtown development through the late 1960s and
early 1970s had its tunnel connection to a transit stop, and its
cluster of commuter-related shops. But the election of the pro-
independence Parti Québecois government in 1976 put a halt to
most large private downtown development for nearly a decade. The
Montreal underground system was left a discontinuous series of
connections radiating out from subway stops, not the hoped-for
continuous network of knotted connections.

By the mid-1980s Quebec separatism had been rejected in a
public referendum, the new government had veered to the right,
and downtown development resumed with a vengeance. In this
latest cycle, the underground pedestrian network became truly continuous, rivaling the streets above. A key north-south linkage was
constructed under the city's major east-west shopping street, rue
Ste. Catherine, and several more are planned. New tunnels connected previously isolated segments, and east-west paths prolif-
erated to the point where much of the corporate core of downtown
Montreal could be traveled without ever venturing outside. Both
underground at the metro and concourse levels and in multileveled
complexes above, there was a veritable explosion of retail space in
downtown Montreal, so much so that the city is now seriously over-
boutiqued. Today, it has been estimated that over a third of all
retail and office space in downtown Montreal is directly linked to
the metro and the underground city, including "1.7 million square
meters of office buildings, 1,400 boutiques, two department stores,
3,800 hotel rooms, 11,500 parking spaces, three concert halls, two
rail stations, and numerous housing units."[12]

The more recent additions to the Montreal system apply few of
the beneficial lessons of Place Ville Marie. Light wells are seldom
incorporated now; materials are cheaper and public spaces less
generous. Sporadic funding and the extreme boom-bust cycles of
the Montreal real-estate market mean that some sections are un-
dersized and others oversized, to accommodate structures that will

never be built. As in the skyway systems, an urban calculus evolved that reduced the underground city to its most essential elements, in the process eradicating its verve and character. The most controversial recent project is Les Promenades de la Cathedrale, a part of the Maison des Coöperants office complex. Here Christ Church Cathedral, a dour but much-loved Gothic Revival church on rue Ste. Catherine, was elaborately pinned and reinforced, and a shopping center was constructed *underneath*, where the crypt had been. In an inversion of the sales of air rights that have made some of the richest congregations in Christendom richer, the church was paid well for the real estate underneath and around its nave. To sweeten the deal, the developer provided a flashy Bible store on the retail concourse; leather-bound scriptures can now compete with clothes and knickknacks in the subterranean marketplace.

Adding architectural insult to urban injury, the new retail zone mimics the spatial order and structural detail of the stone church above. One can now sit in the food fair of Les Promenades with an Orange Julius and an order of Polynesian PoPo balls and gaze upward to the gothic arches hung like scenographic stalactites from the ceiling, pale postmodern echoes of the actual church above. With the eye following the tracery, trefoils, and buttresses, one can contemplate the spiritual lesson of Les Promenades de la Cathedrale: the house of worship as marketing hook. Welcome to the analogous city. The demolition of the church above now must surely follow to complete the cycle.

As in Calgary and Minneapolis, the parallel city in Montreal has had some unintended effects. Street-level pedestrian activity has been reduced on north-south streets where underground passages provide an alternative. Rue Ste. Catharine, though, the major east-west shopping street, has proven itself amazingly resilient, vital even at the height of a Canadian winter. This is the one place in Montreal where all races, all classes, and both poles of this linguistically divided city meet in a happily frenetic parade. Yet while the sheer number of pedestrians is as high as ever, the social and economic makeup of the throngs still walking at street level has changed. Increasingly, Ste. Catharine is a street for those who pass through downtown, rather than those who live or work there.

Not surprisingly, the underground city is altogether a less free-thinking zone than above. When the provincial government banned

English-language signs in an attempt to bolster cultural identity for francophone Quebec, the independent merchants along rue Ste. Catharine risked jail terms by promoting their businesses in the proscribed language. The merchants of the underground city, however, quickly conformed to the new laws, bowing to pressure from shopping-complex owners and retail-chain management, who wanted to avoid confrontation. The mechanisms for social enforcement underground in Montreal are not nearly as obvious as those in Detroit or Minneapolis, but just as effective; many of the shopping centers linked to the underground city, writes Montreal urban planner David Brown,

> effectively screen clientele by keeping a watchful eye out for "undesirables" and "undesirable activity." Occasionally these definitions may go so far as to embrace all non-shoppers and all non-shopping activity. Observations and interviews indicate that people who would like to spend a little time relaxing in these centres must adopt a "resting from shopping" attitude when seated. Even then, the guards at many locations are instructed to move people along when they have sat for more than fifteen minutes.[13]

With residents and office workers increasingly drawn to the parallel analogous city (though only to shop), the ground level, exposed to the climate, is left to casual visitors, desultory shoppers, hangers-on, the young, and the restless. The residual vitality of Montreal's streets has been such that the middle class has not yet been scared away from its most important streets, but one could easily imagine a scenario of rapid decline, particularly if a prolonged recession or rising Quebec nationalism exacerbates social stresses and if additional tunnels provide a more continuous alternative for walkers.

Toronto and Edmonton have also opted for underground cities on the Montreal model, but they are not nearly as extensive. Toronto's civic authorities quickly sensed the unease in the new world underground, and in the early 1980s canceled public subsidies and planning policies promoting them. Edmonton has hedged its bets by switching in the 1980s from underground to overhead Pedways, in keeping with the jumbled architecture and urban planning in that city. Planners and critics in both cities argued that without at least periodic visual connection to the sun or to conventional streets, disorientation is a real problem in the new analogous city, not soluble through design alone.

Meanwhile the recent decline of Toronto's most important north-south street should stand as a warning for the future of Montreal's Ste. Catherine. Over the past decade Yonge Street has gone from lively boulevard to a tawdry series of stratified urban zones with sobriquets like "corporate core," "rough trade," "boys' town," "up-market," and "highway out of town," and whose spatially separated populations mix less than they did. The new Torontonians are a wholly disaggregated series of social, racial, class, and sexual subtypes, without the possibility of contact, divided by occupation, bylaw, habit, or default. Welcome to the tidy but separate rooms of the analogous city.

Perhaps because it is not as rich and obsessed with "world-class" status as Toronto, Montreal is the exception to this sad new rule about the incompatibility of diverse populations in even the most even-handed and just of North American cities. The analogous cities created by bridges and tunnels have been an underestimated means by which the North American city has been spatially zoned into separated and contained populations. It will one day be seen that the rent-a-cop on the concourse effectively zones social space as much as any land-use control, minimum lot size, or municipal edict. An expression of suburbia in the very heart of urban life, the analogous city removes the most powerful, monied, and articulate classes from downtown streets just when their attention and support are needed most.

Luckily, the spread of the analogous city is limited by the extraordinarily high investment it requires, usually provided directly or indirectly by governments. A key reason why there are more urban experiments overhead than underground is that bridges are cheaper than tunnels.[14] An underground city like Montreal's makes economic sense only if a major cycle of intense downtown development is tied to the construction of a subway system; tunneling and underground construction costs are simply too high to consider it otherwise. Since Los Angeles is the only major North American city planning a new heavy-transit system, Montreal is likely to be the most complete exploration of the underground city we will see.

Resisting the Analogous City

In contrast to the assertive symbolism of the theme park, the festival
market, or the ersatz town center, the analogous urbanism of the
underground and overhead city at first seems quiet, benign. Yet it
has the same roots, and its long-term effects may be more profound
than those more obvious targets of debate on the New North American City. Skyways and tunnels are at the forefront of one of the
most important urban processes of the 1990s: the suburbanization
of downtown. One reason for their widespread acceptance has been
that these new passageways have been presented, and broadly accepted, as mere technological fixes to avoid the extremes of climate
or to ease walking. With tunnels and bridges now connecting heretofore isolated islands of new development, retail dollars tend to
be spent within the network, rather than outside. More destruc-
tively, marginal social groups and political activity have been quietly excluded from what now passes for the public domain, and
monoclass, monoform, and decidedly monotonous hermetic archi-
pelagos have been created—all in the name of escaping the blazing
summer sun or the blustering winter wind. Under the guise of
convenience, we are imposing a middle-class tyranny on the last
significant urban realm of refuge for other modes of life, other
values: downtown streets.

The new tunnels and bridges act like the beltways and bypasses
that now ring every major metropolis on the continent; they are
all a movement system, independent of conventional streets, linking
work with shopping with recreation. Like the freeways that slashed
through the cities thirty years ago, these pedestrian networks are
rationalized in public discussion as infrastructure pure and simple,
an amenity for all that will not significantly change the city. With
the advantage of hindsight, we now know that the interstates and
beltways were anything but value-neutral "mere infrastructure";
their impact on nonwhite and inner-city neighborhoods was and
is disproportionately destructive. Political allegiances and connections shaped their location and construction, and they effectively
subsidize the flight of the middle classes from cities to exclusionary-
zoned fortresslike suburbs—what they avoid is as important as
what they connect. Now, what the beltways and interstates accomplished at the regional scale is being replicated in miniature in the

new analogous city of tunnels and bridges—they are extensions of the same sociopolitical processes, the same civic ideologies.

The filtering away of the middle classes from downtown streets removes the last zone of physical contact for the increasing diversity of ethnic and racial backgrounds, life-styles, and values in our cities. The rapidly evolving cultural space of television, computers, and the new communication technologies will never replace the information and economic system which is the vital public street. With climate the code word, and the offensiveness of poverty and epidemic crime the immediate issues, it will become increasingly easy for other cities to follow the lead of Minneapolis, Calgary, and Montreal towards the unintentional—but real—stratification of their social composition.

Dallas is a case in point, demonstrating these disturbing trends in the evolution of the analogous city. The key planner for the Dallas system of bridges and tunnels is the very same traffic engineer who helped propose Montreal's underground city—Vincent Ponte. The *éminence grise* of the analogous city, Ponte went so far as to propose banning pedestrians from parts of Dallas because "one of the chief contributing factors to traffic congestion is crowds of pedestrians interrupting the flow of traffic at intersections."[15] The solution, according to Ponte and other proponents, is to displace virtually all pedestrian activity into the simulated urban realm overhead and underfoot. The problem with the Dallas system is the spatial injustice it has done to the city. While one might try to explain away the social and racial separation of Charlotte or Calgary as the minor inconveniences of small and self-correcting cities, to see it on the scale of downtown Dallas brings the metaphor of spatial apartheid home: the nonwhite, the socially nonconformist, or the politically dissenting are unlikely ever to be allowed to install themselves in the quasiprivate domain of the city's elevated and underground shopping concourses.

Armed with the technocratic rationale of Ponte and an earnest army of civic engineers, traffic-department bean-counters across the continent record the number of cars to clear right turns per green light, building the case for new pedestrian bridges and tunnels. Bridges proliferate in Houston, Denver, and Winnipeg. Baltimore, Cleveland, Boston, and other cities have joined the experiment, or are about to. The reversal in the 1980s of two decades of improved urban amenity will only increase pressure for the construction of the analogous city, because too many of us—especially at the highest level of corporate and political life—have lost faith in the possibility of a socially diverse, multiracial, tolerant, public urban realm. Architects and planners, blinded by their skills and goaded by short-term objectives, have only too readily acquiesced to the analogous city.

It may yet become apparent to all that in losing the social forum of the traditional street to the new analogous city, something important is forever departed. A zone of coexistence, of dialogue, of friction, even, is necessary to a vital urban order; either we must return to the streets, or the analogous city must become more like the real city and the real streets from whence it came. Already, there is evidence of strategies of subversion, and one can never underestimate the potential of urban populations to associate where, when, and with whom they choose, especially where architectural symbolism, security guards, and signs tell them not to. The prostitutes on the Calgary bridges and the overdressed young black men in Detroit are not failures of the analogous city, but harbingers of its possible redemption through use by those who were first excluded. As outside pressures mount, the fantasy of germ-free suburban life maintained within the antiseptic analogous city cannot be maintained, even as the concept of the suburb itself becomes more complex, recombinant, recondite.

Many of the current political and social forces changing the North American city are almost inevitable, the glacial movements of an increasingly icy urban polity. But there is nothing inevitable about the analogous city. Dependent upon large public subsidy, the analogous city is vulnerable to public influence. We must start to question the motives of cities and citizens who find themselves suddenly incapable of dealing with climate, even while they praise the lively street culture of sweltering Cairo, rainy Milan, gloomy London, or icy Stockholm. We should sound alarms at all radical urban interventions that portray themselves as "just" infrastructure, because they have too often proven anything but "just" that. Where the analogous city has been built, we need to find ways of opening it up to a complete and representative citizenry—even to those who threaten, avow causes, or cannot or choose not to consume. We should not sacrifice the life of the polis, that most ancient benefit of the culture of western cities, with meek excuses about private property rights and the desires of people to associate with their own kind.

Recall the Medici gazing from the *corridoio vasariano* onto the fighting in the Florentine streets below. We must, civic and virtuous people all, resist the temptation to fancy ourselves the new Medici, with our continuous sealed walker's highways to art gallery, shopping center, health club, and other splendid palaces of refuge. We must not let our commissioning of grandiose civic centers blind us to life in the surrounding precincts; we cannot build our city of art and poetry alone. We must quit the splendid surroundings of our new bridges to return again to the streets, with all their hectoring danger, their swirling confusion, and their muddled vitality. Or else we must do all we can to bring the culture of the street into the new realm, however dangerous or messy this might be. To do less is to accept a substitute, to live an analogue.

MIKE DAVIS

Fortress Los Angeles: The Militarization of Urban Space

The city bristles with malice. The carefully manicured lawns of the Westside sprout ominous little signs threatening "ARMED RESPONSE!" Wealthier neighborhoods in the canyons and hillsides cower behind walls guarded by gun-toting private police and state-of-the-art electronic surveillance systems. Downtown, a publicly subsidized "urban renaissance" has raised a forbidding corporate citadel, separated from the surrounding poor neighborhoods by battlements and moats. Some of these neighborhoods—predominately black or Latino—have in turn been sealed off by the police with barricades and checkpoints. In Hollywood, architect Frank Gehry has enshrined the siege look in a library that looks like a Foreign Legion fort. In Watts, developer Alexander Haagen has pioneered the totally secure shopping mall, a latter-day Panopticon, a prison of consumerism surrounded by iron-stake fences and motion detectors, overseen by a police substation in a central tower. Meanwhile in Downtown, a spectacular structure that tourists regularly mistake for a hotel is actually a new federal prison.

Welcome to post-liberal Los Angeles, where the defense of luxury has given birth to an arsenal of security systems and an obsession with the policing of social boundaries through architecture. This militarization of city life is increasingly visible everywhere in the built environment of the 1990s. Yet contemporary urban theory has remained oddly silent about its implications. Indeed, the pop apocalypticism of Hollywood movies and pulp science fiction has been more realistic—and politically perceptive—in representing the hardening of the urban landscape. Images of prisonlike inner cities (*Escape from New York*, *Running Man*), high-tech police death squads (*Bladerunner*), sentient skyscrapers (*Die Hard*), and guerrilla warfare in the streets (*Colors*) are not fantasies, but merely extrapolations from the present.

Such stark dystopian visions show how much the obsession with security has supplanted hopes for urban reform and social integration. The dire predictions of Richard Nixon's 1969 National Commission on the Causes and Prevention of Violence have been tragically fulfilled in the social polarizations of the Reagan era.[1] We do indeed now live in "fortress cities" brutally divided into "fortified cells" of affluence and "places of terror" where police battle the criminalized poor. The "Second Civil War" that began during the long hot summers of the late 1960s has been institutionalized in the very structure of urban space. The old liberal attempts at social control, which at least tried to balance repression with reform, have been superseded by open social warfare that pits the interests of the middle class against the welfare of the urban poor. In cities like Los Angeles, on the hard edge of postmodernity, architecture and the police apparatus are being merged to an unprecedented degree.

The Destruction of Public Space

The universal consequence of the crusade to secure the city is the destruction of any truly democratic urban space. The American city is being systematically turned inward. The "public" spaces of the new megastructures and supermalls have supplanted traditional streets and disciplined their spontaneity. Inside malls, office centers, and cultural complexes, public activities are sorted into strictly functional compartments under the gaze of private police forces. This architectural privatization of the physical public sphere, moreover, is complemented by a parallel restructuring of electronic space, as heavily guarded, pay-access databases and subscription cable services expropriate the invisible *agora*. In Los Angeles, for example, the ghetto is defined not only by its paucity of parks and public amenities, but also by the fact that it is not wired into any of the key information circuits. In contrast, the affluent Westside is plugged—often at public expense—into dense networks of educational and cultural media.

In either guise, architectural or electronic, this polarization marks the decline of urban liberalism, and with it the end of what might be called the Olmstedian vision of public space in America. Frederick Law Olmsted, the father of Central Park, conceived public landscapes and parks as social safety-valves, *mixing* classes and ethnicities in common (bourgeois) recreations and pleasures: "No one who has closely observed the conduct of the people who visit [Central] Park," he wrote, "can doubt that it exercises a distinctly harmonizing and refining influence upon the most unfortunate and most lawless classes of the city—an influence favorable to courtesy, self-control, and temperance."[2]

This reformist ideal of public space as the emollient of class struggle is now as obsolete as Rooseveltian nostrums of full employment and an Economic Bill of Rights. As for the mixing of classes, contemporary urban America is more like Victorian England than the New York of Walt Whitman or Fiorello La Guardia. In Los Angeles—once a paradise of free beaches, luxurious parks, and "cruising strips"—genuinely democratic space is virtually extinct. The pleasure domes of the elite Westside rely upon the social imprisonment of a third-world service proletariat in increasingly repressive ghettos and barrios. In a city of several million aspiring immigrants (where Spanish-surname children are now almost two-thirds of the school-age population), public amenities are shrinking radically, libraries and playgrounds are closing, parks are falling derelict, and streets are growing ever more desolate and dangerous.

Here, as in other American cities, municipal policy has taken its lead from the security offensive and the middle-class demand for increased spatial and social insulation. Taxes previously targeted for traditional public spaces and recreational facilities have been redirected to support corporate redevelopment projects. A pliant city government—in the case of Los Angeles, one ironically professing to represent a liberal biracial coalition—has collaborated in privatizing public space and subsidizing new exclusive enclaves (benignly called "urban villages"). The celebratory language used to describe contemporary Los Angeles—"urban renaissance," "city of the future," and so on—is only a triumphal gloss laid over the brutalization of its inner-city neighborhoods and the stark divisions of class and race represented in its built environment. Urban form obediently follows repressive function. Los Angeles, as always in the vanguard, offers an especially disturbing guide to the emerging liaisons between urban architecture and the police state.

Forbidden City

Los Angeles's first spatial militarist was the legendary General Harrison Gray Otis, proprietor of the *Times* and implacable foe of organized labor. In the 1890s, after locking out his union printers and announcing a crusade for "industrial freedom," Otis retreated into a new *Times* building designed as a fortress with grim turrets and battlements crowned by a bellicose bronze eagle. To emphasize his truculence, he later had a small, functional cannon installed on the hood of his Packard touring car. Not surprisingly, this display of aggression produced a response in kind. On October 1, 1910, the heavily fortified *Times* headquarters—the command-post of the open shop on the West Coast—was destroyed in a catastrophic explosion, blamed on union saboteurs.

Eighty years later, the martial spirit of General Otis pervades the design of Los Angeles's new Downtown, whose skyscrapers march from Bunker Hill down the Figueroa corridor. Two billion dollars of public tax subsidies have enticed big banks and corporate headquarters back to a central city they almost abandoned in the 1960s. Into a waiting grid, cleared of tenement housing by the city's powerful and largely unaccountable redevelopment agency, local developers and offshore investors (increasingly Japanese) have planted a series of block-square complexes: Crocker Center, the Bonaventure Hotel and Shopping Mall, the World Trade Center, California Plaza, Arco Center, and so on. With an increasingly dense and self-contained circulation system linking these superblocks, the new financial district is best conceived as a single, self-referential hyperstructure, a Miesian skyscape of fantastic proportions.

Like similar megalomaniacal complexes tethered to fragmented and desolate downtowns—such as the Renaissance Center in Detroit and the Peachtree and Omni centers in Atlanta—Bunker Hill and the Figueroa corridor have provoked a storm of objections to their abuse of scale and composition, their denigration of street life, and their confiscation of the vital energy of the center, now sequestered within their subterranean concourses or privatized plazas. Sam Hall Kaplan, the former design critic of the *Times*, has vociferously denounced the antistreet bias of redevelopment; in his view, the superimposition of "hermetically sealed fortresses" and random "pieces of suburbia" onto Downtown has "killed the street" and "dammed the rivers of life."[3]

Yet Kaplan's vigorous defense of pedestrian democracy remains grounded in liberal complaints about "bland design" and "elitist planning practices." Like most architectural critics, he rails against the oversights of urban design without conceding a dimension of foresight, and even of deliberate repressive intent. For when Downtown's new "Gold Coast" is seen in relation to other social landscapes in the central city, the "fortress effect" emerges, not as an inadvertent failure of design, but as an explicit—and, in its own terms, successful—socio-spatial strategy.

The goals of this strategy may be summarized as a double repression: to obliterate all connection with Downtown's past and to prevent any dynamic association with the non-Anglo urbanism of its future. Los Angeles is unusual among major urban centers in having preserved, however negligently, most of its Beaux Arts commercial core. Yet the city chose to transplant—at immense public cost—the entire corporate and financial district from around Broadway and Spring Street to Bunker Hill, a half-dozen blocks further west.

The underlying logic of this operation is revealing. In other cities, developers have tried to harmonize the new cityscape and the old, exploiting the latter's historic buildings to create gentrified zones (Faneuil Market, Ghirardelli Square, and so on) as supports to middle-class residential colonization. But Downtown Los Angeles's redevelopers considered property values in the old Broadway core as irreversibly eroded by the area's status as the hub of public transportation primarily used by black and Mexican poor. In the wake of the 1965 Watts Rebellion, whose fires burned to within a few blocks of the old Downtown, resegregated spatial security became the paramount concern. The 1960–64 "Centropolis" masterplan, which had envisioned the renewal of the old core, was unceremoniously scrapped. Meanwhile the Los Angeles Police Department (LAPD) abetted the flight of business from the Broadway–Spring Street area to the fortified redoubts of Bunker Hill by spreading scare literature about the "imminent gang invasion" by black teenagers.[4]

To emphasize the "security" of the new Downtown, virtually

all the traditional pedestrian links to the old center, including the famous Angels' Flight funicular railroad, were removed. The Harbor Freeway and the regraded palisades of Bunker Hill further cut off the new financial core from the poor immigrant neighborhoods that surround it on every side. Along the base of California Plaza (home of the Museum of Contemporary Art), Hill Street functions as the stark boundary separating the luxury of Bunker Hill from the chaotic life of Broadway, now the primary shopping and entertainment street for Latino immigrants. Because gentrifiers now have their eye on the northern end of the Broadway corridor (redubbed Bunker Hill East), the redevelopment agency promises to restore pedestrian access to the Hill in the 1990s. This, of course, only dramatizes the current bias against any spatial interaction between old and new, poor and rich—except in the framework of gentrification. Although a few white-collar types sometimes venture into the Grand Central Market—a popular emporium of tropical produce and fresh foods—Latino shoppers or Saturday *flaneurs* never ascend to the upscale precincts above Hill Street. The occasional appearance of a destitute street nomad in Broadway Plaza or in front of the Museum of Contemporary Art sets off a quiet panic, as video cameras turn on their mounts and security guards adjust their belts.

Photographs of the old Downtown in its 1940s prime show crowds of Anglo, black, and Mexican shoppers of all ages and classes. The contemporary Downtown "renaissance" renders such heterogeneity virtually impossible. It is intended not just to "kill the street" as Kaplan feared, but to "kill the crowd," to eliminate that democratic mixture that Olmsted believed was America's antidote to European class polarization. The new Downtown is designed to ensure a seamless continuum of middle-class work, consumption, and recreation, insulated from the city's "unsavory" streets. Ramparts and battlements, reflective glass and elevated pedways, are tropes in an architectural language warning off the underclass Other. Although architectural critics are usually blind to this militarized syntax, urban pariah groups—whether young black men, poor Latino immigrants, or elderly homeless white females—read the signs immediately.

Extreme though it may seem, Bunker Hill is only one local expression of the national movement toward "defensible" urban centers. Cities of all sizes are rushing to apply and profit from a formula that links together clustered development, social homogeneity, and a perception of security. As an article in *Urban Land* magazine on "how to overcome fear of crime in downtowns" advised:

> A downtown can be designed and developed to make visitors feel that it—or a significant portion of it—is attractive and the type of place that "respectable people" like themselves tend to frequent. . . . A core downtown area that is compact, densely developed and multifunctional, [with] offices and housing for middle- and upper-income residents . . . can assure a high percentage of "respectable," law-abiding pedestrians. Such an attractive redeveloped core area would also be large enough to affect the downtown's overall image.[5]

Mean Streets

This strategic armoring of the city against the poor is especially obvious at street level. In his famous study of the "social life of small urban spaces," William Whyte points out that the quality of any urban environment can be measured, first of all, by whether there are convenient, comfortable places for pedestrians to sit. This maxim has been warmly taken to heart by designers of the high corporate precincts of Bunker Hill and its adjacent "urban villages." As part of the city's policy of subsidizing the white-collar residential colonization of Downtown, tens of millions of dollars of tax revenue have been invested in the creation of attractive, "soft" environments in favored areas. Planners envision a succession of opulent piazzas, fountains, public art, exotic shrubbery, and comfortable street furniture along a ten-block pedestrian corridor from Bunker Hill to South Park. Brochures sell Downtown's "livability" with idyllic representations of office workers and affluent tourists sipping cappuccino and listening to free jazz concerts in the terraced gardens of California Plaza and Grand Hope Park.

In stark contrast, a few blocks away, the city is engaged in a relentless struggle to make the streets as unlivable as possible for the homeless and the poor. The persistence of thousands of street people on the fringes of Bunker Hill and the Civic Center tarnishes the image of designer living Downtown and betrays the laboriously

constructed illusion of an urban "renaissance." City Hall has re-
taliated with its own version of low-intensity warfare.

Although city leaders periodically propose schemes for removing indigents *en masse*—deporting them to a poor farm on the edge
of the desert, confining them in camps in the mountains, or in-
terning them on derelict ferries in the harbor—such "final solutions" have been blocked by council members' fears of the
displacement of the homeless into their districts. Instead the city,
self-consciously adopting the idiom of cold war, has promoted the
"containment" (the official term) of the homeless in Skid Row,
along Fifth Street, systematically transforming the neighborhood
into an outdoor poorhouse. But this containment strategy breeds
its own vicious cycle of contradiction. By condensing the mass of
the desperate and helpless together in such a small space, and
denying adequate housing, official policy has transformed Skid Row
into probably the most dangerous ten square blocks in the world.
Every night on Skid Row is Friday the 13th, and, unsurprisingly,
many of the homeless seek to escape the area during the night at
all costs, searching safer niches in other parts of Downtown. The
city in turn tightens the noose with increased police harassment
and ingenious design deterrents.

One of the simplest but most mean-spirited of these deterrents
is the Rapid Transit District's new barrel-shaped bus bench, which
offers a minimal surface for uncomfortable sitting while making
sleeping impossible. Such "bumproof" benches are being widely
introduced on the periphery of Skid Row. Another invention is the
aggressive deployment of outdoor sprinklers. Several years ago the
city opened a Skid Row Park; to ensure that the park could not
be used for overnight camping, overhead sprinklers were programmed to drench unsuspecting sleepers at random times during
the night. The system was immediately copied by local merchants
to drive the homeless away from (public) storefront sidewalks.
Meanwhile Downtown restaurants and markets have built baroque
enclosures to protect their refuse from the homeless. Although no
one in Los Angeles has yet proposed adding cyanide to the garbage,
as was suggested in Phoenix a few years back, one popular seafood
restaurant has spent $12,000 to build the ultimate bag-lady-proof
trash cage: three-quarter-inch steel rod with alloy locks and vicious
out-turned spikes to safeguard moldering fishheads and stale french
fries.

Diego Card

LA Skid Row
Fortified Garbage

Public toilets, however, have become the real frontline of the city's war on the homeless. Los Angeles, as a matter of deliberate policy, has fewer public lavatories than any other major North American city. On the advice of the Los Angeles police, who now sit on the "design board" of at least one major Downtown project, the redevelopment agency bulldozed the few remaining public toilets on Skid Row. Agency planners then considered whether to include a "free-standing public toilet" in their design for the upscale South Park residential development; agency chairman Jim Wood later admitted that the decision not to build the toilet was a "policy decision and not a design decision." The agency preferred the alternative of "quasi-public restrooms"—toilets in restaurants, art galleries, and office buildings—which can be made available selectively to tourists and white-collar workers while being denied to vagrants and other unsuitables. The same logic has inspired the city's transportation planners to exclude toilets from their designs for Los Angeles's new subway system.[6]

Bereft of toilets, the Downtown badlands east of Hill Street also lack outside water sources for drinking or washing. A common and troubling sight these days is the homeless men—many of them young refugees from El Salvador—washing, swimming, even drinking from the sewer effluent that flows down the concrete channel of the Los Angeles River on the eastern edge of Downtown. The city's public health department has made no effort to post warning signs in Spanish or to mobilize alternative clean-water sources.

In those areas where Downtown professionals must cross paths with the homeless or the working poor—such as the zone of gentrification along Broadway just south of the Civic Center—extraordinary precautions have been taken to ensure the physical separation of the different classes. The redevelopment agency, for example, again brought in the police to help design "twenty-four-hour, state-of-the-art security" for the two new parking structures that serve the *Los Angeles Times* headquarters and the Ronald Reagan State Office Building. In contrast to the mean streets outside, both parking structures incorporate beautifully landscaped microparks, and one even boasts a food court, picnic area, and historical exhibit. Both structures are intended to function as "confidence-building" circulation systems that allow white-collar workers to walk from car to office, or from car to boutique, with minimum exposure to the public street. The Broadway-Spring Center, in particular, which links the two local hubs of gentrification (the Reagan Building and the proposed Grand Central Square) has been warmly praised by architectural critics for adding greenery and art to parking. It also adds a considerable dose of menace— armed guards, locked gates, and ubiquitous security cameras—to scare away the homeless and the poor.

The cold war on the streets of Downtown is ever escalating. The police, lobbied by Downtown merchants and developers, have broken up every attempt by the homeless and their allies to create safe havens or self-governed encampments. "Justiceville," founded by homeless activist Ted Hayes, was roughly dispersed; when its inhabitants attempted to find refuge at Venice Beach, they were arrested at the behest of the local council member (a renowned environmentalist) and sent back to Skid Row. The city's own brief experiment with legalized camping—a grudging response to a series of deaths from exposure during the cold winter of 1987—was abruptly terminated after only four months to make way for the construction of a transit maintenance yard. Current policy seems to involve perverse play upon the famous irony about the equal rights of the rich and poor to sleep in the rough. As the former head of the city planning commission explained, in the City of the Angels it is not against the law to sleep on the street per se—"only to erect any sort of protective shelter."[7] To enforce this proscription against "cardboard condos," the police periodically sweep the Nickel, tearing down shelters, confiscating possessions, and ar- resting resisters. Such cynical repression has turned the majority of the homeless into urban bedouins. They are visible all over Downtown, pushing their few pathetic possessions in stolen shop- ping carts, always fugitive, always in motion, pressed between the official policy of containment and the inhumanity of Downtown streets.

Sequestering the Poor

An insidious spatial logic also regulates the lives of Los Angeles's working poor. Just across the moat of the Harbor Freeway, west of Bunker Hill, lies the MacArthur Park district—once upon a time the city's wealthiest neighborhood. Although frequently character- ized as a no-man's-land awaiting resurrection by developers, the district is, in fact, home to the largest Central American community in the United States. In the congested streets bordering the park, a hundred thousand Salvadorans and Guatemalans, including a large community of Mayan-speakers, crowd into tenements and boarding houses barely adequate for a fourth as many people. Every morning at 6 A.M. this Latino Bantustan dispatches armies of sewing *operadoras*, dishwashers, and janitors to turn the wheels of the Downtown economy. But because MacArthur Park is midway between Downtown and the famous Miracle Mile, it too will soon fall to redevelopment's bulldozers.

Hungry to exploit the lower land prices in the district, a powerful coterie of developers, represented by a famous ex-councilman and the former president of the planning commission, has won official approval for their vision of "Central City West": literally, a second Downtown comprising 25 million square feet of new office and retail space. Although local politicians have insisted upon a significant quota of low-income replacement housing, such a palliative will hardly compensate for the large-scale population displacement sure to follow the construction of the new skyscrapers and yuppified "urban villages." In the meantime, Korean capital, seeking *lebensraum* for Los Angeles's burgeoning Koreatown, is also pushing into the MacArthur Park area, uprooting tenements to construct heavily fortified condominiums and office complexes. Other Asian and European speculators are counting on the new Metrorail station, across from the park, to become a magnet for new investment in the district.

The recent intrusion of so many powerful interests into the area has put increasing pressure upon the police to "take back the streets" from what is usually represented as an occupying army of drug-dealers, illegal immigrants, and homicidal homeboys. Thus in the summer of 1990 the LAPD announced a massive operation to "retake crime-plagued MacArthur Park" and surrounding neighborhoods "street by street, alley by alley." While the area is undoubtedly a major drug market, principally for drive-in Anglo commuters, the police have focused not only on addict-dealers and gang members, but also on the industrious sidewalk vendors who have made the circumference of the park an exuberant swap meet. Thus Mayan women selling such local staples as tropical fruit, baby clothes, and roach spray have been rounded up in the same sweeps as alleged "narcoterrorists."[8] (Similar dragnets in other Southern California communities have focused on Latino day-laborers congregated at streetcorner "slave markets.")

By criminalizing every attempt by the poor—whether the Skid Row homeless or MacArthur Park venders—to use public space for survival purposes, law-enforcement agencies have abolished the last informal safety-net separating misery from catastrophe. (Few third-world cities are so pitiless.) At the same time, the police, encouraged by local businessmen and property owners, are taking the first, tentative steps toward criminalizing entire inner-city communities. The "war" on drugs and gangs again has been the pretext for the LAPD's novel, and disturbing, experiments with community blockades. A large section of the Pico-Union neighborhood, just south of MacArthur Park, has been quarantined since the summer of 1989; "Narcotics Enforcement Area" barriers restrict entry to residents "on legitimate business only." Inspired by the positive response of older residents and local politicans, the police have subsequently franchised "Operation Cul-de-Sac" to other low-income Latino and black neighborhoods.

Thus in November 1989 (as the Berlin Wall was being demolished), the Devonshire Division of the LAPD closed off a "drug-ridden" twelve-block section of the northern San Fernando Valley. To control circulation within this largely Latino neighborhood, the police convinced apartment owners to finance the construction of a permanent guard station. Twenty miles to the south, a square mile of the mixed black and Latino Central-Avalon community has also been converted into Narcotic Enforcement turf with concrete roadblocks. Given the popularity of these quarantines—save amongst the ghetto youth against whom they are directed—it is possible that a majority of the inner city may eventually be partitioned into police-regulated "no-go" areas.

The official rhetoric of the contemporary war against the urban underclasses resounds with comparisons to the War in Vietnam a generation ago. The LAPD's community blockades evoke the infamous policy of quarantining suspect populations in "strategic hamlets." But an even more ominous emulation is the reconstruction of Los Angeles's public housing projects as "defensible spaces." Deep in the Mekong Delta of the Watts-Willowbrook ghetto, for example, the Imperial Courts Housing Project has been fortified with chain-link fencing, RESTRICTED ENTRY signs, obligatory identity passes—and a substation of the LAPD. Visitors are stopped and frisked, the police routinely order residents back into their apartments at night, and domestic life is subjected to constant police scrutiny. For public-housing tenants and inhabitants of narcotic-enforcement zones, the loss of freedom is the price of "security."

Security by Design

If the contemporary search for bourgeois security can be read in the design of bus benches, megastructures, and housing projects, it is also visible at the level of *auteur*. No recent architect has so ingeniously elaborated or so brazenly embraced the urban-security function as Los Angeles's Pritzker Prize laureate Frank Gehry. His strongest suit is his straightforward exploitation of rough urban environments, and the explicit incorporation of their harshest edges and detritus as powerful representational elements. Affectionately described by colleagues as an "old socialist" or "street-fighter with a heart," Gehry makes little pretense at architectural reformism or "design for democracy." He boasts instead of trying "to make the best with the reality of things."[9] With sometimes chilling effect, his work clarifies the underlying relations of repression, surveillance, and exclusion that characterize the fragmented landscape of Los Angles.

An early example of Gehry's new urban realism was his 1964 solution of the problem of how to insert luxurious spaces—and high property values—into decaying neighborhoods. His Danziger Studio in Hollywood is the pioneer instance of what has become an entire species of Los Angeles "stealth houses," which dissimulate their opulence behind proletarian or gangster facades. The street frontage of the Danziger is simply a massive gray wall, treated with a rough finish to ensure that it would collect dust from the passing traffic and weather into a simulacrum of the nearby porn studios and garages. Gehry was explicit in his search for a design that was "introverted and fortresslike," with the silent aura of a "dumb box."[10]

Indeed, "dumb boxes" and screen walls form an entire cycle of his work, ranging from the American School of Dance (1968) to his Gemini GEI (1979)—both in Hollywood. His most seminal design, however, was his walled town center for Cochiti Lake, New Mexico (1973): here ice-blue ramparts of awesome severity enclose an entire community, a plan replicated on a smaller scale in his 1976 Jung Institute in Los Angeles. In both of these cases architectural drama is generated by the contrast between the fortified exteriors, set against "unappealing neighborhoods" (Gehry) or deserts, and the opulent interiors, opened to the sky by clerestories and lightwells. Gehry's walled-in compounds and cities, in other words, offer powerful metaphors for the retreat from the street and the introversion of space that has characterized the design backlash to the urban insurrections of the 1960s.

Gehry took up the same problem in 1984 in his design for the Loyola Law School in the MacArthur Park district. The inner-city location of the campus confronted Gehry with an explicit choice: to create a genuine public space, extending into the community, or to choose the security of a defensible enclave, as in his previous work. Gehry's choice, as one critic explained, was a neoconservative design that was "open, but not _too_ open. The South Instructional Hall and the chapel show solid backs to Olympic Boulevard, and with the anonymous street sides of the Burns Building, form a gateway that is neither forbidding nor overly welcoming. It is simply there, like everything else in the neighborhood."[11] This description considerably understates the forbidding qualities of the campus's formidable steel-stake fencing, concrete-block ziggurat, and stark frontage walls.

But if the Danziger Studio camouflages itself, and the Cochiti Lake and Loyola designs are dumb boxes with an attitude, Gehry's baroquely fortified Goldwyn Branch Library in Hollywood (1984) positively taunts potential trespassers "to make my day." This is probably the most menacing library ever built, a bizarre hybrid of a drydocked dreadnaught and a cavalry fort. With its fifteen-foot-high security walls of stuccoed concrete block, its anti-graffiti barricades covered in ceramic tile, its sunken entrance protected by ten-foot-high steel stakes, and its stylized sentry boxes perched precariously on each side, the Goldwyn Library (influenced by Gehry's 1980 high-security design for the U.S. Chancellery in Damascus) projects nothing less than sheer aggression.

Some of Gehry's admirers have praised the Library as "generous and inviting,"[12] "the old-fashioned kind of library," and so on. But they miss the point. The previous Hollywood library had been destroyed by arson, and the Samuel Goldwyn Foundation, which endows this collection of filmland memorabilia, was understandably preoccupied by physical security. Gehry's commission was to design a structure that was inherently vandalproof. His innovation, of course, was to reject the low-profile, high-tech security systems that most architects subtly integrate into their blueprints, and to choose instead a high-profile, low-tech approach that foregrounds the security function as the central motif of the design. There is no dissumulation of function by form here—quite the opposite. How playful or witty you find the resulting effect depends on your existential position. The Goldwyn Library by its very structure conjures up the demonic Other—arsonist, graffitist, invader —and casts the shadow of its own arrogant paranoia onto the surrounding seedy, though not particularly hostile, streets.

These streets are a battleground, but not of the expected kind. Several years ago the *Los Angeles Times* broke the sordid story of how the entertainment conglomerates and a few large landowners had managed to capture control of the local redevelopment process. Their plan, still the focus of controversy, is to use eminent domain and higher taxes to clear the poor (increasingly refugees from Central America) from the streets of Hollywood and reap the huge windfalls from "upgrading" the area into a glitzy theme-park for international tourism.[13] In the context of this strategy, the Goldwyn Library—like Gehry's earlier walled compounds—is a kind of architectural fire-base, a beachhead for gentrification. Its soaring, lightfilled interiors surrounded by barricades speak volumes about how public architecture in America is literally turning its back on the city for security and profit.

The Panopticon Mall

In other parts of the inner city, however, similar "fortress" designs are being used to recapture the poor as consumers. If the Goldwyn Library is a "shining example of the possibilities of public- and private-sector cooperation," then developer Alexander Haagen's ghetto malls are truly stellar instances. Haagen, who began his career distributing jukeboxes to the honkytonks of Wilmington, made his first fortune selling corner lots to oil companies for gas stations—sites since recycled as minimalls. He now controls the largest retail-development empire in Southern California, comprising more than forty shopping centers, and has become nationally acclaimed as the impresario of South-Central Los Angeles's "retail revival."

Haagen was perhaps the first major developer in the nation to grasp the latent profit potential of abandoned inner-city retail markets. After the Watts Rebellion in 1965, the handful of large discount stores in the South-Central region took flight, and small businesses were closed down by the banks' discriminatory redlining practices. As a result, 750,000 black and Latino shoppers were forced to commute to distant regional malls or adjacent white neighborhoods even for their everyday groceries. Haagen reasoned that a retail developer prepared to return to the inner city could monopolize very high sales volumes. He also was well aware of the accumulating anger of the black community against decades of benign neglect by City Hall and the redevelopment agency; while the agency had moved swiftly to assemble land for billionaire developers Downtown, it floundered in Watts for years, unable to attract a single supermarket to anchor a proposed neighborhood shopping center. Haagen knew that the Bradley regime, in hot water with its South-Central constituents, would handsomely reward any private-sector initiative that could solve the anchor-tenant problem. His ingenious solution was a comprehensive *"security-oriented* design and management strategy."[14]

Haagen made his first move in 1979, taking title to an old Sears site in the heart of the ghetto. Impressed by his success there, the redevelopment agency transferred to him the completion of its long-delayed Martin Luther King, Jr., Center in Watts. A year later Haagen Development won the bid for the $120 million renovation of Crenshaw Plaza (a pioneer 1940s mall on the western fringe of the ghetto), as well as a contract from Los Angeles County to build another shopping complex in the Willowbrook area south of Watts. In each case Haagen's guarantee of total physical security was the key to persuading retailers and their insurers to take up leases. The essence of security, in turn, was a site plan clearly derived from Jeremy Bentham's proposed Panopticon—the eighteenth-century model prison to be constructed radially so that a single guard in a central tower could observe every prisoner at all times.

The King Shopping Center in Watts provides the best prototype of this commercial Brave New World for the inner city:

The King Center site is surrounded by an eight-foot-high, wrought-iron fence comparable to security fences found at the perimeters of private estates and exclusive residential communities. Video cameras equipped with motion detectors are positioned near entrances and throughout the shopping center. The center, including parking lots, can be bathed in bright [lights] at the flip of the switch.

There are six entrances to the center: three entry points for autos, two service gates, and one pedestrian walkway. . . . The service area . . . is enclosed with a six-foot-high concrete-block wall; both service gates remain closed and are under closed-circuit video surveillance, equipped for two-way voice communications, and operated by remote control from a security "observatory." Infrared beams at the bases of light fixtures detect intruders who might circumvent video cameras by climbing over the wall.[15]

The observatory functions as both eye and brain of this complex security system. It contains the headquarters of the shopping-center manager, a substation of the LAPD, and a dispatch operator who both monitors the video and audio systems and maintains communication "with other secure shopping centers tied into the system, and with the police and fire departments." At any time of day or night, there are at least four security guards on duty—one at the observatory, and three on patrol. They are trained and backed up by the regular LAPD officers operating from the observatory substation.[16]

The King Center and its three siblings (all variations on the Panopticon theme), as expected, have been bonanzas, averaging annual sales of more than $350 per leasable square foot, as compared to about $200 for their suburban equivalents.[17] Moreover, Haagen has reaped the multiple windfalls of tax breaks, federal and city grants, massive free publicity, subsidized tenants, and sixty- to ninety-year ground leases. No wonder he has been able to boast, "We've proved that the only color that counts in business is green. There are huge opportunities and huge profits to be made in these depressed inner-city areas of America that have been abandoned."[18]

High-Rent Security

The security-driven logic of contemporary urban design finds its major "grassroots" expression in the frenetic efforts of Los Angeles's affluent neighborhoods to physically insulate their real-estate values and life-styles. Luxury developments outside the city limits have often been able to incorporate as "fortress cities," complete with security walls, guarded entries, private police, and even private roadways. It is simply impossible for ordinary citizens to enter the "cities" of Hidden Hills (western San Fernando Valley), Bradbury (San Gabriel Valley), Rancho Mirage (low desert), or Palos Verdes Estates (Palos Verdes Peninsula) without an invitation from a resident. Indeed Bradbury, with nine hundred inhabitants and ten miles of gated private roads, is so obsessed with security that its three city officials will not return phone calls from the press, since "each time an article appears, . . . it draws attention to the city, and the number of burglaries increases."[19]

Recently, Hidden Hills, a Norman Rockwell painting behind walls, has been bitterly divided over a Superior Court order to build forty-eight units of seniors' housing on vacant land outside the city gates. At meetings of the city's powerful homeowners' association (whose members include Frankie Avalon, Neil Diamond, and Bob Eubanks) opponents of compliance have argued vehemently that the old folks "will attract gangs and dope."[20]

Meanwhile, older high-income cities like Beverly Hills and San Marino have restricted access to their public facilities, using byzantine layers of regulations to build invisible walls. San Marino, which may be the richest and most Republican city in the country (85 percent), now closes its parks on weekends to exclude Latino and Asian families from adjacent communities. An alternative plan, now under discussion, would reopen the parks on Saturdays, but only to those with proof of residence or the means to pay daunting use fees. Other upscale areas (including thirty-seven Los Angeles neighborhoods) have minted similar residential privileges by restricting parking to local homeowners. Predictably such preferential parking ordinances proliferate mainly in neighborhoods with three-car garages.

Affluent areas of the City of Los Angeles have long envied the autonomy of fortress enclaves like Hidden Hills and Palos Verdes. Now, with the cooperation of a pliant city council, they are winning permission to literally wall themselves off from the rest of the city. Since its construction in the late 1940s, Park La Brea has been Los Angeles's most successful experiment in mixed-income, high-rise living. Its urbane population of singles, young families, and retirees has always given a touch of Manhattan to the La Brea Tarpits area of Wilshire Boulevard. But its new owners, Forest City Enterprises, hope to "upgrade" the project image by sealing it off from the surrounding neighborhoods with security fencing and NO TRESPASS-ING signs. As a spokesperson for the owners blandly observed, "It's a trend in general to have enclosed communities."[21]

A few miles north of Park La Brea, above the Hollywood Bowl, the wealthy residents of Whitley Heights have won the unprece-dented privilege of withdrawing their streets from public use. Eight high-tech gates will restrict access to residents and approved visitors using special electronic codes. An immediate byproduct of "gate-hood" has been a dramatic 20 percent rise in local property values—a windfall that other residential districts are eager to emu-ulate. Thus in the once wide-open tractlands of the San Fernando Valley—where a decade ago there were virtually no walled-off communities—homeowners are rushing to fortify their equity with walls and gates. Brian Weinstock, a leading local contractor, proudly boasts of the Valley's more than one hundred newly gated neighborhoods, and reports an insatiable demand for additional security. "The first question out of [every buyer's] mouth is whether there is a gated community. The demand is there on a three-to-one basis."[22]

Meanwhile the very rich are yearning for unassailable high-tech castles. Where gates and walls will not suffice, the house itself is redesigned to incorporate state-of-the-art security. An important if unacknowledged motive for the current "mansionizing" mania on the city's Westside—the tearing down of $3 million houses to build $30 million supermansions—is the search for "absolute se-curity." To achieve it, residential architects are borrowing design secrets from overseas embassies and military command posts. For example, one of the features currently in high demand is the "ter-rorist-proof security room" concealed in the houseplan and reached by hidden sliding panels or secret doors. Merv Griffin and his fellow mansionizers are hardening their palaces like banks or missile silos.

But technology is not enough. Contemporary residential security in Los Angeles—whether in the fortified mansion or the average suburban bunker—depends upon the extensive deployment of private security services. Through their local homeowners' associations, virtually every affluent neighborhood from the Palisades to Silver Lake contracts its own private policing; hence the thousands of lawns displaying the little ARMED RESPONSE warnings. A recent *Times* want-ads section contained over a hundred ads for guards and patrolmen, mostly from firms specializing in residential protection. Within greater Los Angeles, the security-services industry is a Cinderella sector that has tripled its sales and workforce—from 24,000 to 75,000 guards—over the last decade. "It is easier to become an armed guard than it is to become a barber, hairdresser, or journeyman carpenter," reports Linda Williams in the *Times*. Although the patrolmen are mostly minority males earning close to minimum wage, their employers are often multinational conglomerates offering a dazzling range of security products and services. As Michael Kaye, president of burgeoning Westec, a subsidiary of Japan's Secom, Ltd., explains: "We're not a security-guard company. We sell a *concept* of security."[23]

What homeowners' associations contract from Westec—or its principal rival, Bel-Air Patrol (part of Borg-Warner's family of security companies, which include Burns and Pinkerton)—is a complete "systems package": alarm hardware, monitoring, watch patrols, personal escorts, and, of course, "armed response" as necessary. Although law-enforcement experts debate the efficiency of such systems in foiling professional criminals, there is no doubt that they are brilliantly successful in deterring unintentional trespassers and innocent pedestrians. Anyone who has tried to take a stroll at dusk through a neighborhood patrolled by armed security guards and signposted with death threats quickly realizes how merely notional, if not utterly obsolete, is the old idea of "freedom of the city."

The LAPD as Space Police

This comprehensive urban security mobilization depends not only on the incorporation of the police function into the built environment, but also on the growing technopower of the police themselves. Undoubtedly the LAPD's pioneering substitution of technology for manpower was in part a necessary adaptation to the city's dispersed form; but it also expresses the department's particular relationship to the community. Especially in its self-representation, the LAPD appears as the progressive antithesis to the traditional big city police department with its patronage armies of patrolmen grafting off their beats. The LAPD, as reformed in the early 1950s by the legendary Chief Parker (who admired, above all, the gung-ho elitism of the Marines), would be incorruptible because unapproachable, a "few good men" doing battle with a fundamentally evil city. *Dragnet*'s Sergeant Friday precisely captured the Parkerized LAPD's prudish alienation from a citizenry composed of fools, degenerates, and psychopaths.

Technology helped foster this paranoid esprit de corps, and virtually established a new definition of policing, where technologized surveillance and response supplanted the traditional patrolman's intimate folk knowledge of a specific community. Thus back in the 1920s the LAPD had pioneered the replacement of the flatfoot or mounted officer with the radio patrol car—the beginning of dispersed, mechanized policing. Under Parker, ever alert to spin-offs from military technology, the LAPD introduced the first police helicopters for systematic aerial surveillance. After the Watts Rebellion of 1965, this airborne effort became the cornerstone of a policing strategy for the entire inner city. As part of its Astro program, LAPD helicopters maintain an average nineteen-hour-per-day vigil over "high-crime areas." To facilitate ground-air coordination, thousands of residential rooftops have been painted with large, identifying street numbers, transforming the aerial view of the city into a huge police grid.

The fifty-pilot LAPD airforce was recently updated with French Aerospatiale helicopters equipped with futuristic surveillance technology. Their forward-looking infrared cameras are extraordinary night eyes that can easily form heat images from a single burning cigarette a mile away, while their 30-million-candlepower spotlights, appropriately called "Night Suns," can turn night into day. Meanwhile the LAPD retains another fleet of Bell Jet Rangers capable of delivering complete SWAT units anywhere in the region. Their training, which sometimes includes practice assaults on Downtown high-rises, anticipates some of the spookier Hollywood images—as in *Blue Thunder* or *Running Man*—of airborne police terror.

But the decisive element in the LAPD's metamorphosis into a Technopolice has been its long and successful liaison with the military aerospace industry.[24] Just in time for the opening of the 1984 Los Angeles Olympics, the department acquired ECCCS (Emergency Command Control Communications Systems), the most powerful police communications system in the world. First conceptualized by Hughes Aerospace between 1969 and 1971, ECCCS's design was refined and updated by NASA's Jet Propulsion Laboratory, incorporating elements of space technology and mission-control communications.

Bunkered in the earthquake-proof security-hardened fourth and fifth sublevels of City Hall East (and interconnecting with the police pentagon in Parker Center), the Central Dispatch Center coordinates all the complex itineraries and responses of the LAPD using digitalized communication to eliminate voice congestion and guarantee the secrecy of transmission. ECCCS, together with the LAPD's prodigious information-processing assets, including ever-growing databases on suspect citizens, have become the central neural system for the vast and disparate security operations, both public and private, taking place in Los Angeles.

The Carceral City

All these technologically advanced policing strategies have led to an invisible Haussmannization of Los Angeles. No need to clear fields of fire when you control the sky; no need to hire informers when surveillance cameras ornament every building. But the police have also reorganized space in far more straightforward ways. We have already seen their growing role as Downtown urban designers, indispensable for their expertise in "security." In addition they lobby incessantly for the allocation of more land for such law-and-order needs as jail space for a burgeoning inmate population and expanded administrative and training facilities for themselves. In Los Angeles this has taken the form of a *de facto* urban-renewal program, operated by the police agencies, that threatens to convert an entire section of Downtown and East LA into a vast penal colony.

Nearly 25,000 prisoners are presently held in six severely overcrowded county and federal facilities within a three-mile radius of City Hall—the largest single incarcerated population in the country. Racing to meet the challenge of the "war on drugs"—which will double detained populations within a decade—authorities are forging ahead with the construction of a controversial state prison in East Los Angeles as well as a giant expansion of County Jail near Chinatown. The Immigration and Naturalization Service, meanwhile, has been trying to shoehorn privatized "microprisons" into unsuspecting inner-city neighborhoods. Confronting record overcrowding in its regular detention centers, the INS has commandeered motels and apartments for operation by private contractors as auxiliary jails for detained aliens—many of them Chinese and Central American political refugees.

The demand for more law-enforcement space in the central city, however, will inevitably bring the police into conflict with developers. The plan to add two high-rise towers with 2,400 new beds to County Jail on Bauchet Street, Downtown, has already raised the ire of developers hoping to make nearby Union Station the hub of a vast complex of skyscraper hotels and offices. One solution to the increasing conflict between carceral and commercial redevelopment is to use architectural camouflage to insert jail space into the skyscape. Ironically, even as buildings and homes become more like prisons or fortresses, prisons are becoming aesthetic objects. Indeed, carceral structures are the new frontier of public architecture. As an office glut in most parts of the country reduces commissions for corporate high-rises, celebrity architects are designing jails, prisons, and police stations.

An extraordinary example, the flagship of the emergent genre, is Welton Becket Associates' new Metropolitan Detention Center in Downtown Los Angeles. Although this ten-story Federal Bureau of Prisons facility is one of the most visible new structures in the city, few of the hundreds of thousands of commuters who pass by every day have even an inkling of its function as a holding center for what has been officially described as the "managerial elite of narco-terrorism." This postmodern Bastille—the largest prison built in a major U.S. urban center in decades—looks instead like a futuristic hotel or office block, with artistic flourishes (for example, the high-tech trellises on its bridge-balconies) that are comparable to Downtown's best-designed recent architecture. In contrast to the human inferno of desperately overcrowded County Jail a few blocks away, the Becket structure appears less a detention center than a convention center for federal felons—a "distinguished" addition to Downtown's continuum of security and design.

The Fear of Crowds

In actual practice, the militarization of urban space tends to race far ahead of its theoretical representations. This is not to say, however, that the fortress city lacks apologists. Charles Murray, ideologue *par excellence* of 1980s antiwelfarism, has recently outlined ambitious justifications for renewed urban segregation in the 1990s. Writing in the *New Republic* (increasingly, the theoretical journal of the backlash against the urban poor), Murray argues that *landlords*—"one of the greatly maligned forces for social good in this country"—*not cops* are the best bet for winning the war on drugs.[25] Given the prohibitive cost of building sufficient prison space to warehouse the country's burgeoning population of inner-city drug-users, Murray proposes instead to isolate them socially and spatially. In his three-prong strategy, employers would urine-test and fire drug-tainted workers at will; parents would use vouchers to remove their children from drug-ridden public schools; and, most importantly, landlords would maintain drug-free neighborhoods by excluding the "wrong kind of person."

Murray advocates, in other words, the restoration of the right of employers and landlords to discriminate—"without having to justify their arbitrariness." Only by letting "like-minded people . . . control and shape their small worlds," and letting landlords pursue their natural instinct "to let good tenants be and to evict bad ones," can the larger part of urban America find its way back to a golden age of harmonious, self-regulating communities. Murray is undoubtedly proud of all the Los Angeles suburbanites rushing to wall off their tract-home *gemeinschafts*.

At the same time, he unflinchingly accepts that the underclass—typified, in his words, by the "pregnant teenager smoking crack" and the "Uzi-toting young male"—will become even more outcast: "If the result of implementing these policies is to concentrate the bad apples into a few hyperviolent, antisocial neighborhoods, so be it." Presumably it will be cheaper to police these pariah communities—where *everyone*, by definition, is a member of the dangerous class—than to apprehend and incarcerate hundreds of thousands of individuals. "Drug-free zones" for the majority, as a logical corollary, demand social-refuse dumps for the criminalized minority. Resurrected Jim Crow legislation, euphemistically advertised as "local self-determination," will insulate the urban middle classes (now including the Cosby family as well) from the New Jack City at their doorstep.

In this quest for spatial discrimination, the aims of contemporary architecture and the police converge most strikingly around the problem of crowd control. Cothinkers of Murray doubtless find the heterogeneous crowd a subversive anathema to their idyll of "like-mindedness." As we have seen, the designers of malls and pseudopublic space attack the crowd by homogenizing it. They set up architectural and semiotic barriers that filter out the "undesirables." They enclose the mass that remains, directing its circulation with behaviorist ferocity. The crowd is lured by visual stimuli of all kinds, dulled by Muzak, sometimes even scented by invisible aromatizers. This Skinnerian orchestration, if well conducted, produces a veritable commercial symphony of swarming, consuming monads moving from one cash-point to another.

Outside in the streets, the task is more difficult. The LAPD continues to restrict the rights of public assembly and freedom of movement, especially of the young, through its mass sweeps and "Operation Hammer," selective juvenile curfews, and regular blockades of popular "cruising" boulevards. Even gilded white youth suffer from the strict police regulation of personal mobility. In the former world capital of adolescence, where millions overseas still imagine Gidget at a late-night beach party, the beaches are now closed at dusk, patrolled by helicopter gunships and police dune buggies.

A watershed in the local assault on the crowd was the rise and fall of the "Los Angeles Street Scene." Launched in 1978, the two-day annual festival at the Civic Center was intended to publicize Downtown's revitalization as well as to provide Mayor Bradley's version of the traditional Democratic barbecue. The LAPD remained skeptical. Finally in 1986, after the failure of the Ramones to appear as promised, a youthful audience began to tear up one of the stages. They were immediately charged by a phalanx of 150 police, including mounted units. In the two-hour melee that followed, angry punks bombarded the police cavalry with rocks and bottles; fifteen officers and horses were injured. The producer of the Street Scene, a Bradley official, suggested that "more middle-of-the-road entertainment" might attract less "boisterous crowds." The prestigious *Downtown News* counterattacked: "The Street Scene gives Downtown a bad name. It flies in the face of all that has been done here in the last thirty years." The paper demanded "reparations for the wounded 'reputation of Downtown.' " The Mayor canceled the Scene.[26]

The demise of the Scene suggested the consolidation of an official consensus about crowds and the use of space in Los Angeles. Once the restructuring of Downtown eliminated the social mixing of groups in normal pedestrian circulation, the Street Scene (ironically named) remained one of the few occasions or places (along with redevelopment-threatened Hollywood Boulevard and the Venice boardwalk) where Chinatown punks, Glendale skinheads, Boyle Heights lowriders, Valley Girls, Marina designer couples, Slauson rappers, Skid Row homeless, and gawkers from Des Moines could still mingle together in relative amity. Moreover, in the years since the Battle of the Ramones, relentless police intimidation has ignited one youthful crowd after another into pandemonium, producing major riots in Hollywood on Halloween night 1988, and in Westwood Village in March 1991 (during the premiere of *New Jack City*). Each incident, in turn, furnishes new pretexts for regulating crowds and "preventing the invasion of outsiders" (as one Westwood merchant explained in a TV interview). Inexorably, Los Angeles moves to extinguish its last real public spaces, with all of their democratic intoxications, risks, and undeodorized odors.

Cities for Sale:
Merchandising History
at South Street Seaport

Tucked beneath the Brooklyn Bridge and an elevated highway, the South Street Seaport looks as if it had been snipped from an old city map and carelessly set down beside the superdeveloped financial district of lower Manhattan. Once considered a leftover space of derelict structures, narrow streets, and abandoned piers, it is today an upscale marketplace catering to employees from the Wall Street area, curious tourists, and urban explorers. An evocation of the city's maritime history and the sights and adventures of its mercantile days, South Street Seaport resembles Quincy Market in Boston, Harbor Place in Baltimore, Fisherman's Wharf in San Francisco, the Riverwalk in New Orleans, and other such waterfront districts that were restructured in the 1970s and 1980s to become leisure-time zones combining shopping and entertainment with office and residential development.

South Street Seaport is a historic tableau with Fulton Street at its center. Crossing a wide roadway, the spectator leaves the modern city of corporate skyscrapers and enters a historic architectural promenade. On the south* is Schermerhorn Row, a block of merchants' countinghouses built in the early nineteenth century, now rehabilitated for boutiques, restaurants, and museum spaces.

---

* Directions in Manhattan are all about 30° off the true north-south axis, but in this area they are more skewed than usual, closer to 45°. Fulton Street runs northwest-southeast, and this stretch of South Street runs northeast-southwest—parallel, confusingly, to the East River. By convention, though, crosstown Fulton is said to run east-west, and South Street north-south.

Across from these red-brick landmarks, a reconstructed cast-iron warehouse and a fancifully recreated Fulton "Festival" Market replace the market sheds that had occupied that spot since 1822. On Water Street, toward the western margins of this eleven-block officially designated historic district, stands the South Street Seaport Museum with its art gallery, library, reception center, and shops selling stationery, books, and charts. Under the elevated East River Drive, which runs above South Street, a boardwalk opens onto the waterfront berths of renovated ships and a brand-new exhibition pavilion with still more shops and restaurants.

In reality, however, the Seaport's imaginary historical museum is everywhere, surrounding the spectator with an artfully composed historic ambience. The rough-and-tumble Fulton Fish Market sheds—the last reminders that South Street Seaport was once a working waterfront—are carefully blocked from view. And, lest the spectator wander too far upriver from this historic tableau and ruminate upon the melancholy ruins and haunting memories of the original waterfront, Richard Haas's enormous trompe l'oeil mural replicating the images of Schermerhorn Row and the Brooklyn Bridge quickly turns attention back toward the tableau.

A tour along the waterfront of Manhattan reveals several such isolated, self-enclosed patches of development, and more are to come: the (proposed) Riverwalk development, a minicity on a platform jutting into the East River; South Street Seaport and the adjacent development of East River Landing; the gigantic skyscraper complex proposed for South Ferry; the miraculous ninety-two-acre landfill of Battery Park City; another platform in the river across from the Jacob Javits Convention Center called Hudson River Center; and finally the reduced but still gargantuan Trump project at Penn Yards, intended to reclaim acres of abandoned waterfront, underused railroad yards, and factories a mile further up the Hudson. Certainly no unified image of the city emerges from this series of disparate scenic views. Nor does a visionary masterplan establish a logical and orderly arrangement of the scenery. New York is no longer a city concerned with such high-Modernist aspirations as providing a broad range of housing, efficient public transportation, or leisure and work spaces for the masses. Indeed, most of the contemporary enclaves along New York's once-forgotten waterfront are postindustrial service centers planned to attract the young ur-

South Street Seaport

ban professionals and double-income childless couples increasingly populating the city. These developments are premixed design packages that reproduce preexisting urban forms: office and residential towers, townhouses and hotels, stores and restaurants, health clubs, performing-arts centers, museums, esplanades, marinas, parks, and squares.

And, crucially, these city scenes do not mean to decontextualize architecture by eradicating all ties to the city's historical past as do Modernist sites such as the United Nations on the East River and Lincoln Center for the Performing Arts on the Upper West Side. On the contrary, these newer sites are laden with historical allusions to the traditional vision of the city: a coherent place of intimate streets, lined with small-scale facades and shopping arcades, ornamented with signs, punctuated by open spaces, trees, lampposts, and benches. The aim is theatrical: to represent certain visual images of the city, to create perspectival views shown through imaginary prosceniums in order to conjure up emotionally satisfying images of bygone times. Architecture and the theater use similar means to design places of pleasure and spectacle, manipulating scenery, ornament, and facades, to underscore the sentiment of their play.

However they may be fused or confused, there is of course always a distinction between the represented image of the city and its reality. In fact, New York's developed pockets are divided by swaths of neglect. But rather than arousing condemnation, this chaotic arrangement and disconnected juxtaposition of city segments is accepted and indeed celebrated as the result of rampant but healthy development. Because each fragment is well composed, it absorbs the spectator's attention, upstaging the neglected in-between spaces. For those who travel along this imaginary architectural promenade, centers of spectacle efface the distinctions between the real cityscape and the show.

The History of the Tableau

This is not the first time that scenographic arrangements of city views and simulated landscapes of consumption have been presented to fascinated audiences. The Paris arcades, glass-covered internal passageways cut through privately owned buildings, first appeared in the early nineteenth century. They, and the department stores that followed them, welcomed consumers to the world of illusion and entertainment: their shimmering interiors of marble, glass, and gold enabled the phantasmagorical world of commodities to substitute a world of dreams for that of reality.

Guy Debord has written that the spectacle is capital accumulated to such a degree that it becomes an image, which T. J. Clark sees as explaining Haussmann's transformations of Paris during the reign of Napoleon III.[1] The new public scenery of boulevards and other architectural landscapes provided the setting for the ostentatious display of wealth. The spectacle was everywhere: the promise of industrial expansion took on mythic proportions, expressed in the era's monumental buildings, the abundance of their decoration, and the size of the crowds they held. Gigantic railroad systems plunged toward the heart of the city, where they burst into magnificent train sheds and cavernous stations. International expositions displayed commodities from around the world in ever-larger exhibition halls surrounded by elaborate fairgrounds and pleasure gardens. To serve the growing market for leisure amusements, certain sections of the city became permanent entertainment grounds, adorned with panoramas, georamas, and winter gardens. Dramatic complexes of theaters, art galleries, and shopping arcades made the comings and goings of every spectator a part of their exuberant show.[2]

In addition to this nineteenth-century spectacle of consumption, these scenographic views recreated the image of an earlier, more manageable city, and so calmed the fears, or at least distracted the gaze, of the viewer. As industrialization and modernization rapidly transformed the cityscape, dioramas and panoramas—literal examples of scenographic art—became popular entertainments and successful commercial ventures. As old traditions were erased before their eyes, the urban spectators of the nineteenth century drew comfort from the art of replicating a bygone reality. Displayed on the circling walls of specially designed theaters, the familiar image of a geometrically framed cityscape, drawn and controlled by the hand of man, calmed anxieties engendered by revolutions and change. Panoramas of contemporary cities experiencing rapid transformation, such as London, Paris, and Berlin, were soon joined by more exotic, even threatening spectacles: Moscow burning, Jerusalem under assault, the marvels of Athens, the mysteries of Cairo, turning the faraway and remote into the close and familiar.

Moving panoramas joined the fixed ones, unrolling their painted scenery across the stage. The most famous of these precinematic events was John Banvard's *Trip down the Mississippi* (1840), which he advertised as the largest painting in the world. Stretched between two large rollers erected on either side of the stage, Banvard's scenery unrolled downriver for one show and upriver for the next. Literal recreations of actual voyages, these picture shows became the newsreels and travelogues of the nineteenth century. The narrators who typically accompanied the shows would retell the adventures experienced by the artists in search of the pictures, embellishing the tales with a variety of stories and artifacts—legends associated with these sites, hyperbolic yarns, paintings of local flora, fauna, and costumed peoples.

One of the most remarkable shows was seen in the London Coliseum, designed by Decimus Burton in 1824 to display panoramas at Regent's Park. A few years earlier, when the dome of St. Paul's Cathedral was being repaired, the artist Thomas Horner climbed its scaffolding and with the aid of telescopes and other measuring devices painted the entire all-encompassing view of London. These formed the basis for his huge panorama, which he hung in the Coliseum. A high platform simulated the scaffolding on St. Paul's, placing the spectator at the center of the carefully illuminated image of London. In the darkened and hushed interior, nothing disrupted the enveloping vision of the panorama, no thing penetrated to destroy the illusion—not the cries of the city, nor its boisterous motions, nor its harsh realities.[3]

This art of the double, an image of the city set up within the space of the city, inaugurates the age of reproduction. Such simulations brought city streets into picture galleries, while the panorama enclosed its spectators, regulated their pleasures, and focused their gaze. The real city, never actually displayed, disappeared from view: its chaos, its class distinctions, its snares and vices—all of these lay outside the circular frame, beyond the horizon that controlled the view. The city's image became the spectacle itself. There was no need for a narrative to embellish this view, for in the panorama the spectator was isolated—her or his perspective privatized—and trained to view the surrounding environment as a disciplined order of things.[4]

There were other spectacles of simulation as well. Tableaux vivants were popular amusements in the eighteenth and nineteenth centuries; then, live performers recreated static scenes from famous paintings or sculpture. Viewed through elaborate picture frames, these "living pictures" sought to imitate the original art work closely enough to strike the spectator with the wonders of reconstruction.[5] Edward Kilyani took the tableau to new heights in New York City in the 1890s. He presented "Queen Isabella's Art Gallery" to fascinated audiences between the second and third acts of Edward E. Rice's popular play *1492*. In order to simulate the effect of marble sculpture, "nude" women, arranged in artful compositions, were placed well to the rear of the darkened black-draped stage and just in front of a painted backdrop. The most popular tableaux mimed well-known paintings of *Diana*, *The Idyll*, or *Psyche at the Well*.[6]

A century later, we seem to be witnessing in the contemporary city a proliferation of fictions and simulations. The nostalgic arts of preservation on display at historic developments like South Street Seaport borrow heavily from the nineteenth-century genres of the exhibition hall, the panoramic spectacle, and the tableau vivant. Both the old forms and the new are arts of commercial entertainment and imaginary travel; both are image spectacles, scenographic visions relying on an art of verisimilitude; and both present a particular reframing of urban reality. Late capitalism has simply replaced the boulevard with historicized street malls and the department store with "festival" markets, which offer the same mix of image and illusion as the nineteenth-century spectacle. This is spectator art, meant to be quickly scanned, not analyzed in detail, where the pleasure of the view suspends critical judgment; it is commercial art as well, expected to entertain for a profit. And now, as in the nineteenth century, a feeling of social insecurity seems to breed a love of simulation.

The Types of City Tableaux

The city tableaux now common in many American and European cities fall into three main categories. First there are historic quarters whose form and preservation are mandated by law, such as the small hilltown of Plaka on the slopes of the Acropolis in Athens, London's West End estates with their famous squares and townhouse streetscapes, the old working-class quarters of Le Marais near the Pompidou Center in Paris, and South Street Seaport.

Second, there are special districts with a strong visual or historical identity whose ambience is controlled by contextual zoning or design guidelines. In New York City, for example, the recycling of gritty Union Square is directed by design codes to conform thematically to the fashionable sense of place produced by pre-1916 skyscraper forms, and the revamping of Times Square is being regulated by lighting and billboard guidelines to revive the aura of the Great White Way. Finally, countless cities have witnessed the proliferation of residential enclaves, shopping malls, festival marketplaces, and theme parks whose visual decor and atmosphere are cleverly managed and staged. These sites range from small-town crossroads, where the general store and the hitching post have been reinstated, to impressive theme parks like Disney World, where the golden era of Hollywood has been reinvented and represented, to whole neighborhoods like Battery Park City.

What characterize these new urban zones are the reiteration and recycling of already-known symbolic codes and historic forms to the point of cliché. Codes control signs, materials, colors, ornamentation, street furniture, and street walls; and codes also dictate the design of public spaces, the types of buildings, and the range of activities. Most important, codes contain a schema or program that generates a narrative pattern, a kind of memory device that draws associations and establishes relations between images and places, resemblances and meaning.

Umberto Eco has contrasted postmodernism's "new aesthetics of seriality" with modernism's preferences for the shock of the new, the presentation of material in an "unexpected and chance manner, embracing originality and enhancing innovation."[7] Serial production involves the artist in the replication of a formal set or known pattern. The era of electronics, Eco suggests, never emphasizes shock, interruption, or novelty but instead values the repeatable, the cyclical, the expected. Inattentive viewing publics, according to Eco, search for relaxation and amusement, and remain indifferent to the stories narrated, relishing instead how well the copy reproduces the original, and how minute variations embellish well-established themes. Cinema and television abound with such solipsistic examples: the "to-be-continued" blockbuster sagas of *The Godfather* and *Rocky*, and the daytime soap operas with their predictable story turns and stock characters. All of these forms intentionally repeat or play with popular narrative patterns; indeed the spectator's pleasure arises partly from knowing what will happen next.

Historic preservations and retro urban designs are literal representations of the past. They too are designed for inattentive viewers, for the tourist or city traveler who browses through these real-life stage-sets scarcely aware of how the relics of the past have been indexed, framed, and scaled. These curious mixtures of reconstituted styles-of-life and fashionable environments have proved effective tourist attractions, and economic-development experts now turn every small-town thoroughfare into Main Street. Vintage villages, regardless of their lack of authenticity, are designed to resurrect local economies. City after city discovers that its abandoned industrial waterfront or outmoded city center contains enormous tourist potential and refurbishes it as a leisure-time spectacles and sightseeing promenade. All of these sites become culinary and ornamental landscapes through which the tourists—the new public of the late twentieth century—graze, celebrating the consumption of place and architecture, and the taste of history and food.

Picture-Writing

These city tableaux manipulate patterns, both architectural and urban. They are endlessly repeated copies—Main Street revitalizations, for example, or warehouse recyclings, or waterfront renovations. Busy creating simulated traditions, urban developers seem intent on stockpiling the city's past with all the available artifacts and relics, thereby obscuring the city's actual history. The homogenized icons in our historic marketplaces reveal the limited stock of images spectators are meant to use to understand American history. "We, all of us here," Peter Handke writes in the voice of an American, "learned to see in terms of historical pictures. A landscape had meaning only if something historical happened in it. A giant oak tree in itself wasn't a picture; it became a picture only in association with something else."[8]

America's historical archive is filled with these pictorial lessons: William Penn and the Peace Tree, George Washington and the cherry tree, Yankee Doodle and his fife and drum, honest Abe Lincoln in his stovepipe hat, Charlie Chaplin struggling against modern times, the mushroom cloud of the atomic bomb. American cityscapes, too, stimulate associated meaning. Everyone knows the meaning of Main Street, USA: the small business community of practical, law-abiding citizens devoted to "free enterprise" and "social mobility." The meaning of the New England village green, with its lofty elms, white clapboard houses, and a simple steepled church, is equally clear: a family-oriented, moral, thrifty, and practical community.[9] New York has its own special collection of pictorial tableaux—most obviously, its skyline, which since the turn of the century has expressed the city's immense commercial force and prosperity.[10] And now Manhattan's reconstructed seaport conveys another distinct story.

Every waterfront tableau, of course, is in some form or another a seafaring tale that places man in a contest against nature, and every seaport festival marketplace is an entrepôt of exotica, an image theater that reflects our desire for the curious and the marvelous. It is this environment of trade and voyages, of mechanical pulleys, levers, and winches, a world charted by optical instruments and balanced by mechanical laws, that is set up before our eyes in the historic tableau of South Street Seaport.

This particular tableau is part of the larger Harbor Park, a nineteenth-century seaport that has been reconstituted as a series of separate museum pieces replicating the lore of the sea and America's immigrant past: The neoclassical buildings that once sheltered retired seamen at Snug Harbor on Staten Island have been restored; the great halls of Ellis Island now let the visitor experience a simulation of an immigrant's first day in America; nearby Liberty Island contains another museum of immigration in the base of the Statue of Liberty. And there are other seafaring places to explore as well: in Brooklyn, the Fulton Ferry Museum that tells the story of the ferries that used to shuttle across the East River, connecting the then-separate cities of Brooklyn and New York; and Battery Park, with its historic fortress, which once protected the city against British naval attack.

On the surface of these tableaux, everything seems steeped in tradition. The way it was has supposedly become the way it is. Yet these nostalgic constructions only refer to history obliquely by appropriating styles of clothing, architectural environments, and furnishings to create a mood through which the past is filtered and perceived. These stylized historical tableaux, on one level, are self-conscious attempts to regain a centered world, to reestablish a mythical base on which American moral, political, and social traditions might stand. Like the "Old Towns" of the East, the "Colonial Villages" of the South, the "Frontier Towns" of the West and the "Trading Posts" of the Northwest, these New York tableaux link the past to the present through visual re-creations that gloss over real social change by capitalizing on the yearnings for lost innocence, heroic feats, adventures, explorations, and conquests. Bluntly put, these dramas of action compensate for present-day failures. The awareness of highways in disrepair, charred and abandoned tenements, the scourge of drugs, the wandering homeless, subway breakdowns and deteriorating buses, visual litter and auditory bombardment—all are erased and ignored in the idealized city tableaux set up before the spectator's eyes and presented as an entertaining show. As the French philosopher Michel Foucault realized, the muffled fiction of history is "a place of rest, certainty, reconciliation, a place of tranquilized sleep."[11]

To travel through American cities is to sense that these gigantic urban regions are disintegrating into unrelated groupings of shopping centers, special zoning districts, and housing tracts, all carved up by highways and multilevel traffic interchanges. That peculiar American place, the historic tableau, proliferating in the centers of these deconstructed cities, is an attempt to arrest this uprootedness, this sense of nonplace, this decomposition into bits and pieces. Regulatory codes govern the spatial configurations of these tableaux: private residential streetscapes are protected from intrusive alterations, public spaces are defended against incompatible designs, and storefronts and commercial signs are restricted to facsimiles. But in fact these tableaux are the true nonplaces, hollowed out urban remnants, without connection to the rest of the city or the past, waiting to be filled with contemporary fantasies, colonized by wishful projections, and turned into spectacles of consumption.

We can continue to puncture holes in our cities' fabric, windows that look back to the past. In these apertures we can simulate the art of travel in time and space through historicized architectural forms and the art of historic restoration. We can also simulate the illusion of travel through video tableaux and pictorial histories that let us "be there" on clipper ships heading for China, or among immigrants passing through Ellis Island.[12] But something will be missing, something closed off, something left out of focus.

City tableaux are the places where a society turns back upon itself to view the spectacle of its own performance and to defamiliarize the habitual by placing it in new contexts and formal arrangements. Spectacle is just that, a bracketed moment, a play within a play, a time in which the act of putting on the show becomes the performance. The spectacle, moreover, is a visual delight intended to immobilize our attention in the act of "just looking." In the scenographic tableaux of our contemporary cities, whether a historic district, a contextually zoned district, or a carefully managed theme park, the act of 'just looking' and enjoying the pure visibility of the show absorbs the spectator's view.

The spectacle is always part of a show, and going to the theater part of leisure-time experience. Devoted to entertainment and wish fulfillment, city tableaux on the margins of reality are designed explicitly for escape and gratification. They emphasize their own lack of seriousness by claiming, as spectacles do, that their business is show business. These tableaux separate pleasure from necessity, escape from reality. They widen the gap between the city on display and the city beyond our view. And in so doing they sever any connection they might have had to the art of building real cities, for, after all, these city tableaux only claim to be special places for fun and entertainment, areas of the city to explore during periods of play, which promise not to burden the spectator with the seriousness of reality.[13]

A Landscape of Perfect Projects

The proliferation of scenic enclaves eventually reduces the city to a map of tourist attractions, which suppresses the continuous order of reality, the connecting in-between places, and imposes instead an imaginary order of things. The spectator is offered no visual image of the metropolitan whole, in all its uneven development; attention is directed to those sites that are perceived as productive or useful, or are engineered to satisfy desires.

During the 1970s and 1980s, the creation of such sites became increasingly important, reflecting fundamental changes in the patterns of consumption, financing, real-estate development, and telecommunication. A network of global cities arose to coordinate the international circulation of capital, goods, labor, and corporations; cities such as London, New York, Los Angeles, and Tokyo became partners in a market that exchanged and distributed not only goods, but also finance, advertising, insurance, fashion, design, art, music, and film. The downtowns of these first-tier cities rapidly became globally oriented financial and business service centers, demanding new office towers, luxury residences, entertainment spaces, and upscale marketplaces.[14]

But the effects of globalization were felt beyond these cities. As computers made capital increasingly flexible in the 1970s and 1980s, able to move instantly from place to place, and as mergers enabled large corporations to scatter the segments of their operations, cities of all sizes, both in the United States and abroad, could compete for investments. Moreover, as computerized information systems made white-collar jobs increasingly portable, America's midsized cities experienced fantastic growth, since they combined the advantages of both town and country, affordable housing and good jobs. A 1989 *Newsweek* report on "Hot Cities" detailed the miraculous rebirth of such cities as St. Paul, Birmingham, Portland (Oregon), Fort Worth, Orlando, Sacramento, Providence, Charlotte, Columbus, and Albuquerque. In particular, *Newsweek* noted that the site-selection committee of Sematech, a computer-chip consortium, reviewed the credentials of 134 cities before locating their new headquarters in Austin, Texas. Apparently only two big cities, Boston and Kansas City, were among the 25 finalists in the competition for livability and good business climate.[15]

In this competitive location game, cities and regions must market themselves: their "imageability" becomes the new selling point.[16] Consequently spatial design codes and architectural pattern languages become increasingly important in selling the look of an upmarket, upbeat environment. In this marketing war, style-of-life and "livability," visualized and represented in spaces of conspicuous consumption, become important assets that cities proudly display.

Since the mid-1970s, most cities' economic-development strategies have been focused entirely on attracting the headquarters of multinational corporations and global financial concerns, and providing all the infrastructure, service, hotels, and convention centers these industries require. In New York, for example, the new landfill of Battery Park City, the massive redevelopment strategy for Times Square, and South Street Seaport were all planned as sites of such conspicuous consumption. Here architects and artists have focused their designs to appeal to the tastes of white-collar workers and upper-middle-class consumers—the new urban populations. But

New York is selling more than just upmarket goods and services. The image campaign sponsored by the Alliance for New York City Business promotes an upbeat vision of "New York Ascendant" in advertisements extolling the virtues of living and working in New York.[17] This ad campaign papers over the expanding gap between the impoverished manufacturing workers and the increasingly well-to-do white-collar workers. If the dualities of wealth and poverty create stressful discrepancies, what better way to sidestep these inequities than by connecting the civic and symbolic traditions of New York's architectural heritage to fictional recreations in such well-designed places as Battery Park City, Times Square, and South Street Seaport?

The spectator who enters the $4 billion Battery Park City on its 92 acres of landfill in the Hudson River may observe that this new architectural tableau is in reality a historically constituted and structured composition. Surrounding the four megatowers housing the World Financial Center, the spectator will find traditional red-brick-and-limestone apartment buildings grouped around vest-pocket parks, a two-mile-long waterfront esplanade connecting a series of parks and coves, plus a superluxurious yacht club and a glass winter garden squeezed between dominating office towers. Governed by a 1979 masterplan, this "urban dream" has recycled architectural elements and styles borrowed from the city's best residential sections, unified by the memory of Manhattan's gridiron street pattern and by the distillation of "Old New York" lighting, signage, and colors. The design codes of Battery Park City are exemplary, for they have so concentrated New York City's landmarks that here one can find the look of prewar apartment houses combined with the views and atmosphere of Brooklyn Heights, reproductions of Central Park lampposts and 1939 World's Fair benches, the inspiration drawn from the private enclave of Gramercy Park as well as the great landscape inheritance of Olmsted's parks.

The organizing principle behind this collection of architectural and urban forms is a nostalgic longing to repossess and return to New York's heyday—the interwar period when the city emerged as an international financial capital in both style and substance. In those glory days, corporate skyscrapers replaced the shorter buildings to become the new symbol of the city's civic pride; stately Beaux-Arts apartment buildings on Park Avenue and Central Park

West, built with high-quality materials and adorned with elaborate ornamentation, spoke of wealth and sophistication. At Battery Park City, the constant evocation of historic imagery recalling the civic values of New York's heroic past offers a reassuring anchor, and thus a justification of the expenditure of public money in an essentially private domain.

The contested Times Square redevelopment is yet another advertising strategy in the campaign to sell "New York Ascendant." Once Times Square was celebrated around the world as a vibrant theater district bathed in a flood of electric lights. A vital crossroads, it combined a communications and media center with a theater and movie district, hotels, restaurants and bars, office towers, and nearby garment showrooms and factories. By the 1980s, most of these elements had declined or moved away, replaced by the night frontier of adult bookstores and novelty shops, crack dealers and prostitutes, cheap movies and seedy bars. Now redevelopers on the side of the angels want to reclaim Times Square from the clutches of vice through the largest urban-renewal project ever undertaken in America. Hence all of the area surrounding 42nd Street and up the Broadway spine is being revitalized as a new office, hotel, and entertainment center, following worldwide real-estate and market trends.

In order to recapture the energy and movement that once characterized Times Square, and consequently to call on popular memory to legitimate this plan, an ordinance now requires that the facade of each new structure be lit up like a giant jukebox, with the tacit assumption that these supersigns will restore the long-lost glitter of the Great White Way. Special design guidelines also legislate the restoration of nine theaters, the renovation of the subway station, and the location of retail outlets on the street floor of skyscraper towers. Redevelopment thus intends to replace the mean streets with an image of old Times Square, as if its aura could be caught under glass. Yet even if all the massive redevelopment towers are forced to simulate a "Times Square look," they can be only cold and distant reminders of the razzle-dazzle that sparked Times Square's fame. Moreover the bulk and height of this purified complex of commerce and culture will certainly destroy the fragile remnants of the incongruous and the unusual that once made Times Square the most provocative spectacle in town.

•

South Street, too, was once an energetic thoroughfare, a street of ships stretching two miles from the Battery to Corlear's Hook, its strip of gallant windjammers a sign of the port's vitality. By the 1930s, however, South Street had become part of the dark urban jungle, a street of dilapidated semivacant structures housing junk shops and cut-rate stores, frequented by seamen and drifters.[18] No matter how brilliant its past, the area around South Street and Fulton Street had turned into a labyrinth of dark narrow streets, congested traffic, and claustrophobic development—a no-man's-land. When the real waterfront died and the real marketplaces were removed, they left a void in which it became possible to reconstruct the mythical ambience of an old seaport.

By the 1950s, it was apparent to the financial and real-estate groups of New York that the once undisputed center of capital below Fulton Street was obsolete, while the midtown area—with its better transportation network, new office towers, and the United Nations—was thriving. The Downtown Lower Manhattan Association, sponsored by David Rockefeller, addressed the need for more parking garages and wider streets, so that the financial district would be easily accessible by car and thus prepared for the next wave of development. This district, the group reported, was forced to reach skyward because it was completely hemmed in by decaying and underutilized districts. In the very shadow of the skyscrapers, the old meat, dairy, and produce market crowded up to decaying piers along the Hudson River. Since the Washington Market no longer primarily serviced Manhattan, the Rockefeller group suggested it could be relocated outside of the city in modernized and efficient warehouses and its space redeveloped more profitably as housing. Over on the East River, the congested narrow lanes south of the Brooklyn Bridge were the logical path along which the financial district itself might expand. Here, the Fulton Fish Market, which now received most of its shipments from trucks, not fishing boats, was another candidate for relocation. Its dilapidated waterfront and city-owned piers could be replaced by a transportation center for the financial district, complete with a heliport and a commercial airstrip.[19]

The New York waterfront continued to decline, and the Rockefeller group began to implement their plans for redevelopment. By 1968, an urban-renewal district was created south of the Brooklyn Bridge in the area surrounding the Fulton Market. On the other side of the island, another urban-renewal district took the place of the Washington Market. The Rockefeller group was also interested in developing the World Trade Center and using the earth from its excavations as landfill to create Battery Park City.

Since 1884, when the original John D. Rockefeller was among the first millionaires to move to the upper reaches of Manhattan, on West 54th Street near Fifth Avenue, the Rockefellers have sought to replace segments of Manhattan with luxury enclaves mixing commercial and cultural development. In the heart of the depression, John D. Rockefeller, Jr., offered New Yorkers Rockefeller Center, the first landscaped skyscraper composition, a self-contained mixed-use luxury development protected from the threatening city and focused internally on a sunken plaza, a series of roof gardens, and subterranean commercial areas. It is not surprising then that the Rockefeller group of the 1960s proposed to redevelop the lower-Manhattan waterfront with six luxury residential-and-office communities, each composed around a waterfront plaza and marina and housing between ten and fifteen thousand residents employed in the financial district.

In the 1960s, a second landscape came into view. Since shipping activity on the waterfront had declined beyond repair, it seemed a splendid time to recapture its glory days by building a maritime museum. Peter Stanford, an advertising executive, formed the Friends of South Street Seaport to create an outdoor museum in memory of the nineteenth-century waterfront with its quaint countinghouses, ship chandleries, and sail lofts.[20] Incorporated as the South Street Seaport Museum in 1967, Stanford's group proposed to preserve a four-block area by turning it into a historical enclave for pedestrians, opening onto the waterfront and replicating the ambience of this former "street of ships." The Seaport group had to move quickly against the development pressures emanating from the Rockefeller group. By the mid-1970s, two different yet complementary landscapes were firmly in place: the Rockefeller group would retain control over the development of the larger waterfront district as a mixed-use, twenty-four-hour-a-day, luxury townscape and the expansion of the financial district, while the museum group would concentrate on restoring the waterfront and reconstructing the historic tableau.

But who would pay for the restoration? The federal government was no longer subsidizing urban renewal, the banks were waiting for better times, and public interest in piecemeal preservation was on the decline. And so another landscape director was called in: in 1976 the city began negotiations with the Rouse Company, the successful shopping-mall and festival-market developers. Rouse proposed, with public assistance, to turn Fulton Street into a pedestrian walk, to construct a pavilion with a historic flavor for restaurants and boutiques on rebuilt waterfront piers, and to reconstruct a new festival food market on the site where the Fulton Market sheds had stood for over 160 years.[21]

An urban-design theory had already evolved out of the Rouse Company's successful marketplace compositions. As mixed-use centers, these small commercial enclaves were developed on the sites of old marketplaces. Preferring the density of historic areas to wide-open shopping malls, the Rouse Company rejected large-scaled, single-use structures like department stores in favor of small retail shops lining pedestrian passageways and open-air shopping promenades in a carefully regulated yet varied visual environment. These preferences fit exactly into the vision of the museum's historic tableau as a quiet retreat from the rest of the city, and they guaranteed that the ambience would be carefully implemented and controlled.[22]

Nevertheless, commercial revitalization, historic preservation, tourism, and the art of simulation do not mix easily. Efforts at historic preservation often take a back seat as development forces gain strength. By the time South Street Seaport opened in 1983, three-quarters of its museum space had been reassigned to Cannon's Walk, lined with shops. South Street Seaport Museum may have begun with a desire to preserve a few seedy taverns, fish stalls, and countinghouses in order to commemorate its great maritime past, but it was also hoped that historic preservation would turn the entire waterfront along the East River into an outdoor museum. Yet aside from a museum whose cultural programs have yet to be fully financed, a few rehabilitated ships, and a multiscreen film *The Seaport Experience*—in which the sights, sounds, and smells of clam hawkers, cobblestones, bells, fog, mist, and sea spray are cleverly simulated—cultural resuscitation seems to have stalled. Development appears to have gained an advantage: Phase One saw Benjamin Thompson's specially designed New Fulton Market Building open in 1983, Phases Two and Three were completed in

1985 with the construction of new pier pavilions and a thirty-four-story office tower called Seaport Plaza. There is more to come.

Brokering Desire

Places like Battery Park City, Times Square, and South Street Seaport are sustained not only by the pleasures of picture-writing, but by the expansion of historical tourism, the desire to "just look" at the replicated and revalued artifacts and architecture of another time. Yet to historicize is to estrange, to make different, so that a gap continually widens between then and now, between an authentic and a simulated experience. Dean MacCannell in *The Tourist* castigates the practice of historic preservation for attempting to "museumize" different life-styles and societies, as well as past works of art and architecture, and thus for increasing the gap between the past and the present.[23] He considers sightseeing a ritual performed to honor this differentiation, for even as many tourists travel in search of art forms displaced from their original contexts and relocated in museums, they catalogue and collect "unique" environments, accumulating what they hope is an "authentic" sense of place and time.

But in both the tourist industry and historic preservation, there seems to be an attempt (not wholly successful) to unify and heighten the sense of the present by emphasizing the break with the past and with tradition, or to justify a particular aspect of the present by emphasizing a related aspect of the past. In the reconstructed seaport, do we concentrate on the ingenuity of the mechanics or the exoticness of the imports, on the wealth of the merchants or the poverty that led the seamen to indenture themselves? Everything is significant. Museums, historic zones, and city tableaux present highly particular stagings of the past.

John D. Rockefeller, Jr., recomposed and restaged reality when he underwrote the restoration of Colonial Williamsburg in the 1920s and 1930s. The controlled re-creation of an eighteenth-century townscape, which simultaneously sought to educate and entertain those with the money and inclination to travel, was largely the product of the restorer's imagination. Michael Wallace describes the mythological purpose of Williamsburg as a townscape dedicated to the memory of the southern planter class, who represented for

Rockefeller the original corporate elite. In memory of this group and at great expense, Rockefeller erected a symbolic environment planned and organized like a well-run corporation, presided over by genteel patricians and earthy craftsmen. The workers and slaves—the ninety percent of the population who actually created the wealth of the original town—never appeared on its stage.[24]

In their desire to solidify the traces of the past into a unified image, to restore an intactness that never was, developers of historicized open-air bazaars and storehouses of heterogeneity like South Street Seaport, where consumers can buy anything from anywhere, have so conflated geographical space and historical time that the actual uniqueness of place and context have been completely erased. These illusionary environments of simulation provide the decor for our acts of consumption. In contemporary times, commodities are no longer marketed for their utility and efficiency alone, but as part of a system of values that gives them added meaning. The further away the commodity seems from the functional, the useful, and the necessary, the more appealing it appears. When the commodity is placed within a system of signs symbolizing entire life-styles and supporting environments, the system itself seeks to increase consumption by suggesting that a particular life-style requires the acquisition of not one but an entire series of goods.[25] Consequently, simulated landscapes of exotic and imaginary terrains, cleverly combining the fantastic with the real, become the ideal background props for our contemporary acts of consumption, set-ups that intensify the commodity's power of seduction.

The cleverly formulated landscapes of Disneyland—meticulously designed to encourage consumption—might be called the original historic-marketplace tableau. Visitors to this fantastical space become the narrators of a story that deceptively harmonizes contradictory elements. In the landscapes of Frontierland, Adventureland, Tomorrowland, even Fantasyland, they compose the stories of how Americans achieved victory over Indians, exotic countries, outer space—in short, over historical memory. At Disneyland, the American way of life is displayed as a universal sign of progress. Symbolically, whatever path the traveler may take, the voyage begins and ends at Main Street USA, where the tourist shops lie. Hence Main Street becomes the center of Disneyland's story, a shrewd commercial tale that tells of consumption American style. By presenting the facades of Main Street, and all its "lands" for that matter, as miniature versions of a fantastic past, Disneyland sparks the visitor's imagination and willingness to buy. Yet it is not the environment that is falsified, for everything in Disneyland is absolutely fantastical, but the fact that Disneyland is quintessentially a landscape for consumption, not for leisure.[26]

In just this manner, South Street Seaport is above all a marketplace, the stage for a particular kind of experience—that of pure desire, where the buyer imagines a fantastical world which the possession of a certain object seems to promise. Indeed, marketplaces are essentially containers of desire and yearnings. Ships and sailors and seaports—what else are they but projections of the desire that propelled men and ships to voyage around the world for that pinch of Madagascar pepper to flavor our meat or that cup of mocha to stimulate our spirits?[27]

There can be no better stage set for the spectacle of capital than a recycled mercantile area. As an aestheticized emblem of New York's mercantile past, South Street Seaport can be considered a kind of collective souvenir of travel and adventure, exotic commodities and trade. And advertising of course has capitalized on this composition, drawing on a set of pleasurable feelings that develop when objects are seen within the nostalgic milieu of a fictionalized seaport marketplace. Nostalgia is a sweet sadness generated by a feeling that something is lacking in the present, a longing to experience traces of an authentic, supposedly more fulfilling past, a desire to repossess and reexperience something untouched by the ravages of time. Yet this past only exists in secondhand form, and the impoverished and partial experience it provides can't help but stimulate more longing and desire. As a possession on display, the souvenir generates a travel narrative. A visible reminder of journeys past, it reawakens the longing for still more trips and adventures. But it also fuels the desire to return home with bags filled with trophies commemorating that innocent and treasured past.[28] And this desire to possess, to appropriate, is of course just what advertising seeks to stimulate, whether the desired objects are historic architecture or commodities for sale.

Consequently the historical ambience of South Street Seaport is carefully orchestrated to channel nostalgic desires. The Rouse Company has guaranteed the rough-and-tumble appearance of this waterfront through its choice of construction materials—granite, corrugated steel, red brick—and through weekly meetings with the museum staff to ensure maintenance of the historic "atmosphere." Every street vendor, outdoor decoration, advertisement, sign, and retail space must conform to the Seaport's overall theme. Signs and ads are carefully controlled: the Seaport's logo is used to identify art galleries, exhibition spaces, and shops while outdoor signs replicate the nineteenth-century style of painted wall signs. The museum has reinterpreted South Street's historical role in a series of permanent exhibits on the relationship between the waterfront and commercial development; a slide show of New York's heroic struggle to become a port of worldwide importance; the restoration of traditional trades such as printing and chart-making that illustrate New York's contribution to maritime technology; and periodic popular festivals that recapture the social and cultural aspects of the sea and the waterfront.[29]

The Seaport, originally intended as a twentieth-century outdoor museum for the people, has consumption at its very core—the money used to preserve its historic structures and maintain the ambience of its street of ships comes from its share of the revenues the street of shops produces.[30] The Seaport, then, is really an outdoor advertisement that narrates a story about trade and commodities, and these narratives of adventure and conquest fill out the more intangible nostalgic desires of the consumer. This subtle form of advertising blurs the distinction between the atmospheric stage-set and the commodities on sale, for its well-constructed historic tableau not only enhances the products on display but locks the spectator into a larger-than-life store/story.

What the Rouse Company and the museum sell to the retailers is access to a particular clientele delivered in the right frame of mind: hence their commercial success depends on how convincing the relationship between environment and commodities appears. Their advertising, which is the entire historical milieu, must gain popular appeal through a reassuring, mildly educational, and entertaining pitch.[31]

Consequently, looking at the architecture of Schermerhorn Row, for example, is indistinguishable from looking at commodities to buy. And what are the commodities? Leisure life-styles are for sale in this seafaring environment; in quick succession the spectator can try on the fantastic gear of a nature explorer, an urban pioneer, a fisherman, a sportsman, a safari adventurer, and a voyager to foreign lands. Like historic architecture and reconstructed historic milieux, clothing and accessories can trigger memory. Even in stylized and generic form, the further these commodities lie from everyday reality—the more they accessorize the fantasy narrative of exploration/discovery/colonization—the greater their allure and the more they seem to address some need for authentic and novel experience. The ultimate souvenir can be discovered at Captain Hook's, a private cave full of ships' bells and seashells, scrimshaw and bric-a-brac, or at the Nature Shop, where bird, fish, and dinosaur artifacts, wind chimes and weather instruments, atlases and globes, telescopes and microscopes, clocks and thermometers, narrate the adventure of mercantile days. In Brookstone's Hardware Store one can purchase an assortment of outdoor games from croquet to badminton, picnic boxes and barbecue grills, travel cases and carrying wheels, and every garden tool a nature-lover might require. Laura Ashley and Williamson's clothing stores evoke a simpler and plainer nineteenth century with their natural dyes and fibers. Items from Abercombie & Fitch still masquerade in the stylized look of colonial imperialism.

But for all the allusions to the maritime past, the Seaport's retailers have less and less connection to it. The first boutiques were small retailers selling specialized items from limited stocks but the current shops have a different profile, dominated by huge chains such as Banana Republic, Laura Ashley, Brookstone, and the Nature Store.

Even history will give way to the imperatives of consumption. Consider the food shops: evoking the Fulton Fish Market, South Street Seaport originally showcased fish and other exotic foods. But when the festival market first opened, the fish and other gourmet fare apparently discouraged masses of visitors from exploring the Seaport's adventure; not until fast food concessions such as the New York Pastrami Factory, Brooklyn Bridge Pizza del Porte, and Burger Boys of Brooklyn took over did the public begin to flock to the festival marketplace. Only the removal of the fish from the fish market finally made the "historic" tableau commercially viable.

In South Street Seaport present-day realities and nostalgic desires collide. Wall Street financial interests looking for new territory wanted to preserve the city's historic waterfront and marketplace

only as stage props for more lucrative enterprises. The urban voyager setting sail against the forces of nature, a theme reiterated
over and over again at South Street Seaport, is a metaphor for the
explorations and colonizations of bygone eras; the memory of those
journeys is used to legitimate the contemporary appropriation of
the city's undervalued margins and their conversion into profitable
leisure-time places.[32] A city of increasing spatial differentiation
results in an ever-widening gap between neglected land and revalued places, between the poor that the market ignores and the
well-to-do that it privileges. Historic preservation and the creation
of atmospheric milieus stabilize this difference between types of
public space—a state not likely to change in the future.

The contemporary spectator in quest of public urban spaces
increasingly must stroll through recycled and revalued territories
like South Street Seaport, city tableaux that have been turned into
gentrified, historicized, commodified, and privatized places. These
areas once existed outside of the marketplace, but now their survival
depends on advertising, and on the production of an entertaining
environment that sells. "Just looking" at these city spaces remains
a pleasurable public experience, but an experience that increasingly
comes down to that moment of association when private desires
become linked to future promises offered by items for sale. On one
level, then, South Street Seaport bears witness to the instrumental
and rational production of a public marketspace where communal
celebrations and festivals still occur, albeit in truncated and mod-
ified form. On another level, however, by targeting the spectator
with narrative style-of-life advertising, the Seaport and other such
compositions speak directly to private fantasies, colluding in the
privatization of public space. These shifts of public and private
spheres are turning the streets and spaces of our cities inside-out.
Public ways and communal spaces are being designed by the private
sector as interior shopping streets within large corporate skyscrapers, or festival markets where public admittance is carefully controlled. The private sphere of nostalgic desires and imagination is
increasingly manipulated by stage sets and city tableaux set up to
stimulate our acts of consumption, by the spectacle of history made
false.

MICHAEL SORKIN

See You in Disneyland

As he was led manacled away after his conviction, serial killer Richard Ramirez, Los Angeles's infamous "Night Stalker," turned to the courtroom audience and snarled "See you in Disneyland." America recognized the turn of phrase from the familiar TV ad that invariably follows the World Series or Super Bowl. After a montage of key plays—with "When You Wish upon a Star" swelling behind—the beaming hero of the game is caught striding off field and asked by the announcer, "What are you going to do now?"

The reply is invariable: "I'm going to Disney World."

Disney World, a theme park of theme parks, is America's stand-in for Elysium, the ultimate reward for quarterbacks and pitchers, the utopia of leisure. And it's not just America's: through those pearly gates in Orlando, Florida, lies the leading purely tourist destination on the planet, welcoming close to 100,000 people on good days, over 30 million a year, a throng that spends nearly a billion dollars each year. These staggering numbers include neither the original Disneyland in Anaheim, California, nor Tokyo Disneyland, nor Euro Disneyland, abuilding by the Marne. Thanks to Disney and like attractions, Orlando has become America's capital of transience, with more hotel rooms than Chicago, Los Angeles, or New York.

But the empire of Disney transcends these physical sites; its aura is all-pervasive. Decades of films have furnished a common iconography on generations. Now there's a television channel too. And years of shrewd and massive merchandising have sold billions of Disney things—videocassettes, comic books, pajamas, paper cups, postcards, and mouse-eared coin purses—which vaunt their participation in this exponentially expanding system of objects. The litter of Disneyland is underfoot in streets from New York to Shanghai. More people know Mickey than Jesus or Mao. Who doesn't live in Disney World?

The literal placemaking began with Disneyland. According to one hagiographer, the idea for the park came to Disney in 1938, on a trip to the Chicago Railroading Fair, where he was invited to don engineer's overalls and climb behind the throttle of a historic locomotive, fulfilling a childhood dream. Later, he built a miniature railroad around his own house, anticipating the rail-ringed parks to come. Another myth of the park's origins, much retold, recounts a visit by the Disney family to a conventional amusement park, and Disney's disgust at its failures of hygiene. These fantasies of transport and cleanliness culminated, one day in 1955, in Disneyland itself, the alpha point of hyperreality.

It was always to have been a utopia. Early publicity limns it:

> Disneyland will be based upon and dedicated to the ideals, the dreams, and the hard facts that have created America. And it will be uniquely equipped to dramatize these dreams and facts and send them forth as a source of courage and inspiration to all the world.
>
> Disneyland will be something of a fair, an exhibition, a playground, a community center, a museum of living facts, and a showplace of beauty and magic. It will be filled with the accomplishments, the joys, the hopes of the world we live in. And it will remind us and show us how to make those wonders part of our lives.

If this evocation is a tad fuzzy, Disneyland's immediate origins are specific. Television paid. Strapped for cash to finance spiraling construction costs, the previously TV-shy Disney cut a deal with ABC, then struggling far behind its two rivals. In return for the network's money, Disney offered his most precious commodity: the mouse. Disneyland and the Mickey Mouse Club were born as twins. The park was, as Thomas Hine has noted, "the first place ever conceived simultaneously with a TV series."

This is the sky above Disney World, which here substitutes for an image of the place itself. Disney World is the first copyrighted urban environment in history, a Forbidden City for postmodernity. Renowned for its litigiousness, the Walt Disney Company will permit no photograph of its property without prior approval of its use. Is there a better illustration of the contraction of the space of freedom represented by places like Disney World than this innocent sky?

Seth Rubin

The coincidence is more than temporal. Television and Disneyland operate similarly, by means of extraction, reduction, and recombination, to create an entirely new, antigeographical space. On TV, the endlessly bizarre juxtapositions of the daily broadcast schedule continuously erode traditional strategies of coherence. The quintessential experience of television, that continuous program-hopping zap from the remote control, creates path after unique path through the infinity of televisual space. Likewise, Disneyland, with its channel-turning mingle of history and fantasy, reality and simulation, invents a way of encountering the physical world that increasingly characterizes daily life. The highly regulated, completely synthetic vision provides a simplified, sanitized experience that stands in for the more undisciplined complexities of the city.

There are more than ample precedents for such weird compendia: circuses, festivals, and fairs have long been with us. Disney is the cool P. T. Barnum—there's a simulation born every minute—and Disneyland the ultimate Big Top. Both circus and Disney entertainment are anti-carnivalesque, feasts of atomization, celebrations of the existing order of things in the guise of escape from it, Fordist fun. Disneyland, of course, also descends from the amusement park, especially that turn-of-the-century blossoming at Coney Island, inspiration to imitator parks from coast to coast. Like Disneyland, Coney Island offered itself as a kind of opposition, an Arden of leisure in symbiosis with the workaday city. Steeplechase Park, Luna Park, and Dreamland established the basic elements of this new machinery of pleasure. Their evocations of travel in time and space, lilliputianization, physics-defying rides, ecstatic relationship to new technology, efficient organizing architecture of spectacle and coercion, and aspirations to urbanism—all harbinger apotheosis at Disneyland.

The most direct ancestor, however, is the World's Fair. These spectacles evolved from the national manufacturing exhibitions that grew with the industrial revolution. Originating late in the eighteenth century, the form climaxed in the Great Exhibition of the Works of Industry of All Nations held in London in 1851 under the enormous glass roof of Joseph Paxton's Crystal Palace. William Thackeray described it in an ode written for the occasion as

A Palace as for a fairy prince
A rare pavilion, such as man

Saw never since mankind began,
And built and glazed.

This giddy positivism also shines through in the inaugural address
of Prince Albert, a Mouseketeer *avant la lettre*:

> Nobody who has paid any attention to the peculiar features of
> our present era, will doubt for a moment that we are living at a
> period of most wonderful transition which tends rapidly to ac-
> complish that great end, to which, indeed, all history points—the
> realization of the unity of mankind. . . . The distances which
> separated the different nations and parts of the globe are rapidly
> vanishing before the achievements of modern invention, and we
> can traverse them with incredible ease; the languages of all nations
> are known, and their acquirement placed within the reach of
> everybody; thought is communicated with the rapidity, and even
> by the power, of lightning. On the other hand, the great principle
> of the division of labor, which may be called the moving power
> of civilization, is being extended to all branches of science, in-
> dustry, and art. . . . The products of all quarters of the globe are
> placed at our disposal, and we have only to choose which is the
> best and the cheapest for our purposes, and the powers of pro-
> duction are entrusted to the stimulus of competition and capital.[1]

The 1851 fair was the first great utopia of global capital. The Prince
Consort's evocation of a world shrunk by technology and the division of labor is the ur-theme of the theme park, and Paxton's
Crystal Palace made this visible by canny means. First, the wealth
of nations was contained under one roof, housed in a single architectural space. And the construction itself embodied the progress
of industry—assembled from a vast number of precisely prefab-
ricated elements, the Crystal Palace was the great early expression
of a manufactured building. Finally, the Palace depicted paradise.
Not only was it laid out like a cathedral, with nave and transept,
but it was also the largest greenhouse ever built, its interior filled
with greenery as well as goods, a climate-controlled reconciliation
of Arcadia and industry, a garden for machines.

Since efficiencies in the manufacture of glass had begun to make
them possible late in the eighteenth century, such large structures
had come to be both stand-ins for the ineffable and zoos for the
menagerie of European colonialism. In the days of the dark satanic

mills, winter gardens became hugely popular places of entertainment and assembly. Those tropical landscapes in Berlin or Brussels helped (along with the popular historical and geographical panoramas) to invent the idea of simulated travel, initiating the great touristic dialectic of appearance and reality. The decline in popularity of these environments toward the end of the century was the result of the spread of railways, which made actual exotic travel possible.

This dislocation is central. Whatever its other meanings, the theme park rhapsodizes on the relationship between transportation and geography. The winter garden evokes distance, the railroad proximity. The flicking destination board at JFK or Heathrow offers—in its graphic anonymity—a real trip to Tangier. The winter garden—the "hothouse"—is all artifice, about inaccessibility, about both its own simulations and the impossibility of being present at the scene evoked: it is not recollective, but a fantastic. At its core, the greenhouse—or Disneyland—offers a view of alien nature, edited, a better version, a kind of sublime. Indeed, the abiding theme of every park is nature's transformation from civilization's antithesis to its playground.

In time, these fairs became differentiated. Soon they embraced a variety of pavilions arranged thematically (manufacture, transport, science, etc.), then national and entertainment pavilions, eventually pavilions sponsored by corporations. From the first, these structures, while impermanent, competed in architectural extravagance. And, as the scope of the fairs grew, the ordering and connection of elements assumed paramount importance. Reaching the scale and density of small cities, the fairs also became models, adopted visionary urbanism as an aspect of their agendas, both offering themselves as models of urban organization and providing, within their pavilions, panoramic visions of even more advanced cities to come. The crucial role played by movement systems within the enlarging fairs was not simply a product of necessity but a paradigm for physical relations in the modern city. And the fairs quickly developed "urban problems," especially in relation to their peripheries. They were conceived as exemplars, and stultifying high-mindedness was a staple. As a result, the fairs often found themselves in symbiosis with disorderly carnivals of more "popular" entertainments just beyond their boundaries, with Little Egypt doing "exotic dancing" on the Midway or strippers plying their trade on the fringes of Flushing.

The years that saw the rise of the great universal exposition also witnessed a flowering of practical utopianism. Although much of the theory originated in Europe, America became the great blank canvas for utopian experiments. Not only were new cities being built at a vast clip, communitarian citizens—Fourierites, Owenites, Shakers, Quakers, Mormons, and other affinity groups—built a breathtaking array of intentional communities. While few of these enterprises can be said to have broken much new ground in terms of the physical life of the city, they did abet an atmosphere of renovation and reform that had direct consequences for urbanism. The contrast between this positivistic, optimist vision of the perfectible future and the increasingly degraded condition of the migrant-swollen industrial city precipitated a range of proposals that took increasingly physical form.

In fact, the 1892 Fair in Chicago—aptly called the White City, for the Fair was the urban analogue of the Great White Fleet that was to convey reform in other spheres—represents a summa of one influential impulse. The City Beautiful movement was the first great model for the new city to be born in America. Its prescriptions—baroque symmetries, monumental beaux-arts architecture, abundant parks and greenery—impressed themselves on scores of cities with frequently vivifying results. The City Beautiful's fascination with sumptuousness, visible order, and parks—with the monumental, "public" aspect of the city—anticipates the physical formula of the theme park, the abstraction of good public behavior from the total life of the city. The dazzling Chicago fair showed the potential for magnificence of such concentrated architectural firepower, and virtually every city in America has a civic quarter, however slight the remnant, created under its influence.

Concurrent with the City Beautiful, the pressure of mass settlement and expanding technology created other visions of regulation, less indebted to formal ideas culled from the past. These visions appeared both in imaginary architectural schemes and in a remarkable literary outpouring: novels about happy technologized utopias, like Bellamy's *Looking Backward*, with its strikingly prescient evocation of a world at leisure. These two expressions

were focused on somewhat different territories. The visionary architectural proposals—many inspired by the development of the
technology of tall buildings—were prompted by the prospect of
skyscraper cities and especially by the intricate movement systems
that would be required to sustain them. The novels, however,
tended to be fantasies about the relations of production, scenes of
happy regulation set in a technologically enabled culture of
convenience.

These imaginings anticipated the urbanism promulgated by
modernism itself, which shows two main strains. The first is the
now maligned rationalist, geometric manner—Le Corbusier its
main apostle—an enormity of regimentation plopped at regular
intervals across a verdant landscape. Le Corbusier's vision has
become the icon of alienation, dislodged from its original status as
challenge to the insalubrious dreariness of the industrial city and
reincarnated as faceless urban renewal and bland 1960s downtowns. It is this version of modernist urbanism that Disneyland's
architectural apologists have in mind when they propose it as a
restorative.

But modernism produced another version of the city, one more
central to Disney's American imaginings. The movement for garden
cities, expostulated by the Englishman Ebenezer Howard in his
1902 screed *Garden Cities for Tomorrow*, stands in approximately
the same relationship to Le Corbusier's Cartesian fantasies as English landscape gardening did to French in the eighteenth century.
The one was a romantic ode to "wild" nature, the other an essay
in submission, nature bent to the paths of order. Both, though,
were versions of the pastoral, embracing the idea that the rena-
turalization of the "denatured" city would strip it of its dread, that
the reversion to the natural would have a salutary effect on human
nature itself.

The garden city is the physical paradigm that presages Disney
space, the park in the theme park. Its ideology embraces a number
of formal specifics. To begin with, these were to be small cities
constructed, ex novo, on the exurban perimeter of existing metropolises, to function as escape valve or release from the tension
and overcrowding of the old city. A picturesque plan—the stuff of
the early suburbs—was as indispensable as the strict regulation of
traffic. Indeed, strategies of movement became the ultimate internal

rationale and formal arbiter of the garden city. These included separation of pedestrians and vehicles and a scale of distances convenient for persons on foot. Formally, the result was generally a single center and a radial plan, united by loops of circulation.

Technology and the garden city conjoined in the two great world's fairs of the 1930s: the 1933 Century of Progress Exposition in Chicago and the 1939 World's Fair in New York City. The Chicago Fair was laid out along a meandering roadway meant to evoke "an evolving incipient roadtown," a garden city. Dispersed along this route—and strongly prefiguring the Disney solution—were a variety of pavilions celebrating scientific advance. Over it all soared the skyride: Chicago was the first fair to absolutely elevate the means of movement as its most visible symbol. The layout of the New York Fair evoked an earlier utopian order, the kind of geometric radiating plan characteristic of ideal communities from the Renaissance through the eighteenth century, inspiration to the garden city. However, New York also boasted two gigantic scale models of cities of the future, which between them embodied those two indispensable ideas of order—movement and the garden.

Both were the products of industrial designers, forerunners of Disney's imagineers. The first, "Democracity," the work of Henry Dreyfus, sat inside the famous Perisphere. Although its center was a jumbo skyscraper, the plan of the city—a constellation of sylvan towns on a green perimeter—was pure Ebenezer Howard. The second—and far more popular, perhaps because visitors rode past it in tiny cabs, Disney style—was Norman Bel Geddes's "City of 1960," designed for the General Motors Futurama. Here was the Corbusian version of modernity, a sea of skyscrapers set in green superblocks, ordered by a Cartesian grid. Of course, the rectilinear interstices swam with swift traffic, cars sailing unimpeded to the cardinal points, motion the fertilizing matrix in which the city grew.

The ideology of the garden city today has been dispersed into a wide variety of environments. Consider Opus, an office complex on the ring highway outside Minneapolis. Promotional brochures describe it as

> an imaginative, innovative development . . . a model for a whole new generation of office parks. Strategically located in southwest

suburban Minneapolis, the beautifully landscaped 450-acre site is ribboned with pedestrian and bike paths, colored with flowers, shaded with trees . . . alive and inspiring. Nestled in acres of meadows, hills, and ponds, Opus is only minutes away from shopping centers, sports stadiums, the international airport, and the downtown business districts of Minneapolis and St. Paul. The site is linked to the interstate system by County Road 18 and Crosstown Highway 62.

A look at the plan for the development elucidates the hype: Opus is the garden city with pedestrians carefully separated from vehicular traffic and picturesque circulation routes organizing lots of different sizes. Yet one thing distinguishes Opus from the garden-variety garden city. Opus is an office development, the residential component an afterthought, a few parcels set aside for outside developers to build limited amounts of housing. Given the character of the work performed in each of the office parcels ("Opus gives new meaning to the word 'work' ") and the location of most services and housing off the site, there's no real reason for the elaborate pedestrian links and the careful grade separations. They do, however, "urbanize" the site, giving it a stature in theory that it lacks in use. The pedestrian system signifies benign mobility, a map of motion without movement. The real links are the highway and airport connections and, more crucially, the invisible telecommunications system that is primarily responsible for enabling the dispersed developments that now figure as the major mode of American urbanism.

The perimeter road in Atlanta, Interstate 285, is often offered as a primal scene for the proliferation of this new exurbia. It developed fast. By 1980, central Atlanta had become a symbol of the Sunbelt reborn. The city had a new profile: a classic central place diagram with a clutch of shiny skyscrapers extruding value straight up at its center. By 1985, however, the pattern had just as suddenly shifted: 4.3 million square feet of office space had been added in the center of town, but 7.6 million had been built in the oxymoronic Perimeter Center at one interstate intersection and 10.6 million had gone up in Cumberland/Galleria at another. Perimeter office space is now predominant overall.

The circulation loop that organizes the building sites within Opus recapitulates the highway loop that arrays Opus and other fringe developments around cities like Minneapolis and Atlanta. The order is centrifugal, about perimeters rather than centers, a logic of dispersion. In such spatial hierarchies, circulation always dominates. First, its requirements are literally the largest. By one standard calculation, 1300 square feet of parking space are required for every 1000 square feet of office on the urban perimeter. The physiognomy of movement orders the most primary issues of architecture, deforming it to its requirements. Like the tail-wagged dog, the workspace at the end of the movement chain seems misplaced, out of sequence, a prisoner of the prodigous life-support system necessary to sustain it in its isolation. This incessant circulation mirrors the circuit of capital—that global chain letter, faithfully accumulating—which these offices on the endless perimeter serve to accelerate. If these new developments seem schematic, it is precisely because they represent, in their primary order, an abstraction: the mobility of the capital that enables them.

The organization and scale of Disney World and the Disneylands is precisely that of the garden city. Located on the urban perimeter, they are, as phenomena, comparable to the office parks at other intersections in the highway system, if sited now for convenience of access by leisure commuters. Internally, they are also ordered according to a strict model. Radiating from a strong center—occupied by the totemic castle of fantasy—the parks are arranged in thematic fiefs (Tomorrowland, Frontierland, etc.), which flow into one another. While the ground plane is given over to pedestrian circulation, the parks' perimeters and airspace are the terrain of elaborate transport systems: trains, monorails, and aerial gondolas.

Movement is ubiquitous and central. Disneyland and Disney World are, in the travel agent's parlance, "destinations." The implication is double, enfolding the acts of traveling and of arriving. The element of arrival is especially crucial, the idea that one is not passing through some intermediate station but has come to someplace where there is a definitive "there." In the larger discourse of travel, these places are vested with a kind of equivalence. The only relevant variable is motion. As the slogan for Busch Gardens, a rival theme park in Williamsburg, Virginia (hard by the first park, Colonial Williamsburg), proclaims—over the *Ode to Joy*—"If you want to see Europe, take a vacation in Virginia. . . . It's all the fun and color of old Europe . . . but a lot closer!" (Not to mention, without pesky Abu Nidal threatening to crimp your pleasures en route!)

Like world's fairs, both Busch Gardens and Disneyland offer intensifications of the present, the transformation of the world by an exponential increase in its commodities. World's fairs are microcosmic renditions of the "global marketplace," transnational shopping malls. At Disneyland, this monumentalized commodity fetishism is reduced to the pith of a haiku. While the nominal international "competition" at the orthodox fair centers on the "best" of national manufacture, the goods at Disneyland represent the degree zero of commodity signification. At Disney World, for example, the "national" pavilions groan with knick-knacks. These are not simply emblems of participation in the enterprise of the higher, global, shopping, they are stand-ins for the act of travel itself, ersatz souvenirs. A trip to Disneyland substitutes for a trip to Norway or Japan. "Norway" and "Japan" are contracted to their minimum negotiable signifiers, Vikings and Samurai, gravlax and sushi. It isn't that one hasn't traveled—movement feeds the system, after all. It's that all travel is equivalent.

Getting there, then, is not half the fun: it's all the fun. At Disneyland one is constantly poised in a condition of becoming, always someplace that is "like" someplace else. The simulation's referent is ever elsewhere; the "authenticity" of the substitution always depends on the knowledge, however faded, of some absent genuine. Disneyland is in perpetual shadow, propelling its visitors to an unvisitable past or future, or to some (inconvenient) geography. The whole system is validated, though, by the fact that one has literally traveled, that one has, after all, chosen to go to Disneyland in lieu of any of the actual geographies represented. One has gone nowhere in spite of the equivalent ease of going somewhere. One has preferred the simulation to the reality. For millions of visitors, Disneyland is just like the world, only better.

If culture is being Disneyfied (and there's no mistaking it!) the royal road there is precisely that: going for a ride. Whatever else they subsume, the Disney zones harbor an amusement park, a compendium of rides offering both kinesis narrativized (a trip, a fantasy voyage) and that mild empirical frisson of going one-on-one with Sir Isaac, testing the laws of everyday physics. The visitor travels in order to travel. Whether experienced at 37,000 feet, on the interstate, or padding between Mike Fink's Keel Boat Ride and Captain Eo in your new Nikes, the main experience—motion—is broadened, extended right back to your front door.

Each Disney park embodies a kind of thematic of transportation. Euro-Disneyland, rising by the Marne, sits athwart a TGV line (the French bullet train—what a ride!), convenient to all Europe. Disney World exists in gravitational relationship to the airport at Orlando. Disneyland, superannuated Shangri-la of the American fifties, is an exit on the LA freeway. In each instance, the park sits as an intensely serviced node on a modern network of global reach. The urbanism of Disneyland is precisely the urbanism of universal equivalence. In this new city, the idea of distinct places is dispersed into a sea of universal placelessness as everyplace becomes destination and any destination can be anyplace. The world of traditional urban arrangements is colonized by the penetration of a new multinational corridor, leading always to a single human subject, the monadic consumer. The ultimate consequence is likely to be the increasing irrelevance of actual movement and the substitution of the even more completely artificial reality of electronic "virtual" space. (As the Frank Zappa lyric puts it, "How can you be two places at once when you're not anywhere at all?") For the moment though, the system still spends its energies on sculpting more physical simulacra.

Consider the trip to the original Anaheim Disneyland. Conceived regionally, in the days before cheap air transport allowed its touristic reach to match its ideological grasp (who can forget poor Nikita Khrushchev's frustration at being denied a visit?), Disneyland was not simply designed for arrival by car, but was—like Los Angeles—begot by the car. One approaches Disneyland only after tooling across the vast Southern California sward of atomization, the bygone suburban utopia of universal accessibility that the automobile was supposed to guarantee.

Whatever else it represents, Disneyland is also a model of Los Angeles. Fantasyland, Frontierland, Tomorrowland—these are the historic themes of the city's own self-description, its main cultural tropes. The genius of the city, however, resides not simply in dispersal but in juxtaposition, the invention of the possibility of the Loirish Bungalow sitting chockablock with the Tudoroid. The view through the framing window of the passing car animates the townscape, cinematizing the city. This consumption of the city as spectacle, by means of mechanical movement through it, precapitulates the more global possibilities of both the multinational corridor created by air travel and the simultaneous electronic everywhere of television. Disneyland offers a space in which narrative depends on motion, and in which one is placed in a position of spectatorship of one's own spectatorship.

While the car may be LA's generator, it's also its "problem," motor of democracy and alienation both, repressor of pedestrianism and its happy random encounters. There's a school (popular along the learnedly kitsch axis of early architectural postmodernism) that exalts Disneyland as a solution to the dissipation of the public realm engendered by cars. This is achieved by relegating cars to a parking periphery, creating an auto-free zone at its center, and using efficient, technologized transport (that charismatic monorail) to mediate.

But this is only half of the story. In fact, Disneyland less redeems LA than inverts it. The reason one circulates on foot in Disneyland is precisely to be able to ride. However, the central experience, by anyone's empirical calculation, is neither walking nor riding but waiting in line. Most of a typical Disney day is thus spent in the very traffic jam one has putatively escaped, simply without benefit of car. Indeed, what's perfect, most ultimately viable, at Disneyland is riding. After hours of snaking through the sun with one's conscientiously well-behaved fellow citizens comes the kinetic payoff: brief, thrilling, and utterly controlled, a traffic engineer's wet dream.

There's a further inversion. Much of the riding at Disneyland —from Space Mountain to Mr. Toad's Wild Ride—takes place indoors. Driving a car in Los Angeles is at once an intensely private and very public activity: on the road, one is both isolated and fully visible. Disneyland surrealizes the ambiguity by making driving domestic, interior, even as it's regulated by being pared of control. Chez Mr. Toad, the line culminates in a quaint Olde English manse through which one is conveyed in . . . a quaint Olde English car. One drives in exactly the only place one expects to walk in the "real" city back home.

Getting to Disney World is a more intrinsically long-distance proposition, involving a long-distance automotive schlep or passage through the global air corridor (visitors are presently divided 50/50 between road and air). Let's say the journey begins at Kennedy Airport in New York. Kennedy is organized along exactly the same ring road principles as Disneyland itself. A big vehicular loop defines a perimeter along which are arrayed the terminals of the various airlines. These buildings—most of which were designed in the late fifties or early sixties—are conceived after the fashion of the national pavilions of the world's fairs of the period, modernist shrines whose signifying tasks are engaged via abstraction rather than representation: expressions of grandeur and consequence rather than any particular evocation of regional particulars. This exaltation of the node differs from the more current paradigm— visible at the airports of Chicago, Atlanta, Dallas/Fort Worth, or Orlando—with their emphasis on the seamlessness of the inter- modal transfer. Indeed, at Kennedy, this primacy of the individual terminal is purchased at the cost of considerable inconvenience to travelers transferring between airlines, and a just-begun recon- struction of the airport aims to transform it with the introduction of a "people-mover" system, a linkage-ride like the Disney monorail.

The original arrangement, however, was suited to its Eisen- howerian age, an airport structured like a suburb, America's own version of the garden city. The suburbs, of course, were predicated on the preeminence of the family, its autonomy expressed by free- standing structures on clearly delineated plots. In a time of con- fidence, the visibility of the economic unit was paramount on the symbolic agenda: at Kennedy, as at Disney, the corporations are surrogates for the family, everybody's big brothers. And Kennedy is likewise afflicted with the same problems of transportation as the suburbs it emulated: difficult to get to, inefficient in its internal connections, dependent on a single mode—the car. At the center of the sea of parking within the Kennedy loop—in the symbolic position occupied by Disneyland's castle, Disney World's geodesic or the 1939 World's Fair Trylon and Perisphere—stand three con- crete chapels, for Catholic, Protestant, and Jewish worship. Under the reconstruction plan, they are to be replaced by a more up-to- the-minute shrine: the central node of the new airport movement system. The obliteration of the three chapels, of course, also ob- viates the question of an absence they so directly beg. While this religious trinity may have been sufficient for the American imperium of the late fifties and early sixties, the accelerated globalism of today does not so easily slough off religions classed simply as Other. Certainly, those chapels had to go if only to avoid the question of the missing mosque. At "Kennedy"—America's leading memorial to the great initiatory act of modern terrorism—mingling Islam and air travel would clearly be too risky.

If airports have become the locale of choice for random terror, they're also arenas for other politics. The Tokyo airport, Narita, is a perennial protest site. Located many miles from the center of Tokyo in an agricultural area typified by small landholdings, Narita's plans to build a long new runway on expropriated farm land have repeatedly fallen afoul of the local left, and numerous, often violent, demonstrations have occurred. From an American vantage point there's something at once quixotic and stirring in this rage on behalf of traditional life in a country that has become the emblem of breakneck modernization and globalized capital. But there's no mistaking the power of the runway, a spirit portal of virtually Egyptian intensity. Like an automatic teller machine, the runway is the point at which a vast, controlling, and invisible skein is made manifest. As each jumbo sets down, tarring its tread-trace in a puff of burnt rubber, the runway becomes rune-way, marker of that inescapable web.

Hartsdale airport in Atlanta is home base to Delta, the current "official" airline of Disney World. As with any fledgling nation-state, hocking its future for a pride of Boeings, an airline completes an indispensable circuit of status, a symbolic minimum apparatus of nationhood. Indeed, the world's most succinct and prospering nation, Singapore, embodies the shrunken vision to perfection. Almost no territory, an intense electronic and travel economy, a superb airline, and a bustling airport linked by modern rapid transit to a compact skyscrapered downtown, orderly to a fault, complete with hygienically retained ethnic and colonial quarters and regulated with scary draconian legality, it's a virtual Disney Nation, deftly substituting Uncle Harry for Uncle Walt. For Disney World, the relationship with Delta both opens another line of penetration into the Real World and affirms its status as perpetually offshore.

Unlike Kennedy, Hartsdale already has an automated "people-mover" transit system to link its terminal concourses. Vaunted as a panacea for urban congestion in the hardware-fixated sixties, the vision was of fleets of small, highly autonomous, "user-friendly" transit cars gliding silently on elevated tracks. People-movers were also seen as a replacement for the freeways—the previous solution—then coming to be viewed as hopelessly destructive to the urban body they were meant to heal. Although people-movers mainly proved too inefficient and expensive for city use, they were just the thing for the more specific and restricted requirements of airports, where exponential growth had stretched the distance from entry to gates to pituitary proportions.

The fantasy that undergirds the science of people-moving is regulation. It's a primal ordering: the Newtonian vision of the universe, bodies intricately meshing and revolving like ticking clockwork, divinity legible precisely in the Laws of Motion. For planners confronted by the irrationality of the city, the addition of computer-regulated, minutely responsive people-movers clearly meant bringing the global-motion net one step closer to the front door. In the space of capital, circulation is politics: its foregrounding at places like Disneyland is analogous to the barrierless vision of free trade that sparked the fairs of the nineteenth century. The driverless people-mover—its motions seemingly dictated by the invisible hand, mechanical creature of supply and demand—is symbol of this economic fantasy of perfect self-government.

On the Hartsdale people-mover, the recorded voice that signals the stops along the loop was originally female. Held to lack authority, it was changed, not to a male voice but to an electronic androgyne. This, then, is a welcome, the signal of an unspecifiable presentness of the system. Gliding to a stop, the car murmurs, "The next stop is terminal A. The color-coded maps and signs in this vehicle match the colors in the terminal." Indeed, the airport has become ("deregulation" notwithstanding) perhaps the most intensively regulated zone of common experience, a more visible version of the more discrete, concealed governings of the Disney Zones. The combined threats of narcotics and terror have given rise to unprecedented levels of policing and surveillance. Credit and passport checks, magnetic screening, irradiation of luggage, baleful agents vetting security "profiles," sniffer dogs: such are the quotidian experiences of air travel. Indeed, every year over a billion people pass through the airport security apparatus, terrified and terribly safe all at once.

•

The global corridor is the modern Panopticon, seething with surveillance. The genius of this system is, however, not just the drill but the invitation, the willingness of its subjects to participate. Take Williams Island, a typical upper-income enclaved community in Miami, advertised by spokesperson Sophia Loren as the "Florida Riviera." Williams offers at least a triple pitch. Its architectural centerpiece is indeed a complex of buildings meant to evoke Portofino or Saint Tropez, all tile roofs, waterside cafes, and bobbing boats. There's also an idealized movement system, consisting of footways and golf carts. In the context of the successive transformations of the garden city, the golf cart is an interesting modification. The cart's the ultimate reconciliation of machine and garden, a benign transport indigenous to leisure. And the golf course itself is a state of nature apt to the age: a vast acreage of greenery scrupulously regulated to support a network of tiny, shallow holes.

But security is the main feature. The first checkpoint at Williams Island is on the far side of a bridge from the mainland. Residents, once recognized, are admitted with a wave. Visitors undergo further scrutiny, and are directed along a succession of additional checkpoints. At buildings' edge, security becomes high-tech. Each resident of the complex has an electronic pass, like a credit card. To move through the sequence of security locks, he or she must insert the card in a slot. A central computer verifies the pass and opens the door. At the same time, a record of the cardholder's movement is printed out at the main guard post. Like the air traveler, the resident submits to an elaborate system of surveillance with the ultimate rationale of self-protection. Here, however, the surrender of privacy is a privilege. Moving through Williams Island recapitulates the larger experience of moving through the global corridor. The security checks, the certifying credit cards and passports, the disciplined, carefully segmented movements, the ersatz geography, the grafted cachet—this is Disneyville.

Arriving at Orlando airport offers the Disney-bound a hint of things to come. There's a brief people-mover ride from satellite to main terminal and a welter of advertising and Disney Reps in the main lobby. However, the cocooning shroud of automated movement stops at the main entrance. To get from the airport to Disney World, a car is required. Indeed, the only way to arrive at Disney

World is by road. This obliges a key ritual of the corridor: the modulation of the means of movement. At the entrance to Disney, the process is inverted: one passes through a customslike toll barrier, thence to relinquish one's car to hotel, campsite, or day-tripper's parking lots and enter the system. The toll booth is also the limit of a monetary zone: within Disney World, visitors can pay either with conventional instruments or with "Disney Dollars." These—exchangeable for U.S. dollars one to one—confer abso-lutely no advantage, no discount, no speculative hedge. They do, however, concretize and differentiate the experience of exchange and boost the counterfeit aura of foreign-ness.

Visitors are welcomed by the mouse. Mickey—hairless, sexless, and harmless—is a summary: as Disney once put it, "Mickey is a *clean* mouse." Talk about a constructed subject—Mickey stands in the same relationship to human subjectivity as Disneyland does to urbanity. Rigorously and completely manipulated, the mouse's outward appearance is affective and cute. As a gloss on human speech, locomotion, and appearance, the mouse offers pratfalling, loopy variation. As an epistemology, Mickey sees things as we do. Mickey, like most cartoon characters, circulates in the cartoon state of nature, a place which collapses the best of Hobbes and Rousseau, a place where life's inevitable brutishness is always played for laughs, where impulses need not be censored because they are ultimately without consequences. The mechanical mouse, product of the animator's assembly line, also confirms a key switch: at Disney, nature is appearance, machine is reality.

Just as the image of the mouse on a million plastic souvenirs confers aura and legitimacy on them, so the vestiges of utopia in the Disney space certifies them as more than amusement parks. For Disneyzone—Disneyland, Disney World, and all the other Dis-ney places—is also a state of nature, offering the fecund commu-nism of abundance and leisure, a true technocratic postindustrial utopia. The industrial army, raised in the nineteenth century and rationalized in the twentieth, is, at Disneyzone, not dispersed but converted to a vast leisure army, sacrificing nothing in regimen-tation and discipline as it consumes its Taylorized fun. Disneyzone completes the circuit of world's fairism by converting the celebra-tion of production into the production of celebration. The pivot on which this transformation turns is the essential alienation of the producer-turned-consumer, his or her dance to the routines of someone else's imagining.

The need for the efficient production of leisure activities has certainly not escaped the official strategizers of our collective future. In his 1976 *Between Two Ages*, Zbigniew Brzezinski warned his patrons of the exigencies to be faced in the coming "technotronic society." Describing the relationship between employers, labor, and the market in this new order, Brzezinski writes that "in the emerging new society questions relating to the obsolescence of skills security, vacations, leisure, and profit-sharing dominate the relationship, and the psychic well-being of millions of relatively secure but potentially aimless lower-middle-class blue-collar workers becomes a growing problem."[2]

The relation between work and leisure is part of the conceptual problematic that kept Disney's most ambitious, most conventionalized, utopian vision, the Experimental Prototype Community of Tomorrow (Epcot) from full fruition. Epcot was prompted by a number of impulses, one of them the literal realization of a full-scale version of the kind of well-regulated one-dimensional urbanism proposed in model form at the 1939 Fair. Perhaps more strongly motivating, however, was Disney's widely reported frustration at events in Anaheim. Like so many world's fairs, Disneyland was beleaguered by an undisciplined periphery: the huge success of the park prompted developers to buy up miles of surrounding countryside, which was promptly converted to a regulationless tangle of hotels and low commerce. For Disney the frustration was double. First, at the millions lost to others who were housing his visitors. (In the first ten years, Disneyland took in $273 million, the peripherals $555 million). And second, the disorder of it all, the sullying of his vision by a sea of sleaze.

Redress, utopia's wellspring, was thus a major motivator for Disney's next go. With guile and stealth he accumulated 28,000 acres of land near Orlando, Florida, for Disney World and its subset Epcot. As intended, the scheme was to embrace both theme park (a clone of Anaheim) and a full-blown community, initially to house his own workers, eventually to include such additional industrial and residential development as he was able to attract. Spake Disney, "Epcot will always be in a state of becoming. It will never cease to be a living blueprint of the future, where people will live a life they can't find anywhere else in the world today." Disney was able to extract extraordinary, unprecedented concessions from the government of Florida, assuring him of virtually complete sovereignty (including rights of policing, taxation, and administration, and freedom from environmental controls) over his domain.

Unfortunately, death intervened before Disney was able to materialize his dream. Its realization was left in the hands of his successors, whose view of the matter was somewhat more jaundiced. Instead of a full-blown "community," Epcot was reduced to the status of simply another theme park. Indeed, it was to become the Disney empire's most literally world's-fairian incarnation. Organized according to the familiar schema—initiatory "main street," loop of attractions—it directly reproduced the components of its predecessor fairs. Materializing the covert agenda of previous Disney Main Streets (where the ITT pavilion lurks behind the malt-shoppe facade), its main street is flanked by the pavilions of major U.S. corporations, each housing some version of a "ride" through a halcyon future. The GM pavilion with its ode to the car also offers up the Epcot theme song, the remorselessly repeated "It's a small world after all." The loop holds the pavilions of eight elected (and subsidizing) nations, an array projecting a sufficient (one from Asia, one from Latin America . . .) compendium of national diversity.

Even Epcot's symbol—a large geodesic sphere—is received. Its lineage proceeds backwards to the tacky Unisphere of the 1964 New York Fair (in which Disney participation was considerable—including an early Animatronic Abe Lincoln) and to Unisphere's own source, the mesmerizing Perisphere that accompanied the complementingly vertical Trylon to the 1939 Fair. In fact, the line extends—via the biospheres of the nineteenth century—back at least as far as the eighteenth-century French architect Boullée's proposal for a vast spherical cenotaph to Isaac Newton, its interior daubed with stars, a representation of the universe which Newton's mechanics had made so newly comprehensible. Epcot's ball is a degenerate—if still viable—totem of universality. In commercials, Mickey stands atop it, waving, an anticolossus.

It somehow seems inevitable that this puny organ of Brzezinskian "psychic well-being" should stand in for the more literal variety that Disney's fuller first vision (actual homes, actual factories) represents. The two possibilities are clearly antithetical, the one destined to annihilate the other. After all, utopia is illusory, a representation. The careful structure of entertainment and social relations (nominal egalitarianism with segmenting opportunities: meals at up- and downscale restaurants; at night you sleep with your class at hostelries ranging from modest to luxe) at Disneyworld relinquishes its power to draw if it fails as an alternative to daily life.

The Disney strategy, then, inscribes utopia on the terrain of the familiar and vice versa. The economy of its representations depends on a careful calculus of degrees of difference. Like any other consumer operation, it thrives on algorithms of both the desirable and the attainable. Thus, its images never really innovate, they intensify and reduce, winnowing complexity in the name of both quick access and easy digestibility. What's being promoted is not the exceptional but rather the paranormal. Just like the real thing, only better.

In an essay on montage, the Soviet film maker Lev Kuleshov describes a scene shot in the early 1920s with the actors Khokhlova and Obolensky:

> Khoklova is walking along Petrov Street in Moscow near the "Mostorg" store. Obolensky is walking along the embankment of the Moscow River—at a distance of about two miles away. They see each other, smile, and begin to walk toward one another. Their meeting is filmed at the Boulevard Prechistensk. This boulevard is in an entirely different section of the city. They clasp hands, with Gogol's monument as a background, and look—at the White House!—for at this point, we cut in a segment from an American film, *The White House in Washington*. In the next shot they are once again on the Boulevard Prechistensk. Deciding to go farther, they leave and climb up the enormous staircase of the Cathedral of Christ the Savior. We film them, edit the film, and the result is that they are seen walking up the steps of the White House. For this we used no trick, no double exposure: the effect was achieved solely by the organization of the material through its cinematic treatment. This particular scene demonstrated the incredible potency of montage, which actually appeared so powerful that it was able to alter the very essence of the material.[3]

Kuleshov called this technique "creative geography." Like genesplicing, the point is to create a new organism from the substance of the old. Indeed, in another famous experiment, Kuleshov used the technique to "fabricate" a new, recombinant woman, from fragments of several "other" women. The question here is whether the perpetrator is Prometheus or Frankenstein. To distinguish monstrosity from coherence, the practice of montage—and the practice of urbanism, its three-dimensional equivalent—requires a theory of juxtaposition. For the cinema, the theory is either about narrative or its interruption, about a sequence of images bound to time. Montage begs the question of the logic of this arrangement. The city is also joined in sequence. Both its construction and its politics devolve on principles of aggregation. The idealization of such principles creates utopia.

As a utopia, Disneyland's innovation lies not in its fantasy of regulation but in the elision of its place-making. Disneyland is the Holy See of creative geography, the place where the ephemeral reality of the cinema is concretized into the stuff of the city. It should come as no surprise that the most succinct manifestation to date of this crossover is the "Disney-MGM Studios" theme park, recently opened at Disney World. Here, the agenda of dislocated authenticity is carried back to its point of origin. The attraction (much indebted to its precursor Universal Studios Tour back in Los Angeles, now also in Orlando) is explicitly about movies, both the space of their realization (the "studio") and about the particular narrative spaces of particular movies.

Although the attraction is in Florida, at Disney World, and although its recreational agenda is precisely to purvey "creative geography," Disney-MGM is at pains to locate itself in a particularly referential space: Hollywood, the locus classicus of movie-making. Main Street's axial introduction is accomplished with an imaginative recasting of Hollywood Boulevard, heavy on the deco. Visitors enter through a gateway borrowed from the now-incinerated Pan-Pacific Auditorium, past a replica of the famous Crossroads of the World tower, a reincarnate Brown Derby, and a welter of familiar Los Angeles architecture, here scaled down and aggregated with an urbanity unknown at the unedited source.

At the head of this axis stands a re-created Grauman's Chinese. No longer exactly a movie palace, however, it's the queuing zone for the main event at the theme park, the Great Movie Ride, a forty-two-minute trip through scenes from well-known Disney and MGM movies, recreated by Animatronic robots. This is a fabulously compact rendition of the larger experience of Disneyfication, the suspension of the visitor in a serially realized apparatus of simulation. Like the global-corridor traveler, the visitor is propelled past a series of summary tableaux which stand in for some larger, sloughed-off, memory of reality. Of course, the Great Movie Ride goes the system one better, mechanically reproducing a mechanical reproduction.

One of the main effects of Disneyfication is the substitution of recreation for work, the production of leisure according to the routines of industry. Now, one of the products of postindustrialism is not simply the liberation of vast amounts of problematic leisure time, it's the reinvention of labor as spectacle, what Dean Mac-Cannell has called "involuted differentiation." The positivist mythos having withered, culture turns in on itself, simply aestheticizing its internal operations, romanticizing especially those bygone. The tourist travels the world to see the wigged baker at the simulacrum of Colonial Williamsburg drawing hot-cross buns from an "authentic" brick oven or the Greek fisherman on the quay on Mykonos, mending his photogenic nets, or the Animatronic Gene Kelly "singing in the rain."

At the movie theme park this spectacle is multiplied. The "work" at Disney World is, of course, entertainment. The 26,000 employees of the place are all considered by management to be "cast-members." Transforming workers to actors presumably transforms their work into play. This plugs nicely into a familiar mode, an endless staple of the talk-show circuit: the performance of some overcompensated Hollywood sybarite talking about his or her "work" as if the activity were somehow comparable to the labors of the assembly line. It's the same grotesque operation found in the seasonal public negotiations (with frequent strikes) of overpaid sports figures which create a themed version of "old-fashioned" labor relations, rendering union-management relations ridiculous by exaggeration.

But the most important aim of this inversion is not to encourage delusional thinking by some harried cafeteria worker at Disney. It's rather to invent the empire of leisure that still differentiates Disneyworld from everyday life. Visitors to the Disney parks, polled about what they like best, cite first the cleanliness, next the friendliness of the employees. This is surely the redemption of the industrial metropolis: hygienic, staffed with unalienated workers apparently enjoying their contributions to the happy collectivity. The movie ride takes this theory of labor a logical step further. One imagines, to begin with, that the Gene Kelly automaton is working for considerably less than scale. The representation goes the "ideal" worker one better: entertaining itself—fun in the first place—has been fully automated.

Consider a further recursion. In all likelihood, as the tram rolls through the Animatronic Temple of Doom, a hundred video-cams whirringly record the "event" for later consumption at home. That tape is an astonishing artifact, unprecedented in human history. If postmodern culture can be said to be about the weaving of ever more elaborate fabrics of simulation, about successive displacements of "authentic" signifiers, then the Japanese family sitting in front of the Sony back in Nagaski, watching their home videos of the Animatronic re-creation of the creative geography of a Hollywood "original," all recorded at a simulacrum of Hollywood in central Florida, must be said to have achieved a truly weird apotheosis of raw referentiality. Interestingly, several years ago, the inventor Nolan Bushnell proposed a further efficiency in this circuit. His notion was to place little self-propelled robots, each with a video eye, in major tourist cities—Paris, Rome, London, perhaps even Disney World. These could then be driven around by folks in Phoenix or Dubuque, giving them the experience of prowling the Champs Elysée, Regent Street, or the Via Veneto, without actually leaving home. But this is just an incremental advance, economizing only on human mobility, still premised on an old notion of the superiority of old-style "reality."

Disney's ahead of this. The Disney-MGM studio tour offers a third order of re-creation, another involuted riff on the nature of place. Part of the complex is a functioning movie studio, affording visitors the authentic frisson of a brush with living stars, an actual "production." Strolling the backlot, tourists might pass down a set for a New York City street. Although this set is constructed in the same way and with the same creatively interpolative geography as nearby "Hollywood Boulevard," the spectator's relationship to it is different. Success here depends on the apprehension of this space not primarily as a zone of leisure (as on the Great Movie Ride or the stroll down the Boulevard) but as a workplace. It's another order of tourism, like watching the muffin-bakers and glass-blowers at Colonial Williamsburg, the addition of the pleasures of voyeurism to those of mere recreation.

If visitors are permitted the pleasure of circulating "backstage" at the movie studio, there's yet a further backstage that remains inaccessible. In true rational modernist fashion, the Disney parks are built on giant platforms. Underneath the attractions, a labyrinth of tunnels provides service and staff circulation for the public activities above. These areas are strictly off limits to visitors although they're often discussed in publicity as one of the keys to Disney's marvelous efficiency, and photographs—daffy shots of giant Mickey Mice padding down fluorescent-lit concrete corridors—are widely disseminated. This subterranean space inevitably conjures up other, more dystopian images, most notably the underworld in Lang's *Metropolis*, its workers trapped in carceral caverns dancing their robotic ballet like Martha Graham on Thorazine.

But—perhaps in part because a man in a mouse costume is a more genial image of dehumanization than a prole in chains—this "servant space" (in Louis Kahn's locution) has a generally happier reputation. It is, in fact, what makes Disneyland "clean." Not simply is this a venue for the efficient whisking away of the detritus of fun—the tons of Popsicle sticks and hot-dog wrappers generated daily—it divides labor into its clean, public face, and its less entertaining, less "magic" aspects. Like the tourist-popular sewers of Paris, this underworld is both alien and marvelous, "peopled" with strange denizens, inconspicuous yet indispensable, supporting the purer city of being above. It is the dream of each beleaguered city dweller: an apparatus for keeping every urban problem out of sight. In fact, though, it reverses the Langian schema. This disciplinary apparatus is not above but underground, a subterranean Panopticon, ready to spring up innumerable concealed passages to monitor and service the vast leisure army toiling at fun up above.

Such reveries of self-discipline are historic. Stuart Ewen cites a variety of sources celebrating the self-modified behavior of visitors to the White City of 1892. "Order reigned everywhere," wrote one, "no boisterousness, no unseemly merriment. It seemed as though the beauty of the place brought a gentleness, happiness, and self-respect to its visitors." Observed another, "No great multitude of people ever showed more love of order. The restraint and discipline were remarkable." And another, "Courtiers in Versailles and Fontainbleau could not have been more deferential and observant . . . the decorum of the place and occasion than these obscure and myriads of unknown laborers." Even Charlotte Brontë, visiting the Crystal Palace in 1851, opined that "the multitude . . . seems ruled and subdued by some invisible influence."[4]

Jeffrey Katzenberg, head of Disney's movie division, suggests that we "think of Disney World as a medium-sized city with a crime rate of zero." Although the claim is hyperbole (petty larceny mainly leads to expulsion from the kingdom, more serious infractions to the summoning of adjoining police forces), the perception is not: the environment is virtually self-policing. Disney World is clearly a version of a town ("Imagine a Disneyland as big as the city of San Francisco," goes a recent ad) And it's based on a particular urbanism, a crisp acceleration of trends everywhere visible but nowhere so acutely elaborated. The problems addressed by Disneyzone are quintessentially modern: crime, transportation, waste, the relationship of work and leisure, the transience of populations, the growing hegemony of the simulacrum.

But finally, Disneyzone isn't urban at all. Like the patent-medicine-plugging actor who advertises his bona fides as "I'm not a doctor but I play one on TV," Disney invokes an urbanism without producing a city. Rather, it produces a kind of aura-stripped hypercity, a city with billions of citizens (all who would consume) but no residents. Physicalized yet conceptual, it's the utopia of transience, a place where everyone is just passing through. This is its message for the city to be, a place everywhere and nowhere, assembled only through constant motion. Visitors to Disneyzone are reduced to the status of cartoon characters. (Indeed, one of the features of the studio tour is the opportunity for visitors to cinematically interpolate themselves into *Who Framed Roger Rabbit?*) This is a common failing in utopian subjectivity, the predication on a homogenized, underdimensioned citizenship. However, it's also true that there's probably no more acquiescent subject than the postindustrial tourist. And there's surely no question that a holiday-maker wants a version of life pared of its sting, that vacationing finds its fulfillment in escape. The Disney visitor seeks and delights in the relationship between what he or she finds and its obverse back home, terrain of crime, litter, and surliness.

In the Disney utopia, we all become involuntary flaneurs and flaneuses, global drifters, holding high our lamps as we look everywhere for an honest image. The search will get tougher and tougher for the fanned-out millions as the recombinant landscape crops up around the globe. One of the latest nodes appears about to be sprung at Surajkund, near New Delhi, where India's first theme park gleams in the eye of the local tourism department. "We have a whole integrated concept of a fun center," as the *New York Times* quotes S. K. Sharma, state secretary for tourism. "Like all big cities, Delhi is getting polluted. It is getting choked with people. People need amusement and clear air."[5]

Marcuse called utopia "the determinate sociohistorical negation of what exists."[6] Disneyzone—Toon Town in real stucco and metal—is a cartoon utopia, an urbanism for the electronic age. Like television, it is a machine for the continuous transformation of what exists (a panoply of images drawn from life) into what doesn't (an ever-increasing number of weird juxtapositions). It's a genetic utopia, where every product is some sort of mutant, maimed kids in Kabul brought to you on the nightly news by Metamucil, Dumbo in Japan in Florida. The only way to consume this narrative is to keep moving, keep changing channels, keep walking, get on another jet, pass through another airport, stay in another Ramada Inn. The only logic is the faint buzz of memories of something more or less similar . . . but so long ago, perhaps even yesterday.

Notes

MARGARET CRAWFORD: **The World in a Shopping Mall**

I am grateful to those who read and commented on this manuscript during various stages of its development—Marco Cenzatti, Kevin McMahon, Diane Ghirardo, and Ed Soja—and to the excellent editing of Michael Sorkin and Sara Bershtel.

1. Gordon M. Henry, "Welcome to the Pleasure Dome," *Time*, Oct. 27, 1986, p. 60. Other descriptions of the WEM include William S. Kowinski, "Endless Summer at the World's Biggest Shopping Wonderland," *Smithsonian*, Dec. 1986, pp. 35–41; Ian Pearson, "Shop Till You Drop," *Saturday Night*, May 1986, pp. 48–56. A more scholarly approach is offered by R. Shields, "Social Spatialization and the Built Environment: The West Edmonton Mall," *Environment and Planning D: Society and Space*, vol. 7, 1989, pp. 147–64.
2. Leonard Zehr, "Shopping and Show Biz Blend in Giant Center at Edmonton, Alberta," *Wall Street Journal*, Oct. 7, 1985.
3. Mary Ann Galante, "Mixing Marts and Theme Parks," *Los Angeles Times*, June 14, 1989.
4. *Newsweek*, June 19, 1989, p. 36.
5. Margaret Crawford, "I've Seen the Future and It's Fake," *L.A. Architect*, Nov. 1988, pp. 6–7.
6. N. R. Kleinfeld, "Why Everyone Goes to the Mall," *New York Times*, Dec. 21, 1986.
7. Central-place theory, developed by geographer Walter Christaller and economist August Losch, provides a hierarchical structure of market

areas according to scale economies, transport costs, and number of household units. See Walter Christaller, *Central Places in Southern Germany* (Englewood Cliffs, N.J.: Prentice-Hall, 1966).

8. John Dawson and J. Dennis Lord, *Shopping Centre Development: Policies and Prospects* (Beckenham, Kent: Croom Helm, 1983), p. 123.

9. Peter Muller, *Contemporary Suburban America* (Englewood Cliffs, N.J.: Prentice-Hall, 1981), pp. 123–30.

10. "Why Shopping Centers Rode Out the Storm," *Forbes*, June 1, 1976, p. 35.

11. Interview with Linda Congleton (president of Linda Congleton and Associates: Market Research for Real Estate, Irvine, Calif.), who uses both of these systems in market analysis for mall development.

12. Kay Miller, "Southdale's Perpetual Spring," *Minneapolis Star and Tribune Sunday Magazine*, Sept. 28, 1986; Kleinfeld, "Why Everyone Goes."

13. William S. Kowinski, *The Malling of America* (New York: William Morrow, 1985), p. 218.

14. "Metropolitan Roundup," *New York Times*, Jan. 29, 1984.

15. William Leiss, *The Limits to Satisfaction* (Toronto: University of Toronto Press, 1976), p. 4; Lewis Mandell et al., *Surveys of Consumers 1971–72* (Ann Arbor: Institute for Social Research, University of Michigan, 1973), pp. 253–62, 274–75.

16. Leiss, *Limits*, pp. 19, 61.

17. Ibid., p. 92.

18. Rachel Bowlby, *Just Looking* (New York: Methuen, 1985), pp. 1–30.

19. T. J. Jackson Lears, in *No Place of Grace* (New York: Pantheon, 1981) has provided a detailed exploration of the characteristic "weightlessness" of Victorian culture, closely linked to the penetration of market values into the educated middle class.

20. Joan Didion, "On the Mall," *The White Notebook* (New York: Simon and Schuster, 1979), p. 183; Kowinski, *Malling*, pp. 339–42.

21. Richard Sennett, *The Fall of Public Man* (New York: Vintage, 1976), pp. 144–45.

22. Muller, *Contemporary*, p. 92; Ryan Woodward, *Beverly Center* (New York: Leisure, 1985).

23. Galante, "Mixing Marts."

24. Ian Brown in the *Toronto Globe and Mail*, quoted in Kowinski, "Endless Summer," p. 41.

25. Michael Demarest, "He Digs Downtowns," *Time*, Aug. 24, 1981, p. 46.

26. Richard Cobb, "The Great Bourgeois Bargain," *New York Review of Books*, July 16, 1981, pp. 35–40.
27. Sennett, *Fall of Public Man*, p. 142.
28. Emile Zola, *Au Bonheur des Dames* (Paris, 1897); Rosalind Williams, *Dream Worlds* (Berkeley: California, 1982); Bowlby, *Just Looking*.
29. Cobb, "Bourgeois Bargain," p. 38; Meredith Clausen, "The Department Store—Development of the Type," *Journal of Architectural Education*, vol. 39, no. 1. (Fall, 1985), pp. 20–27.
30. Edward Bellamy, *Looking Backward* (New York: Penguin, 1982; reprint of 1888 original); Bradford Peck, *The World a Department Store* (Boston, 1900).
31. Didion, "On the Mall," p. 34.
32. Meredith Clausen, "Northgate Regional Shopping Center—Paradigm from the Provinces," *Journal of the Society of Architectural Historians*, vol. 43, no. 2 (May 1984), p. 160.
33. Urban Land Institute, *Shopping Center Development Handbook* (Washington D.C.: Urban Land Institute, 1977), pp. 29–31.
34. David Harvey, *The Urbanization of Capital* (Baltimore: Johns Hopkins, 1985), p. 128.
35. Clausen, "Northgate," p. 157.
36. Kowinski, *Malling*, p. 356.
37. "Shopping Centers," *Dollars and Sense*, July–Aug. 1978, p. 9.
38. Muller, *Suburban America*, p. 128.
39. Paolo Riani, "Metropolis Times Square," *L'Arca*, vol. 29 (July 1989), pp. 43–49.
40. E. B. Wallace "Houston's Clusters and the Texas Urban Agenda," *Texas Architect*, Sept.–Oct. 1984, p. 4.
41. Graham Shane, "The Architecture of the Street" (unpublished manuscript), chapt. 5, p. 10.
42. Mark McCAin, "After the Boom, Vacant Stores and Slow Sales," *New York Times*, June 5, 1988.
43. Richard Nordwind, "Cornering L.A.'s Markets," *Los Angeles Herald-Examiner*, June 28, 1987.
44. Linda Weber, "Protect Yourself from Shopping Mall Crime," *Good Housekeeping*, Mar. 1988, pp. 191–92.
45. Harvey, *Urbanization*, p. 68.
46. David Meyers, "Horton Plaza's Sales Booming," *Los Angeles Times*, Oct. 4, 1987.
47. Michele Beher and Manuelle Salama, *New/Nouvelle Architecture* (Paris: Editions Regirex-France, 1988), p. 44.
48. Robert Brueggmann, Suburban Downtowns Tour, Society of Architectural Historians Annual Meeting, Chicago, April 1988.
49. Ivon Forest, "Les Impacts des Aménagements pour Piétons dans les

Centres Anciens des Villes en France" (M.A. thesis, Laval University, Quebec, 1982), pp. 47–57.

50. I am indebted to the unknown author of the manuscript "The Malling of the Mall" for many insights into the relationship between the museum and the mall. After coming across this manuscript a number of years ago, I have attempted, without success, to track down its author, to whom I would like to express my gratitude for not only stimulating my own thinking on the subject but also for providing useful concepts and examples.

51. "The Malling of the Mall."

52. Jean Baudrillard, in *For a Critique of the Political Economy of the Sign* (St. Louis: Telos, 1981) and subsequent writings, argues that this separation from the economic base has, indeed, occurred.

LANGDON WINNER: Silicon Valley Mystery House

1. For accounts of the life of Sarah Winchester and her house see William R. Rambo, ed., *Lady of Mystery* (Santa Clara: Rosicrucian Press, 1967); Phyllis Zauner, *Those Spirited Women of the Early West* (Sonoma, Calif.: Zanel Publications, 1989); Laura Bergheim, *Weird, Wonderful America* (New York: Collier, 1988).

2. For a portrait of the valley as it once was, see Yvonne Jacobson, *Passing Farms, Enduring Values: California's Santa Clara Valley* (Los Altos, Calif.: William Kaufmann, 1984).

3. Norris writes, "Yes, the Railroad had prevailed. The ranches had been seized in the tentacles of the octopus; the iniquitous burden of extortionate freight rates had been imposed like a yoke of iron." But he concludes that despite the obvious signs of destruction, a greater good was served. "Untouched, unassailable, undefiled, that mighty world-force, that nourisher of nations, wrapped in Nirvanic calm, indifferent to the human swarm, gigantic, resistless, moved onward in its appointed grooves." Frank Norris, *The Octopus: A Story of California* (New York: Bantam, 1958), pp. 437–38.

4. Roger Miller and Marcel Cote, *Growing the Next Silicon Valley: A Guide for Successful Regional Planning* (Lexington, Mass.: Lexington Books, 1987). See also Peter Hall and Ann Markusen, eds., *Silicon Landscapes* (Boston: Allen and Unwin, 1985).

5. Frederick Emmon Terman, "The Electrical Engineering Research Situation in the American Universities," *Science*, vol. LXV, no. 1686 (April 22, 1927), p. 386.

6. Quoted in A. Bernstein et al., *Silicon Valley: Paradise or Paradox?* (Mountain View, Calif.: Pacific Studies Center, 1977).

7. Everett M. Rogers and Judith K. Larsen, *Silicon Valley Fever: Growth of High-Technology Culture* (New York: Basic Books, 1984), pp. 32–34.

8. For a portrait of Hewlett-Packard and its influence upon Silicon Valley see Michael S. Malone, "The Aristocrats," in *The Big Score: The Billion-Dollar Story of Silicon Valley* (New York: Doubleday, 1985), pp. 25–49.

9. James Treybig, quoted in *The Big Score*, p. 285.

10. Brief biographies with photographs of William Shockley, Robert Noyce, and other Silicon Valley luminaries are provided in Carolyn Caddes, *Portraits of Success: Impressions of Silicon Valley Pioneers* (Palo Alto: Tioga Publishing, 1986).

11. For an analysis of the role of military contractors in the development of Silicon Valley, see AnnaLee Saxenian, "Silicon Chips and Spatial Structure: The Industrial Basis of Urbanization in Santa Clara County, California," Institute of Urban and Regional Development, University of California, Berkeley, Working Paper 345, March 1981.

12. The world's first view of many of these devices in action came in the 1991 war in the Persian Gulf. While debates continue about actual effectiveness of weapons like the Patriot and Tomahawk missiles, the immediate public-relations result was to build public and Congressional support for funding of the next generation of electronic weapons. For an analysis of prospects for the high-tech battlefield, see Frank Barnaby, "How the Next War Will Be Fought," in Tom Forrester, ed., *Computers in the Human Context: Information Technology, Productivity, and People* (Cambridge: MIT, 1989), pp. 518–27.

13. This relative position of the United States in international microelectronics is discussed in Michael Borus, *Competing for Control: America's Stake in Microelectronics* (New York: Ballinger, 1988).

14. Descriptions of working conditions in Silicon Valley can be found in Lenny Siegel and John Markoff, *The High Cost of High Tech: The Dark Side of the Chip* (New York: Harper and Row, 1985) and Dennis Hayes, *Behind the Silicon Curtain: The Seductions of Work in a Lonely Era* (Boston: South End, 1989).

15. *The High Cost of High Tech*, p. 149.

16. Quoted in Robert Howard, *Brave New Workplace* (New York: Viking, 1985), p. 136.

17. For a discussion of social bifurcation in Silicon Valley and its consequences, see articles by AnnaLee Saxenian, "Urban Contradictions of Silicon Valley: Regional Growth and the Restructuring of the Semiconductor Industry," in *International Journal of Urban and Regional Research*, vol. 7 (June 1983), pp. 237–61; and "Silicon Valley and Route 128: Regional Prototypes or Historic Exceptions?" in Manuel

Castells, ed., *High Technology, Space, and Society*, vol. 28 of *Urban Affairs Annual Reviews* (Beverly Hills: Sage, 1985), pp. 81–105.

18. *San Jose Mercury News*, editorial, February 27, 1983.

19. Susan Yoachum et al., "Clean Industry, Dirty Water," reprint of a special report (San Jose: *San Jose Mercury News*, 1983). For an account of efforts by environmental groups to confront these problems, see "Ted Smith, Environmental Activist," chapter 18 of Thomas Mahon, *Charged Bodies: People, Power, and Paradox in Silicon Valley* (New York: New American Library, 1985).

20. From guidelines issued by Japan's MITI, quoted by Sheridan Tatsuno, *The Technopolis Strategy: Japan, High Technology, and the Control of the Twenty-First Century* (New York: Prentice-Hall, 1986), p. 128.

21. For a comparison of the Japanese Technopolis plans with efforts to clone Silicon Valley in the United States and elsewhere, see Raymond W. Smilor, George Zozmetsky, and David Gison, eds., *Creating the Technopolis: Linking Technology Commercialization and Economic Development* (New York: Ballinger, 1988).

22. *The Electronic Supervisor: New Technology, New Tensions* (Washington, D.C.: Congress of the United States, Office of Technology Assessment, 1987), OTA-CIT-333.

23. Stewart Brand, quoted in Siegel and Markoff, *The High Cost of High Tech*, p. 204.

24. Rogers and Larsen, *Silicon Valley Fever*, p. 276. For my critique of ideas of this kind, see "Mythinformation," chapter 6 in *The Whale and the Reactor: A Search for Limits in an Age of High Technology*. (Chicago: University of Chicago Press, 1986).

NEIL SMITH: New City, New Frontier

Some of the research for this paper was assisted by National Science Foundation grant SE87-13043, and draws on an earlier essay, "Tompkins Square Park: Riots, Rents and Redskins," published in *The Portable Lower East Side* 6.1 (1989). I would like to thank Kurt Hollander, Sara Bershtel, and Michael Sorkin for valuable comments and criticisms.

1. Michael Wines, "Class Struggle Erupts Along Avenue B," *New York Times*, Aug. 10, 1988.

2. C. Carr, "Night Clubbing: Reports from the Tompkins Square Police Riot," *Village Voice*, Aug. 16, 1988; Sarah Ferguson, "The Boombox Wars," ibid. The poet Allen Ginsberg relates this reaction from a visiting Chinese student who had been in Beijing's Tiananmen Square during the earliest student confrontations with the police. In China

the police "were dressed in cloth like everybody else. He said the contrast was *amazing*, because in China it was pushing back and forth, and maybe batons. But here it was people who looked like they were dropped from outer space with these helmets on, dropped in the middle of the street from outer space and just beating people up, passers-by and householders—anyone in their path. Completely alienated and complete aliens." "A Talk with Allen Ginsberg," *The New Common Good*, Sept. 1988, p. 7.

3. Leslie Gevirtz, "Slam Dancer at NYPD," *Village Voice*, Sept. 6, 1988; David E. Pitt, "PBA Leader Assails Report on Tompkins Square Melee," *New York Times*, Apr. 21, 1989.

4. Bill Weinberg, "Is Gentrification Genocide? Squatters Build an Alternative Vision for the Lower East Side," *Downtown*, no. 181 (Feb. 14, 1990), p. 1a.

5. Sarah Ferguson, "Should Tompkins Square Be Like Gramercy?" *Village Voice*, June 11, 1991; Dinkins is quoted in John Kifner, "New York Closes Park to Homeless," *New York Times*, June 4, 1991.

6. Joel Rose and Catherine Texier, eds., *Between C & D: New Writing from the Lower East Side Fiction Magazine* (New York: Penguin, 1988), p. xi; Jerome Charyn, *War Cries Over Avenue C* (New York: Donald I. Fine, 1985), p. 7.

7. Carr, "Night Clubbing," p. 17.

8. Philip S. Foner, *The Labor Movement in the United States*, vol. 1 (New York: International Publishers, 1978), p. 448. See also Richard Slotkin, *Fatal Environment: The Myth of the Frontier in the Age of Industrialization 1800–1890* (New York: Atheneum, 1985), p. 338. The best account of the riot comes from Herbert Gutman, "The Tompkins Square 'Riot' in New York City on January 13, 1874: A Re-examination of Its Causes and Its Aftermath," *Labor History*, vol. 6 (1965), p. 55.

9. Gutman, "Tompkins Square 'Riot.' "

10. Roland Barthes, *Mythologies* (New York: Hill & Wang, 1972), p. 129; Slotkin, *Fatal Environment*, pp. 16, 21–32.

11. "Ludlow Street." *New Yorker*, Feb. 8, 1988, p. 29.

12. *New York Times*, Mar. 27, 1983.

13. *New York Times Magazine*, Aug. 6, 1989, p. 37.

14. *New York Times*, Feb. 8, 1990.

15. Ibid.

16. Ibid.

17. Slotkin, *Fatal Environment*, pp. 33, 47.

18. Ibid., p. 375.

19. Frederick Jackson Turner, *The Frontier in American History* (New York: Holt, Rinehart and Winston, 1958).

20. "At the positive end . . . are members of the 'civil class,' whose attitudes and behaviors are based on the assumption that the individual good, and hence the neighborhood good, is enhanced by submitting to social norms. At the other extreme are members of the 'uncivil class.' Their behavior and attitudes reflect no acceptance of norms beyond those imperfectly specified by civil and criminal law. Their attitudes may range from indifference to social norms to hostility toward any collective definition of behavior." Philip Clay, *Neighborhood Renewal* (Lexington, Mass.: Heath, 1979), pp. 37–38.

21. Walter Robinson and Carlo McCormick, "Slouching Toward Avenue D," *Art in America*, vol. 72, no. 6 (1984), pp. 138, 158.

22. Roger Ricklefs, "The Bowery Today: A Skid Row Area Invaded by Yuppies," *Wall Street Journal*, Nov. 13, 1988. See also Kim Levin, "The Neo-Frontier," *Village Voice*, Jan. 4, 1983.

23. Robinson and McCormick, "Slouching Toward Avenue D," pp. 138, 158; Nicolas Moufarrege, "Another Wave, Still More Savagely Than the First: Lower East Side, 1982," *Arts*, vol. 57, no. 1 (1982), p. 73; Moufarrege, "The Years After," *Flash Art*, no. 118 (1984), p. 51.

24. Rosalyn Deutsche and Cara Gendel Ryan, "The Fine Art of Gentrification," *October*, vol. 13 (1984), p. 92.

25. Craig Owens, "Commentary: The Problem with Puerilism," *Art in America*, vol. 72, no. 6 (1984), pp. 162–63.

26. Anne E. Bowler and Blaine McBurney, "Gentrification and the Avant Garde in New York's East Village: The Good, the Bad and the Ugly." Paper presented at the Annual Conference of the American Sociological Association, Aug. 1989, San Francisco, pp. 25, 27.

27. Robinson and McCormick, "Slouching Toward Avenue D," p. 135.

28. Craig Owens argues that "Artists are not, of course, responsible for 'gentrification'; they are often its victims" ("Commentary," pp. 162–63). Deutsche and Ryan respond: "To portray artists as the victims of gentrification is to mock the plight of the neighborhood's real victims" ("The Fine Art of Gentrification," p. 104). See also Bowler and McBurney, "Gentrification and the Avant Garde," op. cit.

29. Gwendolyn Wright, *Building the Dream: A Social History of Housing in America* (Cambridge, Mass.: MIT, 1981), p. 123.

30. Regional Plan Association of America, *New York Regional Plan* (New York: RPA, 1929), quoted in Martin Gottlieb, "Space Invaders: Land Grab on the Lower East Side," *Village Voice*, Dec. 14, 1982.

31. Gottlieb, "Space Invaders."

32. Craig Unger, "The Lower East Side: There Goes the Neighborhood," *New York*, May 28, 1984, pp. 32–41; Anthony DePalma, "Can City's Plan Rebuild the Lower East Side?" *New York Times*, Oct. 14, 1988.

33. Frank DeGiovanni, *Displacement Pressures in the Lower East Side*. Community Services Society of New York, Working Paper, 1987, p. 27.

34. Diana Shaman, "Lower East Side Buildings Rehabilitated," *New York Times*, Apr. 1, 1988.

35. Unger, "The Lower East Side."

36. Neil Smith, "Toward a Theory of Gentrification: A Back to the City Movement by Capital not People," *Journal of the American Planning Association* vol. 45 (1979), pp. 538–48; Eric Clark, *The Rent Gap and Urban Change* (Lund: Lund University Press, 1987).

37. Gottlieb, "Space Invaders."

38. Interview with Sam Bass, Brooklyn property manager, 1986.

39. Doug Henwood, "Subsidizing the Rich," *Village Voice*, Aug. 30, 1988, p. 10; see also Peter Marcuse, "Abandonment, Gentrification, and Displacement: The Linkages in New York City," in Neil Smith and Peter Williams, eds., *Gentrification of the City* (Boston: Allen and Unwin, 1986).

40. Interview with Donald Cogsville, president, Harlem Urban Development Corporation, Apr. 20, 1984; Neil Smith and Richard Schaffer, "Harlem Gentrification—A Catch-22?" *New York Affairs*, vol. 10 (1987), pp. 59–78.

41. Lisa Foderaro, "ABC's of Conversion: 21 Loft Condos," *New York Times*, Mar. 22, 1987. For a mapping of the gentrification frontier, see Neil Smith, Betsy Duncan, and Laura Reid, "From Disinvestment to Reinvestment: Tax Arrears and Turning Points in the East Village," *Housing Studies*, vol. 4 (1989), pp. 238–52.

42. Oreo Construction Services, *An Analysis of Investment Opportunities in the East Village* (cited in Richard Goldstein, "Here Comes the Neighborhood," *Village Voice*, Mar. 2, 1982).

43. Leslie Bennetts, "16 Tenements to Become Artist Units in City Plan," *New York Times*, May 4, 1982; Maurice Carroll, "A Housing Plan for Artists Loses in Board of Estimates," *New York Times*, Feb. 11, 1983; Deutsche and Ryan, "The Fine Art of Gentrification," pp. 100–102.

44. Lisa Glazer, "Heavenly Developers: Building Houses for the ~~Poor~~ Rich?" *Village Voice*, Oct. 11, 1988; Matthew Reiss, "Luxury Housing Opposed by Community," *The New Common Good*, July 1988, p. 15.

45. William R. Greer, "The Fortunes of the Lower East Side Are Rising," *New York Times*, Aug. 4, 1985.

46. Quoted in Deirdre Carmody, "New Day Is Celebrated for Union Square Park," *New York Times*, Apr. 20, 1984.

47. Carter Wiseman, "The Housing Squeeze—It's Worse Than You

Think." *New York*, Oct. 10, 1983, p. 54; Nicolas Moufarrege, "Another Wave."

48. Michael Jager, "Class Definition and the Esthetics of Gentrification: Victoriana in Melbourne." In Smith and Williams, *Gentrification*, pp. 79–80, 83, 85.

49. *New York Regional Plan*, quoted in Gottlieb, "Space Invaders," p. 16.

50. Quoted in Unger, "The Lower East Side," p. 41; Gottlieb, "Space Invaders," p. 13.

51. Wills quoted in Peter Marcuse, "Neutralizing Homelessness," *Socialist Review*, vol. 80, no. 1 (1988), p. 70.

52. Friedrich Engels, *The Housing Question* (Moscow: Progress Publishers, 1975 ed.), pp. 71, 73–74.

53. Kristin Koptiuch, "Third-Worlding at Home, " *Social Text*, vol. 28 (1991), pp. 87–89.

54. Cindi J. Katz, "A Cable to Cross a Curse: Everyday Cultural Practices of Resistance and Reproduction Among Youth in New York City," *Socialist Review* (1991, forthcoming); "Sow What You Know: The Struggle for Social Reproduction in Rural Sudan," *Annals of the Association of American Geographers*, vol. 81, no. 3 (1991, forthcoming).

55. Koptiuch, "Third-Worlding at Home." See also Tom Wolfe's desperate depiction of New York as a Third World beyond the control of the white upper-middle class: *Bonfire of the Vanities* (New York: Farrar, Straus, and Giroux, 1987), p. 7, *inter alia*.

56. Harold M. Rose, "The Future of the Black Ghettos," in Gary Gappert and Richard V. Knight, eds., *Cities in the 21st Century*, Urban Affairs Annual Reviews, vol. 23 (Beverly Hills: Sage, 1982), pp. 139, 148.

EDWARD W. SOJA: Scenes from Orange County

1. From an advertisement for *The Californias*, "a free 144-page travel guide that takes a fresh look at California," published by the California Office of Tourism.

2. Allen J. Scott, "New Frontiers of Industrial-Urban Development: The Rise of the Orange County High Technology Complex, 1955–1984," chapter 9 in *Metropolis: From the Division of Labor to Urban Form* (Berkeley: California, 1988), pp. 167–71.

3. Umberto Eco, *Travels in Hyperreality*, trans. William Weaver (San Diego: Harcourt, 1986), p. 13. Other quotations in this section are taken from pp. 18, 40–41, 43–46, 58.

4. *Orange Coast*, July 1990, p. 46.

5. Interview with Richard Milhous Nixon, *Orange Coast*, July 1990, p. 77.
6. This and subsequent quotations are from Leon Whiteson, "Campus by Design—UC Irvine Hopes to Avoid Boring, Boxy Buildings and Add a Degree of Sophistication As It Expands," *Los Angeles Times*, Dec. 12. 1988.
7. Jean Baudrillard, *America*, trans. Chris Turner (London: Verso, 1988), p. 8.
8. Maria L. La Ganga, "Mixing It Up in Irvine—City's First Bar Carries the Official Stamp of Approval for Style, Location, Appeal," *Los Angeles Times*, Dec. 12, 1988.
9. "The Sky's the Limit! Steel and Concrete Fly as Developments Boom," *Airport Business Journal*, Sept. 1984, p. 18.
10. Jean Baudrillard, *America*, p. 7.
11 Allen Temko, "The Fine Sound and Flawed Design of a Grand Orange County OCPAC," *Los Angeles Times*, Dec. 20, 1987.
12. Baudrillard, *America*, p. 28.
13. Peter Halley, "Notes on Nostalgia," in *Peter Halley Collected Essays 1981–1987* (Zurich: Bruno Bischofberger Gallery, 1988), p. 135.
14. Mark Landesbaum and Heidi Evans, "Mission Viejo: Winning Is the Only Game in Town," *Los Angeles Times*, Aug. 22, 1984.
15. See M. Moskowitz, M. Katz, and R. Lovering, eds., *Everybody's Business—The Irreverent Guide to Corporate America* (New York: Harper and Row, 1980), p. 52.
16. James S. Granelli, "Brokerages Find a Gold Mine in Leisure World," *Los Angeles Times*, Feb. 2, 1986.
17. George Frank, "Urban Sprawl: A New Foe Surrounds the Military," *Los Angeles Times*, Dec. 24, 1988.
18. For an elevated tour of the military ramparts that are beaded along the sixty-mile circle that defines, radiating out from the central city, the Greater Los Angeles Region (GLARE), see Chapter 9 in Edward W. Soja, *Postmodern Geographies* (London: Verso, 1989).
19. Fred Grumm, "Make-Believe Sunshine in the Shadows of San Onofre," *Los Angeles Times*, Oct. 11, 1987.
20. Frank, "Urban Sprawl."
21. Richard Beene and John Broder, "Fire at TRW Delays Final Testing of Alpha Laser, Key 'Star Wars' Weapon," *Los Angeles Times*, Jan. 29, 1988.
22. Reported in the Los Angeles *Daily Journal*, Mar. 24, 1987.

TREVOR BODDY: Underground and Overhead

1. William H. Whyte, *City: Rediscovering the Center* (New York: Doubleday, 1988), p. 199.
2. Charles Moore, "You Have to Pay for the Public Life," in *Perspecta*, nos. 9–10 (1965), pp. 57–106.
3. Richard Sennett, *Palais Royal* (New York: Knopf, 1986), p. 86. Sennett pursues the same theme in his *Fall of Public Man* (1977). His implicitly anarchist approach to urban issues was prefigured in his *Uses of Disorder* (1970).
4. Le Corbusier, *Towards a New Architecture*, trans. Frederick Etchells (London: Architectural Press, 1927), p. 59.
5. There is, of course, a similar disease by which European architects and planners remake themselves and their cities in a New World mold, but that is best left to another essay.
6. Judith Martin, quoted in the special Skyways issue of *Design Quarterly*, no. 129, p. 21.
7. Jaquelin Robertson, "Private Space in the Public Realm," ibid., p. 7.
8. William H. Whyte, *City* (New York: Doubleday, 1988), p. 203.
9. When Canada underwent mandatory conversion to the metric system in the 1970s the system mercifully got special dispensation to avoid being called the Plus Four-Point-Six.
10. Jan Morris's essays on Canadian cities, with perceptive comments on the analogous realms of Calgary, Toronto, and Montreal, are collected in *City to City* (Toronto: Macfarland, Walter, and Ross, 1990).
11. "Vincent Ponte—A New Kind of Urban Designer," *Art in America*, vol. 57 (Sept.–Oct., 1969), p. 66.
12. David Brown, "The Indoor City: From Organic Beginning to Guided Growth" in Bryan Demchinsky, ed., *Grassroots, Greystones, and Glass Towers* (Montreal: Vehicule Press, 1989), p. 72.
13. Ibid., p. 77.
14. The commitment Montrealers feel to their underground city, and to urban design issues in general, was apparent in the immense hue and cry precipitated in 1986 by the proposed construction *of a single elevated bridge over one downtown street*. A developer had proposed a pedestrian bridge over McGill College Avenue to connect two multilevel retail complexes. One of the widest streets downtown, McGill visually connects Mount Royal with the harbor as no other does. A superbly orchestrated citizen's protest, led by Canadian Centre for Architecture director Phyllis Lambert, was ultimately successful in replacing the bridge with *a tunnel underground*, and it is unlikely that another developer will propose an elevated walkway in Montreal,

no matter how expensive or inefficient in terms of retail layout a tunnel might be.

15. Vincent Ponte, quoted in William H. Whyte, *City*, p. 198.

MIKE DAVIS: Fortress Los Angeles

1. National Committee on the Causes and Prevention of Violence. *To Establish Justice, to Ensure Domestic Tranquillity* (Final Report; Washington D.C.: USGPO, 1969.)
2. Quoted in John F. Kasson, *Amusing the Million* (New York: Hill and Wang, 1978), p. 15.
3. *Los Angeles Times*, Nov. 4, 1978.
4. Ibid., Dec. 24, 1972.
5. N. David Milder, "Crime and Downtown Revitalization," *Urban Land*, Sept. 1987, p. 18.
6. Tom Chorneau, "Quandary Over a Park Restroom," *Downtown News*, Aug. 25, 1986.
7. See "Cold Snap's Toll at 5 as Its Iciest Night Arrives," *Los Angeles Times*, Dec. 29, 1988.
8. Ibid., June 17, 1990.
9. "The old socialist" quote is from Michael Rotundi of Morphosis. Gehry himself boasts: "I get my inspiration from the streets. I'm more of a street fighter than a Roman scholar." (Quoted in Adele Freedman, *Progressive Architecture*, Oct. 1986, p. 99).
10. The best catalogue of Gehry's work is Peter Arnell and Ted Bickford, eds., *Frank Gehry: Buildings and Projects* (New York: 1985).
11. Milfred Friedman, ed., *The Architecture of Frank Gehry*, (New York: 1986), p. 175.
12. Pilar Viladas, "Illuminated Manuscripts," *Progressive Architecture*, Oct. 1986, pp. 76, 84.
13. See David Ferrell's articles in the *Los Angeles Times*, Aug. 31 and Oct. 16, 1987.
14. Ibid., Oct. 7, 1987.
15. Jane Bukwalter, "Securing Shopping Centers for Inner Cities," *Urban Land*, Apr. 1987, p. 24.
16. Ibid.
17. Richard Titus, "Security Works," *Urban Land*, Jan. 1990, p. 2.
18. Buckwalter, "Securing," p. 25.
19. *Los Angeles Daily News*, Nov. 1, 1987.
20. Interview, Fox News, Mar. 1990.
21. *Los Angeles Times*, July 25, 1989.
22. Jim Carlton, quoted in *Los Angeles Times*, Oct. 8, 1988.

23. Quoted in *Los Angeles Times*, Aug. 29, 1988.
24. Interviews with LAPD personnel; also Don Rosen, "Bleu Thunder," *Los Angeles Herald Examiner*, May 28, 1989.
25. Charles Murray, "How to Win the War on Drugs," *New Republic*, May 21, 1990, pp. 19–25.
26. *Los Angeles Times*, Sept. 22 and 25, 1986.

M. CHRISTINE BOYER: Cities for Sale

The themes in this essay are elaborated in the author's forthcoming book: *The City of Collective Memory: Its Historical Imagery and Architectural Entertainments.*

1. Guy Debord, *Society of the Spectacle*, no. 34 (Detroit: Black and Red, 1983); T. J. Clark, *The Painting of Modern Life: Paris in the Art of Manet and His Followers* (London: Thames and Hudson, 1985), pp. 9, 23, 78.
2. Susan Buck-Morss, *The Dialectics of Seeing: Walter Benjamin and the Arcades Project* (Cambridge: MIT, 1989), pp. 89–91.
3. Richard Altick, *The Shows of London* (Cambridge: Harvard, 1978); Renzo Dubbini, "Views and Panoramas: Representations of Landscapes and Towns," *Lotus*, no. 52 (1986), pp. 98–111.
4. Altick, *Shows of London*, pp. 136, 147, 188.
5. Jay Caplan, *Framed Narratives: Diderot's Genealogy of the Beholder* (Minneapolis: Minnesota, 1985).
6. Jack W. McCullough, "Edward Kilanyi and American Tableaux Vivants," *Theatre Survey*, vol. 16 (1975), pp. 25–41.
7. Umberto Eco, "Innovation and Repetition: Between Modern and Postmodern Aesthetics," *Daedalus*, Fall 1985, pp. 161–84.
8. Peter Handke, "Short Letter, Long Farewell," quoted in Jerome Klinkowitze and James Knowlton, *Peter Handke and the Postmodern Transformation* (Columbia: Missouri, 1983), p. 44.
9. D. W. Meining, "Symbolic Landscapes," in *The Interpretation of Ordinary Landscapes* (New York: Oxford, 1979), pp. 165–67.
10. "The Sky-line of New York (1881–1897)," *Harper's Weekly*, vol. 41 (Mar. 20, 1897), p. 292.
11. Michel Foucault, *The Archaeology of Knowledge*, trans. A. M. Sheridan Smith (New York: Pantheon, 1972), p. 14.
12. "Video Cassettes Bring History to Life," *New York Times*, Jan. 4, 1986.
13. Andrew Britton, "Blissing Out: The Politics of Reaganite Entertainment," *Movie*, nos. 31–32 (1986), pp. 1–42; and M. Christine Boyer,

"The Return of Aesthetics to City Planning," *Society*, vol. 25, no. 4 (May–June 1988), pp. 49–56.

14. David Harvey, *The Condition of Postmodernity* (New York: Basil Blackwell, 1989).

15. "America's Hot Cities," *Newsweek*, Feb. 6, 1989, pp. 42–50.

16. John K. Ryans, Jr., and William L. Shanking, *Guide to Marketing for Economic Development: Competing in America's Second Civil War* (Columbus: Publishing Horizons, 1986).

17. *New York Ascendant* is the title of the report of the Commission on the Year 2000 (New York: Harper and Row, 1988).

18. *The WPA Guide to New York City* (New York: Pantheon, 1982), pp. 80–84.

19. James Felt and Co., Voorhees, Walker Foley & Smith, *Recommendation for a Redevelopment Study of Lower Manhattan South of Fulton Street*, June 12, 1950; David Rockefeller, John D. Butt, *Lower Manhattan Recommended Land Use Redevelopment Areas and Traffic Improvements* (New York: Lower-Manhattan Association, 1958); "Back to the Waterfront: Chaos or Control?" *Progressive Architecture*, vol. 47, no. 8 (Aug. 1966), pp. 128–39; New York City Planning Commission, *The Lower Manhattan Plan* (New York: NYC Planning Commission, 1966); and Hilary Silver, "The Last Frontier: Politics and Redevelopment on the New York Waterfront" (unpublished paper, 1988).

20. Nancy Bloom and Jo Ellen Freese, "Planning for the Preservation of South Street Seaport" (unpublished paper, Columbia University, 1977). This report was based on interviews with Robin Burns of the Office of Lower Manhattan Development, Brian McMahon of the New York State Maritime Museum, and Peter Standford of the National Maritime Historical Society, on various published reports and deeds, and on articles from the *New York Times* (Dec. 17, 1966, Oct. 15, 1967, Mar. 28 and Dec. 18, 1968, June 11, 1970, and July 30, 1973). See also Harold R. Snedcof, *Cultural Facilities in Mixed-Use Development* (Washington: Urban Land Institute, 1985).

21. Rouse Company, McKeown & Franze, the Ehrenkrantz Group, *The Final EIS Statement: Seaport Market Place*, Sept. 1980.

22. Ronald M. Blatman, "The Misuse of Mixed-Use Centers," *Real Estate Review*, vol. 13, no. 2 (Summer 1983), pp. 93–96.

23. Dean MacCannell, *The Tourist: A New Theory of the Leisure Class* (New York: Schocken, 1976).

24. Michael Wallace, "Visiting the Past," in Susan P. Benson, Stephen Brier, and Roy Rosenzweig, eds., *Presenting the Past* (Philadelphia: Temple, 1986), pp. 148–49.

25. Gail Faurschou, "Obsolescence and Desire: Fashion and the Com-

modity Form," in H. J. Silverman, ed., *Philosophy and the Arts* (New York: Routledge, 1990), pp. 234–59.

26. Louis Marin, *Utopics: Spatial Play* (Atlantic Highlands, N.J.: Humanities Press, 1984), pp. 203–19; Umberto Eco, *Travels in Hyperreality*, trans. William Weaver (New York: Harcourt, 1983), p. 43.

27. Rachel Bowlby, *Just Looking: Consumer Culture in Dreiser, Gissing, and Zola* (New York: Methuen, 1985), pp. 18–24; Philip Fisher, *Hard Facts: Setting and Form in the American Novel* (New York: Oxford, 1985), p. 133.

28. Susan Stewart, *On Longing: Narratives of the Miniature, the Gigantic, the Souvenir, the Collection* (Baltimore: Johns Hopkins, 1984), pp. 23, 135, 147.

29. Ellen Fletcher, "Museum Program Plan," Aug. 7, 1984, and Snedcof, *Cultural Facilities*.

30. "South Street Seaport Museum Planning Conference," Nov. 7, 1968. Instead of paying real-estate taxes and rent to the city, the Rouse Company offered to pay the museum the greater of either $3.50 per square foot or 15 percent of its rental income from its retailers. In addition, after paying for its operating costs and debt service, and expecting at least a 15 percent return on its investment, commercial revenues will be shared equally with the museum. In return, the museum will share its rental income with the city and the state, from whom it actually leases the property. Snedcof, *Cultural Facilities*; Rouse Company, et al., *Final EIS Statement*.

Public money has leveraged private investment in the South Street Seaport thus: Public development costs, a total of $61.05 million (restoration of museum block, $4.3 million; Fulton Fish Market improvements, $3.3 million; stabilization and rehabilitation of Schermerhorn Row, $10 million; infrastructure improvements and construction of waterfront streetscape, $23 million; and construction of pier platform and pedestrian mall, $20.45 million); private development costs, a total of $289.5 million (Seaport Plaza office building, $176 million; development of three blocks fronting Fulton Street [Market, Museum, and Telco blocks], pier pavilion, and retail improvements of Schermerhorn Row, $102.5 million; development of the multiscreen theater, $3 million; and development of rental office space in the museum and Schermerhorn Row, $8 million). Compiled from South Street Seaport Museum files by Snedcof, p. 173.

31. Sut Jhally, *The Codes of Advertising: Fetishism and the Political Economy of Meaning in the Consumer Society* (New York: St. Martin's, 1987), pp. 130–31; Sut Jhally, "The Political Economy of Culture," in Ian Angus and Sut Jhally, *Cultural Politics in Contem-*

porary American Society (New York: Routledge, 1989), pp. 65–81.
32. Neil Smith presents the same argument using the "pioneer" and the "frontier" as the metaphorical devices in "Gentrification, the Frontier, and the Restructuring of Urban Space," in Neil Smith and Peter Williams, eds., *Gentrification of the City* (Boston: Allen and Unwin, 1986), pp. 15–34.

MICHAEL SORKIN: See You in Disneyland

1. "Inaugural Address of the Prince Consort Albert, May 1, 1851," quoted in Wolfgang Freibe, *Buildings of the World Exhibitions* (Leipzig: Editions Leipzig, 1985), p. 13.
2. Zbigniew Brzezinski, *Between Two Ages: America's Role in the Technotronic Era* (New York: Viking, 1976), quoted in Collettivo Strategie, *Strategie* (Milan: Macchina Libri, 1981) included in Tony Solomonides and Les Levidow, eds., *Compulsive Technology: Computers as Culture* (London: Free Association, 1985), p. 130.
3. Lev Kuleshov, "Art of the Cinema," in Ronald Levaco, *Kuleshov on Film: Writings by Lev Kuleshov* (Berkeley: California, 1974), p. 52.
4. Stewart Ewen, *All Consuming Images: The Politics of Style in Contemporary Culture* (New York: Basic Books, 1988), pp. 204–5.
5. *New York Times*, February 10, 1990.
6. Herbert Marcuse, "The End of Utopia," in *Five Lectures* (Boston: Beacon, 1970), p. 69.

The Contributors

TREVOR BODDY teaches architectural history, theory, and design at Carleton University in Ottawa. He is the author of *The Architecture of Douglas Cardinal* and a collection of essays, *Canadian Architecture in the Twentieth Century*.

M. CHRISTINE BOYER is a professor of architectural history and urbanism at Princeton University. She is the author of *Dreaming the Rational City*, *Manhattan Manners*, and forthcoming, *The City of Collective Memory*.

MARGARET CRAWFORD is chair of the History and Theory of Architecture program at the Southern California Institute of Architecture. She is the author of *Designing Company Towns*.

MIKE DAVIS teaches urban planning and political economy at the Southern California Institute of Architecture and UCLA. He is the author of *City of Quartz*, nominated for the National Book Critics Circle Award, and *Prisoners of the American Dream*.

NEIL SMITH teaches in the geography department at Rutgers University. He is the author of *Uneven Development: Nature, Capital and the Production of Space* and is coeditor of *Gentrification of the City*.

EDWARD W. SOJA teaches urban and regional planning at UCLA. He is the author of several books on African development and, more recently, on the economic and spatial restructuring of the Los Angeles region. In

1989, he published *Postmodern Geographies: The Reassertion of Space in Critical Social Theory.*

MICHAEL SORKIN, an architect and writer, teaches at Cooper Union, the Southern California Institute of Architecture, Yale, Harvard, and Columbia and is the author of *The Exquisite Corpse.* For ten years, he was the architecture critic of the *Village Voice.*

LANGDON WINNER teaches political theory at Rensselaer Polytechnic Institute. He is the author of *Autonomous Technology* and *The Whale and the Reactor: A Search for Limits in an Age of High Technology.*